Zaha Hadid's Paintings

Desley Luscombe

# Zaha Hadid's Paintings

## Imagining Architecture

LUND HUMPHRIES

First published in 2024 by Lund Humphries

Lund Humphries
Huckletree Shoreditch
Alphabeta Building
18 Finsbury Square
London EC2A 1AH
UK
www.lundhumphries.com

*Zaha Hadid's Paintings: Imagining Architecture*
© Desley Luscombe, 2024
All rights reserved

ISBN: 978-1-84822-684-5

A Cataloguing-in-Publication record for this book is available from the British Library

All rights reserved. No part of this publication may be reproduced, stored in a retrieval system or transmitted in any form or by any means, electrical, mechanical or otherwise, without first seeking the permission of the copyright owners and publishers. Every effort has been made to seek permission to reproduce the images in this book. Any omissions are entirely unintentional, and details should be addressed to the publishers.

Desley Luscombe has asserted her right under the Copyright, Designs and Patents Act, 1988, to be identified as the Author of this Work.

Copy edited by Jacqui Cornish
Designed by Mark Thomson
Set in The Future and Martina Plantijn
Printed in Estonia

Front cover image: Zaha Hadid Architects, *MAXXI: Museum of XXI Century Arts, Sketch Painting*, Rome, Italy, 1999, Zaha Hadid Foundation. See page 133.
Back cover image: Zaha Hadid, 1994, cibachrome print © Steve Speller / National Portrait Gallery, London

This book is printed on sustainably sourced paper.

Frontispiece:
**Zaha Hadid Architects**
*The Peak, Divers*, Hong Kong, China, 1983
Acrylic and watercolour on paper,
180.3 × 104 cm (71 × 41 in)
Zaha Hadid Foundation

Contents

Acknowledgements 7

Introduction: Experimentation Through Painting 9

1 From Lines to the Tactile Surface:
 *Malevich's Tektonik* to 59 Eaton Place 15

2 Pictorial Space and the Transformation of Architecture:
 The Peak 37

3 Politicising the Urban Character of London:
 Grand Buildings 57

4 Body, Sensation and the Immaterial in Architecture:
 Office Building on Kurfürstendamm 70, Berlin 75

5 Spatial Force – Architecture as Urban Impact:
 Vitra Fire Station 95

6 From the Networked Object to the Fluidity of Histories:
 MAXXI, Rome 115

Conclusion: Of Painting and Architecture 137

Notes 140
Selected Bibliography 151
Index 154
Picture Credits 158

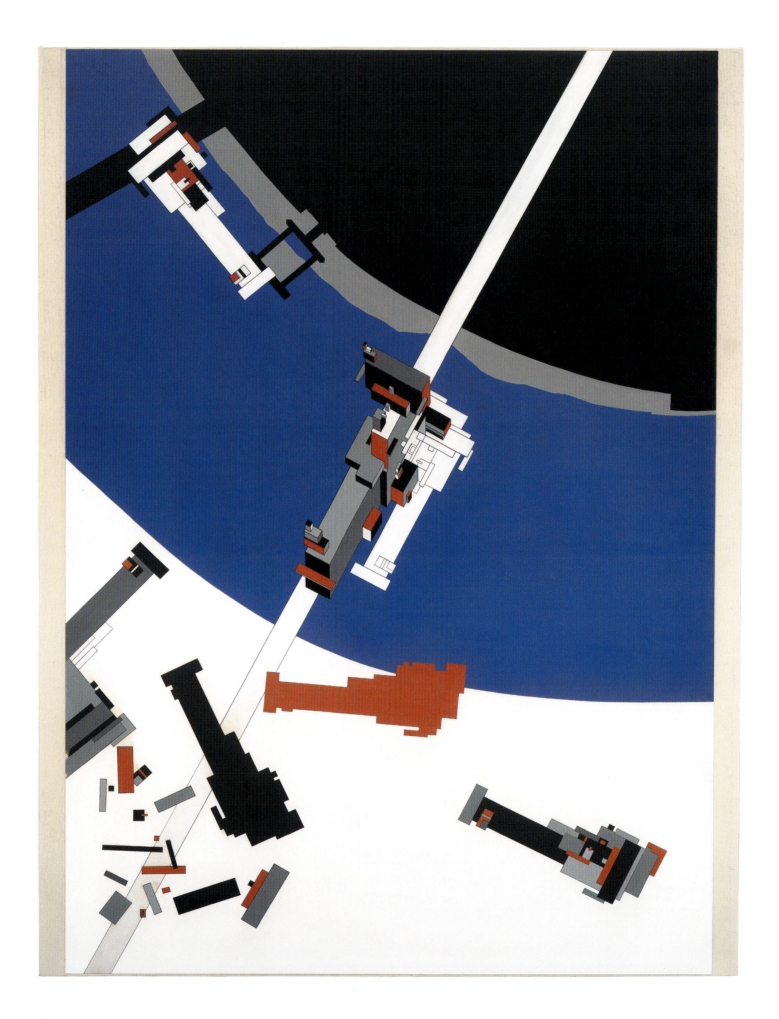

## Acknowledgements

This book would not have been possible without the support of many individuals and institutions. I am indebted to those who were close friends of Zaha Hadid and those who worked with her during the period between 1976 and 1999. Each freely gave of their time to discuss their experience of her early career. Fundamental to analysis was their recall of how each painting was created, as well as other office practices. Their information and shared reminiscences have been invaluable. Those contributing are listed here in alphabetical order: Nicholas Boyarsky, Paul Brislin, Antonio de Campos, Nicola Cousins, Jonathan Dunn, Kristin Feireiss, Paolo Flores, Wendy Galway, David Gomersall, Edgar Gonzalez, Sand Helsel, Kar-Hwa Ho, Manon Janssens, Justyna Karakiewicz, Simon Koumjian III, Nan Lee, Mya Manakides, Brian Ma Siy, Graham Modlen, Patrik Schumacher, Piers Smerin, Henry Virgin, Madelon Vriesendorp, Camilla Ween, Peter Wilson, Michael Wolfson, Woody Yao and Zoe Zenghelis.

Thanks also go to Alfred Siu and Ronald Lu who introduced me to the history of The Peak Leisure Club Competition, Hong Kong; to Alexander Lavrentiev for his permission to include the photographic works created by Alexander Rodchenko; and to Nicholas Boyarsky for his permission to use images from the Alvin Boyarsky Archive.

The office of Zaha Hadid Architects (ZHA) and the Zaha Hadid Foundation (ZHF) were very helpful in allowing me access to the images included within this publication and other supporting materials in preparation of this manuscript; their permissions to use the paintings and supply the images have been invaluable. I thank particularly Jane Pavitt, Serena Lawrance and Catherine Howe of ZHF and Manon Janssens and Henry Virgin of ZHA for their support. In addition, thanks go to Edward Bottoms of the Architectural Association School of Architecture, London, who provided guidance through archival material and photographs from their collection.

In the process of refining images suitable for this publication, I would like to thank Finn Marchant and Robin Murphy from the University of Technology Sydney who provided the technical support; the Faculty of Design, Architecture and Building for their financial support of the research; and finally, my colleagues and friends for their time and critique, in guiding me through the process of writing. They include Rosemary Aitken, Andrew Benjamin, Leo Campbell, Stan Fung, Niall Hobhouse, Flavia Marcello, Charles Rice, Olivier Solente and Helen Thomas, and Susie Walsh for her editorial assistance.

1
**Zaha Hadid**
*Horizontal Tektonik, Malevich's Tektonik*,
London, United Kingdom, 1977
Acrylic on paper, 128 × 89 cm (50⅜ × 35 1/16 in)
San Francisco Museum of Modern Art,
San Francisco

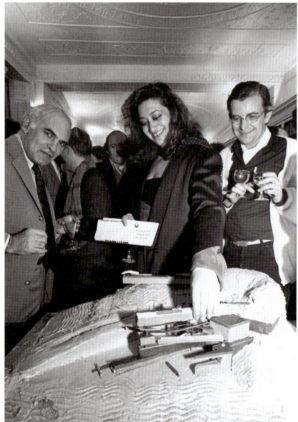

# Introduction: Experimentation Through Painting

*My drawings are not the building. They are drawings about the building. They are not an illustration of a final product. You have to look at them like a text – they are a language.*
Zaha Hadid[1]

Zaha Hadid (1950–2016), the winner of the Pritzker Architecture Prize and the RIBA Royal Gold Medal, remains a significant force in architecture (fig.2). The origins of her international standing can be traced in part to the unique way she developed architectural ideas through drawing and painting. This book aims to contextualise and examine selected paintings, revealing a continuing exploration of architecture's spatial potential. Comparing their visual attributes with examples from fine art, this analysis directs readers to see elements within each composition as connected, portraying a spatial logic of complex architectural thought. Hadid's process of visual thought emerges as experimental, developing a sophisticated agenda for architecture that was both highly theoretical and expressively visual. Within the dynamic and abstract linear effect of her paintings, there is a reimagining of the potency of architecture.

The act of technical drawing in architecture has traditionally been understood to be an objective system whereby each work can be correlated with all others within a 'set' of drawings. Architectural practice structured these representations through strict conventions combining orthography (plan, elevation and section), perspective and three-dimensional isometric or axonometric views.[2] The linear force of the technical drawings associated with architectural designs sat as a pivot between ideas and a realised building.[3] These drawings were considered a truth-telling, bringing the recording powers of the hand, the observations of the eye, and the intellectual work of the mind into alignment, so that architects could transfer their ideas to the understanding of others for a building's realisation. It was in response to Enlightenment thinking that 'presentation' drawings were introduced into architectural practice, reasserting a yet to be realised architecture within a perspectively 'natural' and objectively understood world. In this sense the inclusion of human figures and coloured tonality, within architecture's scenography of the natural, embraced the viewer into a belief structure that was morally guided. Drawing inscribed a way for replicating a world order within architecture's material reality.

Zaha Hadid's paintings infer different origins, emerging from the abstract spatiality of the colour and planes of pictorial space. While architect Lebbeus Woods was to recall their 'systematic and obsessively analytical construction' as drawings, her paintings radicalise any sense of normalcy or the objectivity offered by architecture's traditional practices.[4] They introduce visual metaphors for architectural thought. The question arises, was her manner of painting simply equivalent to a developing representational 'style', one that remained consistent throughout her career? This book argues that her approach to painting presents a powerful alternative to that claim. Her paintings embed the experimental and expressive potential of art to radically critique the disciplinary values of architecture

2  Zaha Hadid, top left and bottom right: 150th Architectural Association Auction to Benefit Student Bursaries, Saatchi Gallery, 1997; middle left: the opening of *Planetary Architecture Two*, 1983, the Architectural Association School of Architecture Archives; bottom left and top and middle right: Hadid painting in the studio, from the studio in early 1987, and in Milan at the launch of *Project for Red Sofa* 1989, Private Collection

of their time. Experimentation requires a changing emphasis that prompts engagement with the discourses of contemporary interest rather than inscribing a consistency through image-making guided by style. Within this understanding, the architecture depicted in Hadid's paintings remains emergent and not easily objectified by conventional expectations. When her ideas are explored, each resulting image accepts a distinctive purpose: where abstract pictorial compositions – and the spatiality implied by surface juxtapositions of colour, tone and linearity – introduce ideas that envisage architecture as worthy of intellectual upheaval. They prompt thought and a response from the viewer that is beyond the apprehension of an architectural and material reality.

Central to Hadid's architectural inquiry was how early 20th-century artists had explored the nature of the two-dimensional surface of painting. From childhood she had a broad general knowledge of Western painting traditions reinforced by her family's visits to galleries and discussions with her father.[5] Her studies at the Architectural Association had increasing interest in the paintings of Suprematism and the Russian avant-garde. But Hadid's sources were also eclectic and idiosyncratic. Friends remember examples of watching Alfred Hitchcock films over and over for their sense of light and space where she would suddenly disappear to return to a painting. Others remember her collections of spacecraft toys hung above the sink in her kitchen or the pens she collected, those ones with models of ships or buildings floating within their encasing covers.[6] These elements register a way of thinking prompted by memories, each metaphorically meaningful to her architectural consideration.

Hadid's paintings complicate what is meant by 'the architectural' as a disciplinary construct. Considering her paintings as a type of theoretical discourse, she described them as if working like language. However, the paintings do not strictly work like language, for while there is a layer of narrative, they structure a distinctively *visual* logic. Within this book, each chapter focuses on the implications of this logic and their architectural propositions for single architectural projects. The paintings are well known through numerous exhibitions and publications and have been seen many times – yet not really 'seen' as the subject for a broad-based critical analysis. Readers of this book may have understood them as a form of branding, but perhaps will have rarely questioned the context or the complex layering of their visual imagery – and how they illustrate theoretical responses to the architectural debates of the period. This book aims to slow down and look more closely at the selected images. It directs readers to see elements within each composition as connected, unifying the visually complex spatial logic of a radical architecture.

Each project when resolved into a series of paintings embeds a sense of temporality, of being vitally engaged within theoretical discourses that can be dated and contextualised. The paintings to be analysed in depth include selections from the projects: Malevich's Tektonik (1976–77); The Apartment at 59 Eaton Place, London (1981–82); The Peak Leisure Club, Hong Kong (1982–83); The Grand Buildings Competition, Trafalgar Square, London (1985); Office Building on Kurfürstendamm 70, Berlin (1986); Vitra Fire Station, Weil am Rhein, Germany (1989–93); and the Museo Nazionale delle arti del XXI secolo (MAXXI), Rome (1999–2009). These projects are key to the development of Hadid's architectural experimentation prior to her practice expanding under the influence of computers. Many paintings from these projects anticipate the new concepts exercised by that change while remaining handcrafted. It is also at this time that the structure of the office moved from being a small 'studio' to the current existing large architectural and design practice.

Selection of paintings within the projects is focused on the delivery of specific ideas rather than any attempt at a complete cataloguing of her work. Refining selection further, each painting included was completed close to the time of the initial design. For many projects, paintings continued to be produced over coming years. Two examples reveal the implication of changes that were introduced over time. The first is the *Malevich's Tektonik* painting series, the earliest of which was completed while Hadid was a student at the Architectural Association in London. There are several iterations for this painting. Each is titled slightly differently. They have differing sizes and were completed for different settings. What changes significantly is their portrayal of the importance of architectural drawing within the final painted imagery, with later copies changing to emphasise colour over line. Even this small change is significant. For this reason, I have used the earliest consideration of the work dated July 1976. It represents the level of thought of that time. A second example is commonly called *Day Night Grand Buildings* or simply *Grand Buildings*, which was completed for an exhibition at the Max Protetch Gallery in New York in 1987, while originating from the project called Grand Buildings completed in 1985. The compositional structure of this painting differs from those originally completed and 'speaks' to concerns of that later period. It is thus considered beyond the precise interests of the paintings completed immediately after the architectural competition of that title. The focus of that chapter remains on those earlier paintings.

Each painting examined will undergo a close interpretive analysis, beginning with visual descriptions that aim to reveal how within their compositional structures architectural ideas become layered and relational. Precedent images are compared, whether from the early 20th-century movements of Suprematism, Futurism and Surrealism, or from photography and other media, or from examples found in Renaissance and Baroque art and architecture. The paintings for each of Hadid's projects use specific techniques to refine their visual and theoretical attention, illustrating responses to changing debates in the architectural discipline and its settings. Each painting sees architecture's future as open ended, revealing how a continuing critical engagement with its disciplinary settings becomes pivotal to her intellectual renewal.

When paintings for a particular project are considered together as an integrated group, their combined propositions take on complex interdependencies not achieved through text, nor through single representations. Unlike text's linear formation, Hadid's paintings reveal how their compositional strategies have the capacity to activate idiosyncratic inquiry from each viewer. There is a distinction made between viewing at a distance and that where the focus is closer and more considered. As the viewer engages with these paintings across multiple images within an exhibition, their collective complex structuring prompts the reception of ideas over time and observation, where viewer responsiveness anticipates an 'apprehension' of the architecture without the expectation of a predetermined meaning.[7] The paintings infer a complex network of ideas bridging between architecture's formal description and painting's pictorial effects. This book's exploration is of a uniquely compelling relationship, of two integrated – yet often quite distinct – activities of architecture and painting.

Important in this book's inquiry is the particular way each painting was created and how it developed as an object in itself. Many interviews with Hadid's assistants informed analysis and are used to provide explanations of techniques and the approaches developed specifically for each artwork. Their multiple voices recognise Hadid's distinctive contribution to many of the paintings and the trust that she developed with them. Their knowledge supports this investigation, coalescing with visual interpretation to reveal how each painting embodies her subtle and unique ways of thinking about architecture. Within her studio environment, Hadid maintained a unique command of approach across her team, seeing their support as fundamental to an exploration and communication of her developing approach to architecture. Each team member recounted the impact of the numerous yellow Post-it® notes of tiny drawings that would appear on their work overnight.[8] They knew their role was to interpret these into drawings. Piers Smerin, who joined the team toward the end of 1983 when he was still a student, revealed in an aside, 'Everyone was equal, but everyone thought they were her favourite! She had that ability.'[9]

Chapter 1 examines the distinctive transformation by Hadid of architecture's technical drawing conventions. Her approach, initiated in the methods introduced by Elia Zenghelis and Rem Koolhaas when Hadid was a student, is explored through the painting *Malevich's Tektonik* and its implications for her first commissions. Of note is the issue of spatial 'grafting'. This is a term used by Zenghelis and Koolhaas in the requirements for students within their design task. It established both spatial and representational constructs within Hadid's projects that are unique. These ideas were fundamentally radicalised in the paintings completed for her brother's apartment: the project called 59 Eaton Place. In a move from drawing to painting, its paintings portray a precise set of experiments, adapting techniques from architecture while enabling a new spatiality from painting to be inscribed. Through painting, spatial fracture, inversion and distortion each became central to Hadid's critique of architecture's spatial potency.

Chapter 2 focuses on four paintings from her winning submission for The Peak Leisure Club, Hong Kong. They form a visual inquiry introducing the implications of Suprematist painting for her architecture and how these sat within other influences. The imagery of these paintings presents an idea of the temporality of the 'experiencing eye' influenced in part by Kazimir Malevich's notion of non-objective 'pictorial space'. The paintings reveal the potency of architecture's spatial role, particularly within a changing conception of the city as metropolis. Hadid's responses to questions of architectural space are framed as visual dialogues when paintings are paired. In the manner of a dialogue, alternative propositions offer each viewer an understanding of the breadth as well as the relational precision of her questioning of architecture's programmatic potential.

In Chapter 3 there is a focus on the series of paintings for the project Grand Buildings, London. As a collective, these paintings expand the implications of Hadid's earlier subverting of perspectival techniques seen in paintings for 59 Eaton Place. Perspective was not a technique that was commonly used in Suprematism. Traditionally, perspective techniques were bound within Euclidean geometry's concepts of a quantifiable space and the objective assumption of an external 'truth'. In Hadid's paintings for Grand Buildings, even though each painting is visualised and structured using perspectival conventions, any transference of this conceptual rigidity was avoided. Working like the notion of the 'photo stills' produced by Alexander Rodchenko, and Malevich's emphasis on sensation, Hadid's paintings for Grand Buildings emphasise the fragmented nature of sensation. It was also through Hadid's engagement with the exhibition *Les Immatériaux* in Paris at the Centre Pompidou, only months prior to the completion of her paintings for Grand Buildings, that their unique application of technique showed synergies with the approach taken by the exhibition's curatorial director, the philosopher Jean-François Lyotard. Through depictions of a series of ephemeral 'snapshots', the renewal of the historic city centre of London is politicised. New programs for the city are informed by individual experiences of the urban context as opposed to the monumentality of a city's ancient buildings and the order imposed by their symbolic axes. Hadid's paintings for Grand Buildings define an urban potential, with new sight lines and pedestrian movements across historic divisions. Each painting's fragmented view introduces a new dynamic aimed at liberating the cultural importance of areas, like Trafalgar Square in London, from the prescribed referencing of its imperial past.

Chapter 4 examines the paintings for the Office Building on Kurfürstendamm 70 in Berlin, where Hadid's focus expands her inquiry of the importance of sensation for architecture's urban presence. This project was undertaken at a time when Hadid was involved with discussions concerning immaterial effects on urban environments. Her paintings develop synergies specific to the writings of Paul Virilio. Each painting questions the inevitability of architecture's material form and its capacity to deliver meaning. They examine sensation in architecture at differing speeds. For Hadid speed remained important for the consideration of architecture's spatiality – but also its registration of surface through materials. In the paintings for Kurfürstendamm, Hadid presented architecture's situation in urban space as the juxtaposition of three speeds – the instantaneous, the idealised (static) and the sequential.

Chapter 5 examines paintings from Vitra Fire Station, Germany. These paintings emerged just after the exhibition *Deconstructivist Architecture* at MoMA in New York in 1988. It is a period when Hadid responded to questions related to the core propositions of deconstruction and contemporary architectural debates surrounding the writings of Jacques Derrida. In the Vitra paintings there is a visual transformation of architecture's role in the city, now becoming politically/critically potent within the layered and complex physical and intellectual contexts of its settings. Evidenced in the paintings for Vitra, architecture's material expression 'deconstructs' key aspects of the visual indicators of social and political boundaries defining urban space. Accepting the complicated nature of the 'ground's' territorial force, the Vitra Fire Station is visualised in an act of destabilising the political force of national borders by reinscribing their linear forms as motifs within its architecture. Existing and remnant lines of force in the environment are reworked as visual diffusers of the authority they once held.

Chapter 6 turns to the conjoined characteristics of architectural space, form and geometry in historic Rome. The paintings for the MAXXI project anticipate the powerful agency of recently emerging digital technologies on the geometries of the city. Early schematic designs, evidenced within the submitted panels for the competition, reveal Hadid's growing experimentation with fluid non-Euclidean geometries. For the paintings for the MAXXI these geometries become networked within the historic geometries of Rome's urban form. What is revealed through a close analysis of the paintings is the potency of Hadid's experimentation when placed beside Rome's historic examples of Donato Bramante and Francesco Borromini's architecture. Rome is considered a model for continuing urban experimentation, where architecture's changing spatial geometries situate the historical within the future typologies of the city.

The chronology informed by each project reveals how Hadid's focus on architecture grew increasingly interpretive. A back-and-forth approach, between the two-dimensional surface of painting and the material form of architecture, presented an illustration of how her own interpretive gaze modified over time. While each painting remains unique to the specificity of the site and program of a single project, as an oeuvre, the collective strength of these paintings portrays a complex and developing way of thinking about architecture's diagrammatic presence, understood through its spaces and material forms, its conceptual scale of operation and relationship with natural settings, and its impact on the visual and social constructs of cities.

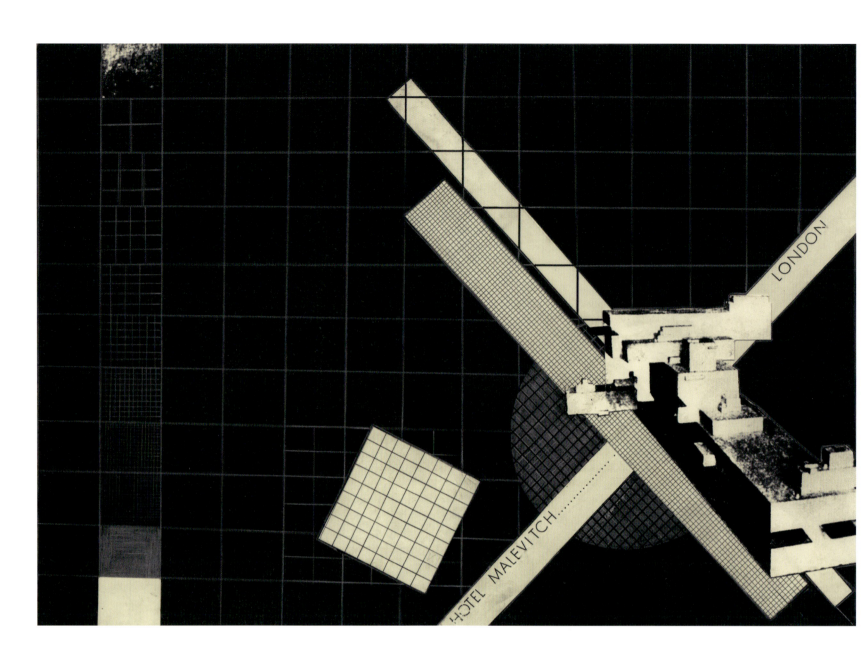

3
Zaha Hadid
*Malevich's Tektonik*, *Presentation Title Page*,
London, United Kingdom, 1976–77
Mixed media collage,
29.7 × 42 cm (11 11/16 × 16 1/2 in)
Zaha Hadid Foundation

# 1 From Lines to the Tactile Surface: *Malevich's Tektonik* to 59 Eaton Place

What is it when a viewer 'apprehends' architecture in their mind from its drawings? Architectural drawings have been considered a special case in artistic practices because they prompt the viewer to imagine something not directly present, to be 'apprehended' not as a result of observation of an external object but from the partial information these drawings provide.[1] Many of Zaha Hadid's architectural drawings were undertaken with this aim in mind, but others are unique, adding the effects of painting to develop a different supposition. These paintings extend the role of architectural drawing to question the broad agenda of what a consideration of architecture might mean in its many contexts. When, as an architectural student, she presented her scheme for the assignment called 'Tektonik' summarily using a single painting, its distinctiveness and radicality were clearly recognised. It 'pictured' an architecture in its physical setting, but through the influence of painting any definition of architecture's spatial and material consequences remained elusive. This image engaged the viewer to develop questions rather than imagine the clarity of an architectural 'object' as realised. Hadid's assessors wrote in her 'Session Report': 'Zaha's performance . . . was like that of a rocket that took off slowly to describe a constantly accelerating trajectory. Now she is a PLANET, in her own inimitable orbit.'[2]

Hadid studied at the Architectural Association London (AA) and in the 1975/76 academic year her tutors Elia Zenghelis and Rem Koolhaas had developed a complex project brief for their teaching Unit. Its task required students to work together in small groups to use a 1920s sculpture created by Russian avant-garde artist Kazimir Malevich – one of his *Arkhitekton*, 'mutating' its form to respond to the architectural scale, size and urban intensity of London.[3] Overlaying the brief requirements was the demand that students were to work in the manner of the Surrealist practice of *Le Cadavre Exquis*, by 'grafting' each other's individual component designs without full knowledge of the other's.[4] However, because of illness, Hadid had completed the project alone. As a result, her design and its application of spatial 'grafting' had the power to shock architectural audiences.[5]

Initially, the representation of her scheme took the form of a portfolio of black and white drawings (figs 3 and 4). The scheme's signature coloured painting, *Malevich's Tektonik*, dated and signed 'Zaha July 1976', is modelled on attributes of one drawing in the folio, adapting its formal complexity through the colouration and compositional strategies of Suprematist paintings (fig.5).[6] Copies and developments of this painting have been displayed since that time as if symbolising the origins of Hadid's architectural thinking. From the many examples, comparison with *Horizontal Tektonik,* dated 1977 and held in the San Francisco Museum of Modern Art, prompts discussion of its dating and the distinctiveness of her earliest painting (fig.1).[7] Comparing her 1976 *Malevich's Tektonik* with the later *Horizontal Tektonik* reveals many similarities; however, the distinctive use of planar colour and abstraction in relation to the drawn line in the earlier example becomes a defining attribute of her approach as a student. The earlier *Malevich's Tektonik* was not a static application of the conventions of architectural drawing, but by retaining

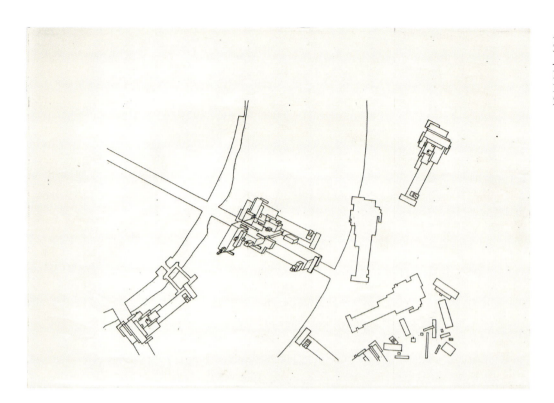

4
**Zaha Hadid**
*Malevich's Tektonik, Axonometric*,
London, United Kingdom, 1977
Ink on paper, 29.7 × 42 cm (11 11/16 × 16 1/2 in)
Zaha Hadid Foundation

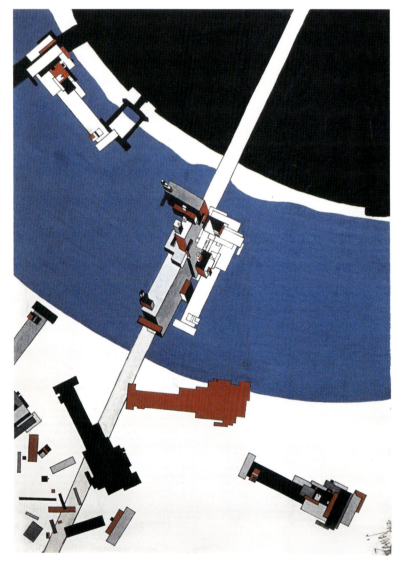

5
**Zaha Hadid**
*Malevich's Tektonik*,
London, United Kingdom, 1976
Acrylic on card, 42 × 60 cm (16 1/2 × 23 5/8 in)
Zaha Hadid Foundation

the dominant lines of a technical architectural drawing, it reflected an openly challenging consideration of architecture, its space–form relations, and issues that affect architecture's role as an urban artefact.

### Architecture's Lines: *Malevich's Tektonik*

The 'Tektonik' project required students to develop 'a form of urbanism appropriate to the final part of the 20th Century', exploiting the unique cultural possibilities of high density living.[8] Zenghelis and Koolhaas's aim for their teaching Unit was for students to form a connection between 'ideology and architecture', delivering 'standards against which . . . the existing can be "measured" and critiqued'.[9] Koolhaas explained his method of *Le Cadavre Exquis* through the design strategies evident in Le Corbusier's *Voisin Plan for Paris* (fig.6).[10]

Koolhaas claimed that Le Corbusier's project had simply 'grafted' the new development as one organism onto another – the city – 'in deliberate ignorance of its further anatomy'.[11] Koolhaas's term 'grafted' was specifically applied to affirm there was no smoothing of the edge conditions or sympathetic architectural contextualism in the process of this insertion. His desire for the project 'Tektonik' was that by taking a focus on London, students would more critically engage with their own environment close at hand, 'grafting' their responses without being swayed by historical contexts that might diminish experimentation.

Hadid's 1976 painting *Malevich's Tektonik* explains the conceptual force of Zenghelis and Koolhaas's expectation for the student projects that year. With abrupt clarity, her final scheme placed Malevich's sculpture *Alpha Arkhitekton* onto London's Hungerford Bridge. In her memory of the time, Hadid has spoken of hearing Zenghelis lecture on Russian Constructivism in her first year at the AA in 1972/73.[12] She also mentions the importance of Suprematist and Russian avant-garde art being heightened prior to 1975 because of a 'show' that had occurred.[13] The most likely candidate for this locally was *Tatlin's Dream: Russian Suprematist and Constructivist Art 1910–1923* at Fischer Fine Art Gallery, local to the AA in London, showing from November 1973 to January 1974.[14] Response to this exhibition dominates the magazine *Studio International* in the March/April edition of 1975, a copy of which is held at the library of the Architectural Association. A second potential 'show' was a major retrospective of Malevich's paintings in the exhibition *Malevich as a Counterrevolutionary*, at the Solomon R. Guggenheim Museum, New York, in 1973–74.[15] While it remains unclear which was the focus of Hadid's comment, the brief that Zenghelis and Koolhaas developed ignited Hadid's further interest. She was to describe her response as a proposition to 'superimpose the Tektonik on the Hungerford Bridge on the chance'.[16]

Following the representational strategies of Suprematism, that year her final scheme used the axonometric techniques of architectural drawing, outlining its forms with geometrically precise black ink lines (fig.7). Even in the first black and white renderings of this drawing there is a clarity given to the surfaces of the forms, where selected planes are rendered in solid black, drawing attention to the form's spatial modulation. The effect retained the geometric purity of the sculpture's contiguous surface and was without the confusion of depicting architectural elements like windows, structure or materials.

In much the same manner as Koolhaas interpreted from the Voisin project of Le Corbusier, Hadid's drawings superimposed an 'architecture' as if 'grafted' onto an existing urban setting. However, while retaining the linear attributes of drawing, it is through the addition of colour in her painting that this message becomes nuanced.

6
Le Corbusier
*Voisin Plan for Paris*, photograph of model,
Paris, France, 1925
Fondation Le Corbusier, Paris

7
Zaha Hadid
'Tektonik in Thames', (detail) *Architectural Association School of Architecture, Projects Review 1975–76*, London, United Kingdom, 1976
Print
The Architectural Association

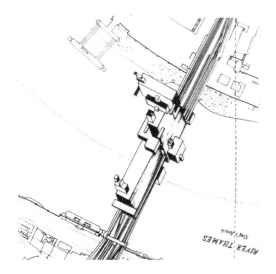

Hadid's limited Suprematist palette of red, tones of grey, and black on a white, blue and black ground introduces a continuity across the pictorial surface emphasising the possibility of visual networks implicit to painting.

While there are precedents for the self-assured nature of this act of 'grafting' in Malevich's own photographic collage *Arkhitekton in Front of a Skyscraper* from 1924, Hadid's resolution transformed the idea of collaging into a spatial and architectural act with its combination of architectural drawing with painting (fig.8).[17] Through an understanding of Le Corbusier's 'graft' at Voisin, her *Malevich's Tektonik* painting registers not just the disjuncture between collaged elements, but through the act of insertion itself, the scheme spatially transformed London.

As the backdrop to the scheme, the city of London as a potent source of architecture and infrastructure is not used as an historical prompt for new development. Reinforcing a simplicity that belies reality, the city's forms become recognisable only through a viewer's knowledge of shapes such as Festival Pier and the Thames River. The cardinal directions of North, South, East, West have been inverted for the painting, with the abstracted form of Central London located at the bottom of the composition. The conceptual complexity of London's geographical and social division signified by the curving linearity of the Thames is now black and white, forming an opposition that reinforced commonly held values.

Within this compositional structure, Malevich's *Alpha Arkhitekton* is portrayed with each facet and plane made distinct through changes of hue and tone controlled within the linearity of the drawing. Beside it is a wire-framed drawing that mirrors the imagery of the *Arkhitekton* on the bridge and extends this emphasis. It suggests an impossible shadow cast onto the river or a further architectural program, flipped and located just below the water's surface. The precise flat colouration of the forms of the bridge's *Arkhitekton*, in red, black and grey tones, directs the viewer's eye to other similar plan shapes at Festival Pier, and then diagonally toward other 'floating' shapes located on the lower part of the composition. This implied connection visually crosses the diagonal made explicit by the extensions of Hungerford Bridge across the complete picture. Onto this 'X', and central to the composition itself, is Hadid's Hotel Malevich, London.[18]

The painting's configuration is further complicated by coloured fragments haphazardly strewn on the northern shore of the Thames where Charing Cross Station, the Embankment and the Strand are currently located. Replacing their programs are silhouettes of the 'Arkhitekton', scattered and coloured in red and black, and set beside a further collection of small, coloured fragments. They have not yet been assigned any programmatic purpose: their forms are placed as if ready for application in the same way as one might set out pieces before completing a jigsaw puzzle.

The viewer of this painting is encouraged to move their gaze across the full composition, an act countering the clarity and purpose of an architectural drawing. However, because of its relatively small size (inferred by the thickness of the drawn line), the actual line work of the drawing, created by using Rotring Rapidograph drafting pens, remains an important part of this 1976 painting. It is an attribute not seen in later larger-scaled copies, including the 1977 version. While colour prompts an engagement across the pictorial surface, it is these lines so importantly bordering each surface profile that underpin the architectural force of the imagery.

Between the emphasis on line in *Malevich's Tektonik* and the layered planarity of paintings for the project 59 Eaton Place, Hadid's manner of representation underwent a significant transformation, introducing a consideration of what painting offered to architecture as a locus of thought. Many of Hadid's early projects, even though becoming more expressive in their drawing, continued to distil the relationship where the architectural drawing remains explicit to a delivery of

8
Kazimir Malevich
*Arkhitekton in Front of a Skyscraper*, 1924
Photograph, *Praesens* 1, 1926
Getty Research Institute

meaning within each painting. It is the strength of the drawn line that dominates their compositions. Examples can be seen in the paintings for The Museum of the Nineteenth Century (1977) and the Irish Prime Minister's Residence (1979) projects, where the linearity required by technical architectural drawing remains dominant, and colour while intensely applied is used only to support their outline. Colour is used to infill the spaces between lines rather than compete with the line's architectural references. Selected colours when repeated across the pictorial composition engage the viewer's interest without supplanting the dominance of drawing.

This approach changed significantly in the paintings for the project known as 59 Eaton Place. Here, the hierarchy between architectural drawing and the act of painting is blurred. In the Eaton Place paintings, the application of colour focuses on the tactile qualities of architecture's surfaces, often removing the presence of drawing altogether. Within the three Eaton Place paintings, Hadid explores painting's conventions and techniques as having implications beyond the scope of technical drawing in architecture.[19] Conceptually, something changes through this process of development. Within the precise graphic explorations embedded in these paintings, architectural spatiality is revealed as having attributes beyond the conventions of drawing.

### The Tactility of the Painted Surface in Architecture's Spatial Inquiry: 59 Eaton Place

Zaha Hadid's project 59 Eaton Place was a reconsideration of an existing residential interior. The clients, Hadid's brother Foulath, his wife and their daughter, aimed to reconfigure their home, a maisonette split over three levels of a large heritage-listed townhouse located in Belgravia. Hadid's family, still associated with Baghdad and Iraqi life, but to a lesser extent its politics, had long connections with Britain.[20] Foulath and his family were living primarily in London while travelling for business between Iraq, North America, Morocco and Europe. Hadid explained her family context saying: 'I came from . . . a background that believes in internationalism and an open view of the world . . . I come from a tradition of modernism, a tradition of looking forward and trying to do things in a very progressive way.'[21]

Work on the design of the project began in 1980 and was Hadid's first significant commission in her new Studio Zaha Hadid. Explaining this in an early interview, she said: 'My office is really more of a studio which I think is important. I have always thought the problem with most practices is that there is almost no connection between practice and ideas like there is in school, and I really wanted a studio where you could test ideas.'[22]

Though the project was never realised, it was visualised in 1981 within three large-scaled paintings for the exhibition *Planetary Architecture* held at Galerie van Rooy in Amsterdam.[23] The three large paintings for 59 Eaton Place have the secondary titles *Plot of Internal Elements*, *Aerial Perspective of the Master Bedroom and Library*, and *Three Towers: the Flamboyant, the Suprematist, the Clinical*.[24] These paintings were included in other exhibitions throughout 1982: the Architectural Association School of Architecture's exhibition *Larger than Life: Cedric Price: The Home / Zaha Hadid: 59 Eaton Place*[25] and the exhibition *British Architecture 1982*, held at the Royal Institute of British Architects, London.[26]

The paintings were generated by hand as drawings, transferred to large sheets of paper and then painted with acrylics. Their complexity can partly be attributed to the working environment of Hadid's office. Nan Lee joined Hadid's team as the first colourist and specialist painter. She recalls interviewing for her job in 1981 by completing a very large painting over the big table in Hadid's mews house well into the night 'with Zaha painting opposite', equally engaged in the painting.[27] Many of those working with Hadid in this period remember fondly the collaborative nature of the work.[28] It is best summed up by Jonathan Dunn who recalls:

> Along with two other people in the studio, I would translate Zaha's sketches which were dynamic, vast strokes of the pen... For 59 Eaton Place I was trying to attach some of the reality of this Grade II listed building to the scheme. Then, through a series of initial studies, paintings, you know, in acrylics, watercolour, and drawn using Rotring Rapidograph pens, we extended ideas. These went through a series of stages, with Zaha coming in and looking at them, and sometimes tearing bits off or marking over the top, we would develop these 'sketches' to a point where they became more and more coherent, and, more and more detailed. You could almost call them maquettes for the final painting. We got to a point where it was going to happen! And then we would draw onto big sheets of cartridge paper. And this was it, it was going to be the painting... The only real influence we had over her was of a painterly or artistic nature. But this was minor. The intellectual property was hers. Yes, of course, we had ideas, and there was a lot of talking that went on amongst the group. But there was no doubt, when it went on the page it was either the right colour or the wrong colour. It was either the right fenestration, or line, or shape, or it wasn't, there didn't seem to be any middle ground in her mind.[29]

In the paintings for 59 Eaton Place, through the expressiveness enabled by painting, Hadid undid the essential bond in architecture between its conventions of orthographic drawing of plan, elevations and sections and its traditional humanist values of aesthetics, social order and material tectonics.[30] These three paintings register a point of change in Hadid's exploration of painting's agency in her architectural thought.

### Spatial Reversals and the Isometric: *59 Eaton Place, Plot of Internal Elements*

The painting *59 Eaton Place, Plot of Internal Elements* uses isometric projection techniques to portray a three-dimensional 'view' of the scheme's plans, extending an understanding of the interior's form and furnishings (fig.9). In the overall composition, however, this documentation is a small component. Its imagery is almost overwhelmed by the painting's compositional detail and colouration.

Because of this detail, and when viewed at a distance, the painting's most obvious visual effect comes from the three distinctive bands of background tones, diagonally cutting across its composition. Each tone builds a different narrative emphasis for imagery. The tone of the lower third, coloured a warm grey, portrays reminders of the London townhouse exterior facade, showing windows, doors and other entry elements. Their repetitive and semi-abstracted grid-like formation exaggerates flatness rather than the modulation of surfaces in the classical details and divisions of the actual building. The middle third has a darkened grey tonality, a diagonal flat band of coloured grids, outlined and separated by regular linear divisions of a lighter tone. These grids extend each side of the isometric drawing of the maisonette, but because of their varied tonality, the inner section of each appears to have vast depth. Their light-toned grid-like divisions are also abstractly

9
Zaha Hadid Architects
*59 Eaton Place, Plot of Internal Elements*,
London, United Kingdom, 1981
Acrylic on paper, 158 × 97 cm (62¼ × 38³⁄₁₆ in)
Zaha Hadid Foundation

suggestive of the wall patterns of the townhouses in plan with their alternating orientations. The upper third of the composition adopts a different pictorial function. Its deep teal-grey colouring is modulated from dark to light across the background, giving the impression of a void-like backdrop behind the tableau of scenes below. Over its vast space, small elements extend from the central imagery, as if hovering unconnected to the interiors.

Onto this tripartite division, the detail of each compositional band is intricately coloured with an abstract arrangement of small shapes that become independently networked. What is important in any attempted apprehension of its architecture in the mind is that viewers will be encouraged to engage intimately, moving in to focus on details when close. It is here that viewers will become aware of spatial inversions that were not so important at a distance. In the lower third of the painting, when close, the abstracted facade elements portrayed have the potential to be interpreted as if projected from different geometric orientations – where the grid of windows comes forward toward the viewer, suggesting the windows float in a void with their grid-like formation projected onto the isometric's flat horizontal absence. Or, alternatively, they can be perceived as falling downward toward the base of the painting, lying flat on the implied facade surface. The effect introduces an Escher-like instability to the image.[31]

Part of this illusion is aided by a juxtaposition between the stripped-back facade-like elements and the pictorial 'ground'. This 'ground' fills the complete pictorial field in this section of the painting. While it has a surface-like quality, emulating the facade of the 19th-century London terrace, its void-like qualities dislodge any ease of its comprehension as a building. Visual information appears precisely defined yet unreal, changing the way viewers engage. There is an intentional move away from seeking the drawing as architectural information to a focus on the painting's sense of surface. By including architectural elements, their fragmentation and floating bring a spatial slippage or movement that introduces a potentially distinct consideration of architecture. In response, viewers might question how this schema relates to the object-like status of the architecture of Belgravia, where traditionally its forms have been conceived as historically detailed, substantive and solid.

Spatial illusions continue in the middle third of the composition where the main living floors of the scheme are portrayed. Their interior details are shown throughout the isometric drawing that is central to this area. Further attributes of the interior, like basement levels and reflected ceiling plans, fill the containment of the grid-like divisions either side. However, there is a spatial deception at play in the way that both upper and lower levels of the scheme have been incorporated in a single plane within this area of the painting. The footprint of the upper floor of the maisonette has been flipped in both directions, extending the surfaces of the lower levels toward an imagined street to the rear of Eaton Place (figs 10 and 11). Those with knowledge of this location and its street patterns would understand that this is not the mews at the rear of the property. Instead, in this rendition of Eaton Place the interior of the upper floor conforms with its now-inverted street plan. Here the master bedroom of the scheme, known to be directly inside the Eaton Place facade, is located at the furthest point of the imagery. The seamlessness of these two interiors, and their 'bridging' of distinctly different spatial planes, is negotiated pictorially by flattening a depiction of the internal elevation of the rear wall, used here to cover the width of the idealised rear lane.

The resulting imagery supports the illusion of spatial continuity between the differing levels of the maisonette. It provides a reminder that our own memory of interior settings is as much supported by personal experiences of the distances travelled and connections made in our own domestic spaces, as it is reflected within

10
Zaha Hadid Architects
(detail) *59 Eaton Place, Plot of Internal Elements*, London, United Kingdom, 1981
Acrylic on paper
Zaha Hadid Foundation

the dominating spatial logic and separations of architecture's traditional drawing conventions.

When hung, the painting reaches over two metres in height, details stretch above eye-height and beyond the visual reach of many viewers. Much of the detail of this central band of imagery becomes lost within the complexity of the composition. What is illustrated by bringing these plans together is an impossible spatial resolution, even though each element is precisely portrayed and is locatable with reference to other drawings. Through the selection of colours, elements begin to perform particularly painterly functions, extending the complexity of Hadid's architectural strategy. For example, in the representation of the lift core, steps and fitments, there is a level of conformity to the expectations of architectural drawings; however, it is through colour and texture that the pictorial and spatial strategy of the painting's imagery emerges. This is evidenced in the repetition of specific colours, for example the colour vermillion. Occurring in just three locations across the painting, its full chromatic value stands out against each background. In the lower third of the composition, it is used in an entry path. Within the middle section, vermillion occurs in the interior on a bench surface associated with the library. Thirdly, it is used to colour a small triangular fragment associated with peripheral wall elements to the left of the main interiors. This colour's extension through tone provides further connections with the pale dusty pinks that are used in steps, windows, interior fittings and a screen in the main bedroom. In recognising these relationships, each viewer is guided to engage with the painting in a different way, rather than seek only its architectural knowledge.

The proximity of different colours becomes suggestive of visual networks within the painting's composition that are spatially meaningful. Vermillion, like other colours, draws attention to the idea of potential relationships in the architecture, referencing in the mind of the viewer as they negotiate the painting's composition and the architecture's implied spatial complexity. What is suggested by these attributes of the painting is that visitors to this imagined apartment will pass the colour vermillion on the entry, and then see it referenced again at other stages throughout the interior.[32] Such information builds up in the mind, inviting consideration of the spatial potential of architecture as distinct from its formal containment through room divisions and their functions. In the process of inquiry, the viewer is drawn toward certain spatial affects, as colour draws attention to connections that might otherwise have been left unseen.

This effect from colour combines with the spatial inversion evident within the painting's depiction of 'flipped' floor plans. It is commonly known that isometric and axonometric drawing techniques have the capacity to present spatial inversions in what they depict. It is also a common understanding in architecture that drawing a cube using isometric projection can increase the ambiguity of its spatiality.[33] In the mind of the viewer, the cube can invert, appearing to be either concave and above, or convex and below their gaze. The use of this as part of the architectural intent has a distinctive history. It was a technique used by Peter Eisenman throughout the drawings of his House projects, carried out in the mid-1970s, and continuing to the mid-1980s.[34] He had argued that the abstraction enabled by the axonometric and isometric projection supported an investigation of architecture at a conceptual level.

The effect was best known in architectural debates through the Suprematist drawing, *Axonometric Projection of the Proun Room* of 1923 by El Lissitzky (fig.12). The implications of its convex/concave illusions and their tie to isometric and axonometric projection became clear in the installation of the room at the *Great Berlin Art Exhibition* in 1923.[35] Art and architectural theorist Yve-Alain Bois has

11
Zaha Hadid Architects
(detail) *59 Eaton Place, Plot of Internal Elements*, London, United Kingdom, 1981
Acrylic on paper
Zaha Hadid Foundation

12
El Lissitzky
*Axonometric Projection of the Proun Room Installed at the Greater Berlin Art Exhibition*, 1923
Print, ink on tracing paper,
44.3 × 59.9 cm (17⁷⁄₁₆ × 23⁹⁄₁₆ in)
Centre Canadien d'Architecture /
Canadian Centre for Architecture

argued that by the early 20th century, the conventions defining both isometric and axonometric drawings inferred a distinct spatiality outside the naturalism of perspectival representation. He explained how both Malevich and Lissitzky had recognised the isometric and axonometric drawing technique as embodying the potential for 'irrational space'.[36] It raises the question of whether Hadid's interest for architecture came as a result of this type of inquiry.

In Hadid's painting *Plot of Internal Elements*, because of this capacity within the conventions of the isometric, the visual understanding of back/front and interior/exterior becomes fluid in a pictorial as well as an architectural sense. Spatial slippage, reinforced by colour or tone and texture, extends Lissitzky's ideas as having implications for the conceptual structuring of architectural space. Hadid's interest in repeating and extending his experimentation identifies her interest in revealing an alternative spatial interaction able to be embedded within architecture. The complex layering of ideas in her painting creates a level of critique of architectural traditions of representation, highlighting the importance of sensate responses within the spaces of the maisonette. Rather than reinforce the authority of architectural drawing practices, the painting's use of colour, tone and surface texture describes a spatial tension developing between a yet to be realised building, its graphic representation, and how viewers are invited to respond to painting's visual effects.

### Spatial Distortion and the Perspective:
*59 Eaton Place, Aerial Perspective of the Master Bedroom and Library*

Hadid's descriptive title *Aerial Perspective of the Master Bedroom and Library* returns the expectations of the viewer to the apparent norms of perspectival representation, a move perhaps at odds with the exploration of the previous isometrically generated painting (fig.13). In one sense the subject of this painting could be considered as a form of natural scenography. But the more the painting is examined, the more this potential seems to evaporate.

13
**Zaha Hadid Architects**
*59 Eaton Place, Aerial Perspective of the Master Bedroom and Library,*
London, United Kingdom, 1981
Acrylic on paper, 201.3 × 112 cm (79¼ × 44 in)
Zaha Hadid Foundation

As explained by the title, the painting uses perspectival techniques, but it does so while introducing a level of expressiveness and distortion not usual in architectural uses of this technique. The subtlety of these changes directly effects viewer expectations for the purpose of this view. The painting's composition relies on a single vanishing point that locates the viewer's downward gaze toward the floor plan, seeing directly into the two main rooms of the upper floor. Vertical distortion, stretching the height of walls, furniture and fitments within their interior, creates an effect on this space in much the same way as Alice (in Wonderland) would have imagined being depicted after drinking from a certain bottle that implored her to 'Drink Me!'[37] By being raised above this distorted scene, the viewer is presented with an equally distorted sense of their own 'reality' as they seem to propel away from the scene. When comparing this strategy to other examples from the fine arts, this type of exaggerated stretching of form can be observed in Salvador Dalí's *The Temptation of St. Anthony* of 1946 (fig.14). Its animals and buildings alike are extended unnaturally as they rise above the ground. But, in this example, the grounded position of the viewer reinforces an embodied action – as St. Anthony shuns the advancement of his ever-insistent temptations.

This effect opens questions related to the architectural purpose of Hadid's *Aerial Perspective of the Master Bedroom and Library*. The imagery of the architecture's surfaces and textures in this scene expands around the viewer both repelling and attracting further inquiry. There is a certain hedonism within the sumptuous tactility of each rendered surface, the soft silk canopy, and a textured wall reminiscent of leather, each contrasting with harsher surfaces of metal and glass. Unlike typical architectural drawings, their appeal directly engages an emotional response from the viewer, informed by their own memories and sensations as they recognise the feel and distinctive aroma of materials they have encountered, rather than the architecture's objective verity.

This type of pictorial effect 'speaks' to the viewer and introduces specific expectations for their reaction. In part the compositional structuring of this painting critiques the conventions usual in historic examples of architectural drawing. Historian Martin Jay has claimed that since the early Renaissance, representations using perspectival techniques have been considered as equivalent to the objectivity of vision: presenting a rational and geometrically verifiable documentation of a 'realistic' scene.[38] Albrecht Dürer's image of the draughtsman's relationship with the scene they are drawing is well known. Its spatial construct from the eye of the draughtsman to the object being considered is a 'singular' and continuous geometry – defined within the strict empiricism of mathematical relationships (fig.15).

In a theoretical discussion of these early techniques in painting, Martin Kemp has shown that within art and architectural representation, the eye was implied

14
Salvador Dalí
*The Temptation of St. Anthony*, 1946
Oil on canvas, 90 × 119.5 cm (35 7/16 × 47 in)
Musées Royaux des Beaux Arts, Brussels, Belgium

15
Albrecht Dürer
*Draughtsman Making a Perspective Drawing of a Reclining Woman*, ca.1600
Woodblock, 7.7 × 21.4 cm (3 × 8 7/16 in)
The Metropolitan Museum, New York

16
Robert Blemmell Schnebbelie
*Perspective of Burlington Arcade*, London, 1827
Black ink and coloured washes on paper,
21.5 × 27.5 cm (8½ × 10¹³⁄₁₆ in)
Drawing Matter Collections, Somerset

as the viewing 'mechanism', through which perspective's mathematically derived geometries work to describe a scene's verity as empirically measured evidence.[39] This logic insists on the idea that there is a naturalism within the perspectival 'view', where the position of objects portrayed reflects what the eye observes. In architecture, perspectival 'correctness' supports an aesthetics of decorum in the realised architecture's response to order in society and its institutions.[40]

In architectural practice, this illusion of accuracy has influenced the application of perspective techniques.[41] Since the Renaissance, perspectival geometries have been thought of as having a mathematical integrity, bringing together a yet to be realised building with an existing reality. The geometry defining the horizon line and picture plane determined the eye's association with the ground, and sets up the image's angle of orientation and ground condition.[42] As a technique, the application of perspectival geometry in architectural representation develops an agreed distortion in the objects portrayed, to give the impression of a consistent and measurable spatial depth diminishing toward infinity.[43] Leon Battista Alberti's writing on architecture at this time emphasised that through drawing, the architect 'desires his work to be judged . . . according to certain calculated standards'.[44]

By comparison, an example from the architect Robert Blemmell Schnebbelie, *Perspective of Burlington Arcade*, London, drawn in 1827, shows the continuing importance in architectural drawing to focus predominantly on these 'calculated standards' (fig.16). Within the complexity of this image there is an attempted naturalism introduced by depicting the new architecture within its urban context and by the application of colour and tone, adjoining buildings and the inclusion of the human figures. However, the resulting view reinforces accuracy of measure providing an understanding of architectural form, scale and materiality to reinforce the appeal of the arcade, bringing natural light into the deep recesses of its interior. These are all attributes that anticipate the reality of the building within its setting and enable the viewer to appreciate its economic and social benefit: its moral decorum.

Two 17th-century paintings usefully illustrate how Hadid's perspectival structuring changes this emphasis and moves imagery away from the verifiability of the drawn line in architecture to the spatiality availed by painting. An initial step is that Hadid's imagery in *Aerial Perspective of the Master Bedroom and Library* takes the focus away from perspectival verity by introducing linear effects that divert viewer attention. This type of visual strategy can be compared with the example of Tintoretto's *Removal of the Body of Saint Mark* of 1562–66 (fig.17). In his exploration of the Tintoretto painting, James Elkins draws attention to the purposeful elongation of the depth of the background setting and weighting of the scene in the foreground to one side of the composition.[45] In his view, this visual strategy was used to direct the attention of viewers away from the centrality of the perspectival view and toward its unfolding narrative. The viewer is encouraged to negotiate the spatiality of this painting and its meaning rather than passively position themselves as a reflection of the scene's 'decorum'.

A second example illustrates how these painterly effects have architectural implications. Andrea Pozzo's painted ceiling for the nave of the Church of Sant' Ignazio di Loyola in Rome, has introduced anamorphic geometries to exaggerate spatial depth, stretching the images of figures and their architectural settings to give the impression of a space many times higher than the architectural reality (fig.18).[46] It is a schema that relies on strict geometry, but one requiring this geometry to appear as if the spatiality of the world is exaggerated, encouraging viewers to find an optimal location, where the view conforms to the logic of their vision.

When comparing Hadid's perspectival composition with these visual strategies developed from painting's techniques, certain approaches are clarified reinforcing viewer interpretations of her imagery. As noted earlier, implied within her painting the viewer floats above the ground at a distance. What they perceive is a world strangely exploding in depth away from what was expected. Like Pozzo's ceiling this has been structured using a precise geometry. Yet, when close to Hadid's painting, each viewer's attention will be directed to the fabric and sensual materiality of furnishing and fitments within this 'dream-scape'. A vertically stretched four-poster bed is portrayed with a soft grey silk canopy, then vertically aligned above this in the painting is an intricately textured screen rendered in a grid of browns and black – as if made of leather or fine timbers – and opposite is a wall unit enclosing a deeply recessed plunge bath in earthy shades. Their sensory reminders of softness are offset by the starkly rendered cobalt blue fins that define the entry of the master bedroom.

This effect continues within the library space in the middle of the composition, where there is a black marble table lined with veins of white and grey, a dramatically stretched black wall unit with a grid of openings contrasting with its mechanised yellow table, and the red bench unit opposite. These main 'events' depict hard surfaces and contrast with the intricate colouring of the library shelving located on a walkway linking the master bedroom to the spa and gym. Further up the painting's expanse is the yellow glass-block wall of the spa and gym that distorts beyond the spatial controls of perspectival representation. In combination, these deliver an extraordinary collection of sensations, where each element of the painting has a precision that suggests a tactility which highlights their sensuality.

A further series of strategies from painting are apparent when Hadid's painting is displayed in a gallery. They rely on attracting the viewer's attention away from the painting's vanishing point. Their gaze will follow lines, shapes and suggested directionality to grasp a meaning implied by what they are guided to see. Like imagery in the Tintoretto painting, there is the initial magnetic pull of the vanishing point attracting the viewer's attention toward the empty centre of the bedroom – a move then countered by the detail of the composition. In this spatial diversion, the visual 'weight' introduced by the darkness of the wall-tones

17
Jacopo Tintoretto
*Removal of the Body of Saint Mark*, 1562–66
Oil on canvas, 397 × 315 cm (156¼ × 124 in)
Gallerie dell'Accademia, Venice

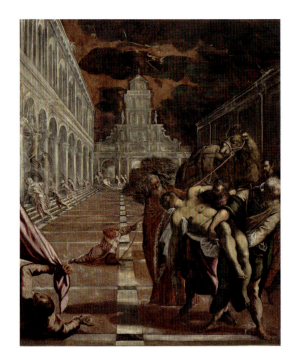

18
Andrea Pozzo
Central Nave, Sant'Ignazio di Loyola,
fresco ceiling, Rome, 1685

either side of the composition, and the apparent u-shape occurring with the visual integration of the facade wall, become dominant. The darkness of the hue surrounding the floor provides an atmospheric weight to the lower section of the image, encouraging the viewer to move their attention between side walls, and to register the room's containment. This effect 'moves the eye' around the composition while purposefully avoiding the static nature of perspectival representation in architecture.

It references the visual impact of a near horizontal 'cut' across the painting, aligned with the top of the dividing wall between the bedroom and library. Extending to the right perimeter of the painting it 'cuts' across a darker shadow behind the wall. On the left, it calls attention to the chevron of dark grey tone that expands from the imagined vanishing point. Both elements direct the viewer's gaze to leave the painting's boundary as they counter the pull of the vanishing point. It is only through the introduction of balance in the form of the perpendicular lightly rendered floor surface, defining the passage leading to the spa and gym, that attention is directed back to explore further attributes central to the architecture. Here, attention shifts again to small areas of detailed chromatically pure colour. These colours, including red, yellow and blue, influence the viewer's gaze to travel across the image, reinforcing its two-dimensional diagrammatic effect. They work pictorially to network relationships. Included are the yellow tiled wall of the gym, the red of the bench of the library, the blue of the bedroom entry fins, the multicoloured bookshelves and the yellow of the adjustable table in the dining room. As a group, the use of colour acts to disrupt the geometric controls of perspectival drawing conventions, and influence the viewer's attention to wander across the pictorial surface.

Through an emphasis on the colouration of surfaces, their shading and the juxtaposition of dark and light tonality, Hadid introduces spatial effects that are more explicitly available from painting. By making viewers prolong their engagement with the process of inquiry, to resolve the competing 'forces' within this painting's imagery and its pictorial construction, there is an acceptance developed between architecture and the possibility of spatial experimentation.

## The Dissection of Architectural Space:
## 59 Eaton Place, Three Towers:
## the Flamboyant, the Suprematist, the Clinical

In contrast to *Plot of Internal Elements*, the painting *Three Towers: the Flamboyant, the Suprematist, the Clinical* takes on a distinctive visual logic (fig.19). While they both use isometric techniques, *Three Towers* illustrates the isometric's relation to the architectural section rather than its plan. In its compositional structure, elements are separated where selected interior volumes and forms have been isolated and spaced across the pictorial field. Commonly known as an 'exploded' isometric, this type of drawing had more common uses in mechanical or industrial engineering, where these drawings document the relationships between components to order and aid their assembly. However, within the imagery of the interior of Hadid's scheme this nomenclature is more idiosyncratic and prompts questions of how it supports architectural understanding, to ask: what is being pulled apart, and for what purpose?

In this painting, there are clear references to architecture being considered as a series of fragments to be assembled, but their reassembly is not about the apprehension of their form as a building. To respond to the question above, each attribute of the painting becomes important. Viewed from left to right, the painting begins with a depiction of a public road, understood through its colour against a dashed yellow centre line. It is followed by the vertical front wall of the townhouse, stripped from attachment to floors and viewed from the interior. Beyond this is a juxtaposition of elements inferring possible internal fittings and architectural features. The architecture becomes less explicit as the viewer's attention moves to the right, where, for example, a series of 'punctured' holes are shown at a different scale to the main isometric 'section', and a flattened horizontal black wall with regular openings is represented at the base of the composition.

Each element of the painting requires the attention of viewers to assign meaning, thereby reassembling parts in the mind in order to personally resolve their architectural implications. While there are many indicators of architecture evident throughout the composition (steps, walls and furniture, for example), their meaning is obfuscated with the introduction of differing architectural scales suggesting a conceptual disjuncture between what would be expected of technical drawing and painting's capacity to express through colour, abstraction and/or precise visual metaphors.

In some areas there is a distinctive and purposeful retention of the linear effects of architectural drawing. This can be seen in the outline of stairs and edges of aerial passageways. However, in other areas there is no sense of the drawing, and the painting dominates with the extent of surfaces defined only by their juxtaposition of changing shades – as in the internal surface of the front facade or the changing profile of the blue ceiling/wall element in the dining room. Where outlines occur, they are retained for specific purposes and are not continuous. Instead, the emphasis in this painting is on the impact of planes and surfaces rather than the linear instrumentality of an architectural section. Drawn lines are precisely controlled throughout the composition and take a supportive role to the effect of colour and tone.

Other attributes reflect painting's influence. There is, for example, the 'removal' of floors in particular rooms, changes in the correlated levels between spaces, and the importance given to certain surfaces over any portrayal of architectural verity. Elements are isolated and layered, in one sense informing viewers of their modulation, but with little consequence for architecture. The painting's name

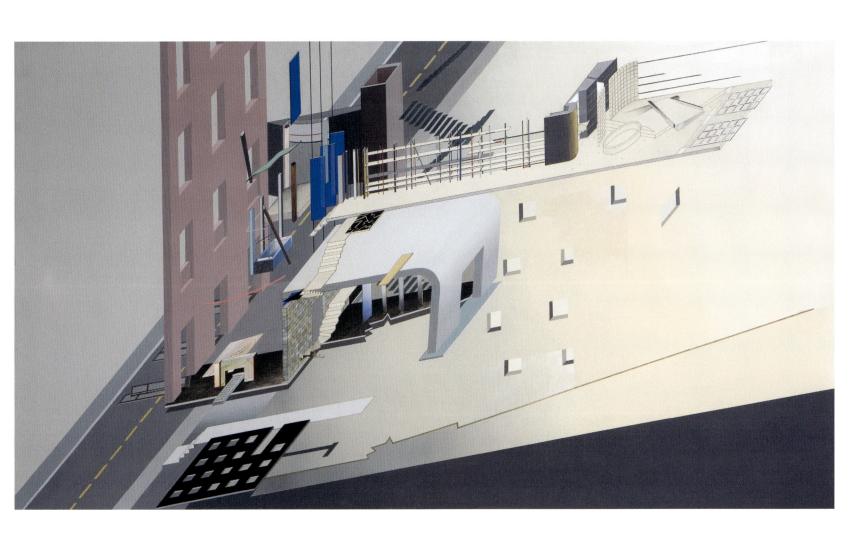

19
**Zaha Hadid Architects**
*59 Eaton Place, Three Towers: the Flamboyant, the Suprematist, the Clinical*, London, United Kingdom, 1981
Acrylic on paper, 106 × 189 cm (41¾ × 74½ in)
Zaha Hadid Foundation

20
Salvador Dalí
*Le rêve de Vénus* (*The Dream of Venus*), 1939
Oil on canvas on 4 Masonite® boards, totalling
240 × 480 cm (94½ × 189 in)
Hiroshima Prefectural Art Museum, Hiroshima

21
Yves Tanguy
*Je vous attends* (*I Await You*), 1934
Oil on canvas, 72.39 × 114.3 cm (28½ × 45 in)
Los Angeles County Museum (LACMA),
Los Angeles

provides some way of interpreting the strangeness of these effects. When Hadid responded in interviews, she suggested three vertical conditions, three 'towers' that define an understanding of the maisonette. At one stage, she explains these as the 'front', 'back' and 'middle' in a very perfunctory manner.[47] What is argued here is that the metaphors used in the title of this painting reveal much more in relation to the architecture. There are, after all, no towers evident in this painting. By using terms in the title like 'the Flamboyant', 'the Suprematist' and 'the Clinical' there is an added interpretive layer over the painting's architectural intent. These terms suggest intensions that guide each viewer to question its spatial relationships beyond any immediate formulation of its architecture in the mind.

As the title implies, the composition of *Three Towers* is more the amalgam of spatial and interpretive layers that can be 'read' throughout its imagery, depending on the lens taken. Reading the titles in reverse order, the term 'clinical' can be seen to reinforce the idea of the forensic: something disassembled for interrogation or dissection. It is an attribute revealed, for example, through the distinct and precise clarity and isolation of architectural elements, whether illustrated by the pink front wall, the powder blue ceiling and wall element at the centre of the composition, or the flooring edge-profiles and staircases that join their particular spaces. Each is precisely and clinically separated for display. They are dissected.

22
Zaha Hadid Architects
(detail) *59 Eaton Place, Three Towers: the Flamboyant, the Suprematist, the Clinical*, London, United Kingdom, 1981
Acrylic on paper
Zaha Hadid Foundation

The forms and shapes of this painting, depicted as if protruding against a flattened background, have an echo of Surrealism. Exploring comparison through paintings such as Dalí's *Le rêve de Vénus* of 1939, or Yves Tanguy's *Je vous attends* of 1934 (figs 20 and 21), suggests how Hadid introduces a metaphysical messaging by isolating objects within vast empty backgrounds, separating them from any sense of contextual reality. While Dalí relied on viewer recognition of strange juxtapositions such as melting clocks, giraffes and lobsters, Hadid used similar strategies to bring together walls, bathtubs and steps. Each attribute of her painting prompts the viewer to similarly question whether there is a higher meaning underpinning the precise juxtaposition of elements. While Tanguy abstracts his 'characters' within his painting, their isolation–connection become powerful indicators. Fundamental in the metaphysic of both examples is the background where vast void-spaces are depicted through their muted shades.

Reflecting these Surrealist strategies, Hadid's painting gives a unique status to each element of the architectural foreground and strips the background of detail. The strategy is compounded with the introduction of differing scales of representation, confounding ease of apprehension of their architectural imperative, while precisely relating elements through the tension of their juxtaposition. When interpreted through the clinical, the imagery of her painting invites questions of meaning as if there is a higher structure of connectivity and order to be attained within its understanding of architecture. In a similar manner to Dalí's and Tanguy's, Hadid's painting introduced the juxtaposition of interrelated, yet independent, narratives prompting consideration as if metaphysical dream states can become potent in architecture.

The second of Hadid's descriptive 'towers', termed 'the Suprematist', initiates a response that is more familiar and expected. However, to understand the consequences of her use of Suprematism requires a necessary aside and comparison. Through her early career, Hadid had returned to the paintings of Kazimir Malevich in their comparison with those of Piet Mondrian, to explain her interest in spatial balance. Malevich's abstract notion of the 'space' within a painting, as distinct from the visual structure inferred by perspectival realism, grew increasingly important to Hadid, but it also drew specific reference to Mondrian.[48] She saw in Malevich's Dynamic Suprematism a sense of pictorial balance defined by a 'cessation of movement', where elements coalesce through abstract spatial inter-dependencies and implied force.[49] By comparison, Mondrian's retention of the orthogonally 'bound' space of the pictorial surface was problematic for Hadid. Malevich's abstraction was seen by Hadid to be more aligned with a conceptual movement of planes and spatial layering. She explained that Malevich's painting was closer to a filmic freeze-frame, suggesting movement as distinct from the static painterly abstraction and orthogonal balance of Mondrian.[50] Interpreting Malevich's paintings, Hadid proposed an architectural equivalency to focus on the 'differences between linear space which is cellular and a linear space which is fluid'.[51] She recognised that in his work, when elements coalesced within painting's sense of pictorial depth, an abstract and dynamic system of balance was introduced that for her had architectural implications.

For Hadid, the evocation of movement in painting could inform the three-dimensional fluid spatiality of architecture. Her response to this implied movement abounds in the details of the painting, where architectural meaning parallels that of the painting's networked spatiality, abstract curvilinearity and colour dynamics. One detail from the painting is an example of how these dynamics bring ideas from painting into the architecture (fig.22). Within its spatial structure, fixed shapes are represented as if they float within an anti-gravitational field where the removal of floors reinforces possible spatial connections across multiple levels of the architecture. Erasures invite investigation of how and why resulting visual juxtapositions are retained. By using Suprematist compositional tactics the painting forms a series of these relationships between the lines, shapes and colours, each directing attention to implied visual connections and the dynamic potential of architecture's interior spaces.

Another example is the use of the hue cobalt blue and its tonal variations. It is used consistently throughout the three major paintings in this set, to reinforce a dynamic sense of balance from which other elements are measured for their comparative tension. In this painting, cobalt blue is used to define small, discrete architectural elements, enough to trigger their plausible cohesion as a group. Lighter shades of the same hue extend this cohesion outward. In the foreground, one of these pale blue forms depicts an element incorporating both a thickened ceiling and a wall of the dining room.[52] It has a distinctive 'familial' tie to the vertical fins on architectural levels above and below. As a group these blue elements develop a dynamism for the architecture and encourage the recognition of new spatial connections that infer Dynamic Suprematism. The dominance of this type of effect in the painting underpins the idea that the spatiality of its architecture should not be considered through simple utilitarian terms such as wall, floor or ceiling. The use of colour affords a level of visual 'power' to the compositional strategies of the painting as well as projecting this into architectural meaning.

When the idea of the 'flamboyant' is explored, Hadid had emphasised it as a suggestion of material tactility, bringing a parallel between painting's expressiveness and architectural space–form relationships. She noted that the term flamboyant described the use of silk and stone, for example.[53] It is through the sensuous textures of material in the architecture that its effect could be equated to flamboyant. This attribute can be interpreted throughout the painting: the bedpost is rendered as if defined by its timbered grain, its silk cover is spatially modulated in pale blue, the fins dividing the room are coloured a bright, cobalt blue and suggest the transparency of glass, a similar colour used for the bath becomes water-like, its end and the fireplace in the main room have been marbleised and set against contrasting details, the dark brown carpet of the ground-floor living room suggests its plushness, and the wall between the downstairs living spaces has been given a texture reminiscent of a light stone or glass block.

In conclusion, with each of these 'towers' there are a series of implicit and explicit prompts for viewers to follow in their mind's reassembly of each element as architecture. Viewer understanding of the co-dependency between notions of abstraction, technical clarity and the sensuality of the interior reinforces memories of sensations in experiencing interiors of their own past. In this sense, the imagery of this painting moves away from the logic of architectural representation to emphasise the possibility of its spatial and material affect, individualised within each viewer's reception. Viewers are encouraged to 'play the games' of each 'tower', whilst also being confronted with their own new sense of distancing from what they observe.

When considering the three paintings for 59 Eaton Place, there is a marked transformation from the emphasis on architectural drawing so pronounced in *Malevich's Tektonik* (1976) and continued in subsequent projects. The Eaton Place paintings each focus on a traditional type of architectural drawing, destabilising its conventions through techniques more available in painting. This process changes the nature of representation and its relation to architecture. It is a practice that sets Hadid apart from the painting that had emerged within OMA, where, of the collaborating four directors, Elia Zenghelis and Rem Koolhaas had focused on architecture and their partners, Madelon Vriesendorp and Zoe Zenghelis, had painted. Hadid had been an addition to OMA from the late 1970s and continued as a director until some time during the early 1980s. Traces of their approach remained within her paintings – especially in the selection of colour and some attributes of visualisation so evident in the work of Vriesendorp and Zenghelis. However, from the time of the *59 Eaton Place* paintings, and her exhibition *Planetary Architecture* at Galerie van Rooy in 1981, Hadid worked to unify the acts of thinking about architecture with those of thinking through painting.

For Hadid, through painting, architectural representation and the power of its drawing conventions are reconceived, and architecture becomes embedded within the sensation of spatial tensions and pictorial effects. There is an implied frisson between forms, colours, textures and materials that idiosyncratically mirrors viewer memories and experiences. In the paintings for 59 Eaton Place, the inversion of power relationships between architectural drawing conventions and painting's capacity to introduce surface effects, linear networks and spatial dynamism, strengthens Hadid's critique of architecture's traditions. These paintings necessitate each viewer to discover an architectural potency within each painting's sinuous imagery. They present as puzzles, their imagery always remaining partial and co-dependent like architectural drawing, but now adding further affect. In any attempted resolution or apprehension of architecture in the mind, viewers will understand that these paintings retain a sense of something beyond the reach of comprehension and toward the slightly ephemeral and spatially abstract in architecture.

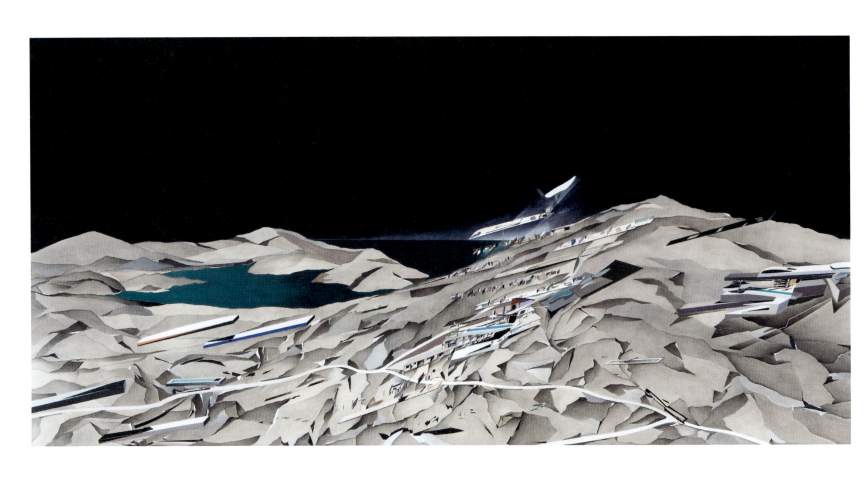

23
Zaha Hadid Architects
*The Peak, Exploded Isometric*,
Hong Kong, China, 1983
Acrylic and watercolour on paper,
104.2 × 205.7 cm (41 × 81 in)
Zaha Hadid Foundation

# 2 Pictorial Space and the Transformation of Architecture: The Peak

During the early 1980s under the chairmanship of Alvin Boyarsky, young architect-educators at London's oldest school of architecture, the Architectural Association (AA), became increasingly successful in international architectural competitions. Of note were Rem Koolhaas and Elia Zenghelis, founding directors of the Office for Metropolitan Architecture (OMA), Bernard Tschumi, and Zaha Hadid.[1] By their success, this group had validated the school as an incubator for new and experimental practices in architecture. Their winning schemes had each challenged the profession's long-held values, offering new approaches that re-engaged with prevailing concepts of modernity.[2] In their reaction to architectural Postmodernism, they developed new methods for articulating complex propositions focused on renewal of cities and of architecture's space–form relationships. Their graphic submissions in these competitions were often constrained by the number and type of drawings dictated by the conditions of entry. However, these architects each extended the communication of their ideas through publications of further writing and the exhibition of drawings in emerging architectural galleries, such as Aedes in Berlin, Max Protetch in New York, and Galerie van Rooy in Amsterdam.[3]

Within this milieu, Zaha Hadid used the communicative and expressive agency of painting as distinct from text or other graphic media. She embraced both the idea of the exhibition and painting's spatial engagement with viewers. This became Hadid's signature way for communicating ideas about her architecture. Her first presentation of paintings had been associated with OMA's *Sparkling Metropolis* exhibition at the Solomon R. Guggenheim Museum in New York in 1978.[4] This was followed by a series of small group exhibitions and the solo exhibition *Planetary Architecture*, held at Galerie van Rooy, opening in late 1981.[5]

Hadid's second solo exhibition, *Planetary Architecture Two*, was at the invitation of Boyarsky, to be held at the AA, opening in November 1983.[6] It was one of a series of new events for Boyarsky as chairman of the school, and was coupled with the publication of a catalogue – luxuriously produced as a large format, boxed folio of images with additional introductory essays and interviews.[7] Hadid's *Folio II, Planetary Architecture Two*, was in the schedule of publications, following only months after Daniel Libeskind's exhibition and catalogue, *Folio I, Chamber Works: Architectural Meditations on Themes from Heraclitus*.[8] The publication of these box sets continued over coming years, as did the exhibitions, further highlighting the intellectual scope of the AA as an institution attracting the interest of international architects who equally supported architectural experimentation through drawing and image.[9]

Boyarsky's invitation to Hadid to mount the exhibition prompted her to create a series of large paintings of her recently winning scheme for The Peak Leisure Club in Hong Kong (The Peak). Her original competition entry had consisted of just six black and white A1-sized sheets of drawings in accordance with the competition submission requirements.[10] While a subsequent series of small, semi-abstract 'views' had been completed for the Hong Kong magazine *Vision, Architecture + Design* published in April 1983, the large format paintings were completed for the AA exhibition.[11] Travelling to Hong Kong to receive the winning prize, Hadid met with the entrepreneur for the new club, Alfred Siu, and inspected the site to further develop the scheme for application to local authorities.[12] Her approach to the architecture of The Peak – now made more specific following experiencing the unique urban setting of Hong Kong, the site, and Siu's varying requirements – developed in tandem with the exhibition paintings during the subsequent seven months.[13]

Hadid and her assistants all worked on the paintings during this period of intense production. The role of painting was to support and enable Hadid to test ideas. Camilla Ween, a fellow student at the AA who had been a friend of Hadid's since the early 1970s, suggested that the process from drawing to painting grew from 'Zaha's dialogue with painting. She liked to explore through painting.'[14] Ween explained the internal nature of the act of painting for Hadid, saying: 'Painting was a means for her to explore a distinctive way of thinking about architecture. I never got the sense that she wanted the painting to communicate something about her project to the rest of the world. It was for her own exploration.'[15] Despite Ween's comments, through exhibition, these paintings would be understood for their visual intrigue and communicative value.

For the original Peak Architectural Competition submission in 1982, Hadid's team included her ex-students Alastair Standing, Jonathan Dunn, Marian van der Waals and Michael Wolfson.[16] Dunn, who had worked with Hadid since the competition for the Irish Prime Minister's Residence in 1979, explained that his own distinctive expertise for the project had emerged from his ability to translate her preliminary sketches and paintings into precise technical orthographic and isometric drawings, and in that process maintain the visual emphasis she required. He recounted the drama of the final hours before the competition submission:

> We worked night and day on The Peak competition. And the day before the deadline, we took an A1 sized Rotring pen drawing, which took days and days, to a printer. And the printing machine, somewhat ironically, tore the drawing in half. When Michael Wolfson and I took it back to Zaha, she went ballistic and said, 'Right, forget it, we're not presenting this, the game's up, let's all go to bed and forget about it.' Michael and I quietly disobeyed her and went with newly completed drawings to the late opening post office in London . . . We managed to get the scheme posted and registered and off to Hong Kong. And, later when we told her what we had done, we were both thrown out of the studio, thrown out the house, and told never to come back again. And that's what happened. Two weeks, maybe three weeks later . . . I got a phone call, I literally had not spoken to Zaha, as she was so cross with us, and she says, 'you know, you're not going to believe what's happened'. I said, 'I have no idea what happened Zaha.' So, she said 'we won The Peak competition. So, get your ass back here.'[17]

Wolfson had transferred in his third year to the AA and had been tutored by Hadid in his fourth year.[18] Remembering the atmosphere of Hadid's teaching Unit, he recalled: 'Everyone knew her background, and OMA's. They were interested in constructivist and Russian ideas of early modernism . . . we were looking at futurist manifestos and the Russian manifestos, just to get an idea of where that was coming from.'[19]

After the competition, his key role for The Peak was to interpret Hadid's ideas into drawings for the base imagery for many of the paintings.[20] He recalled the following period of productivity in the days before Hadid's trip to Hong Kong following the win: 'I just never had time to get involved with painting. It was always, "Do another drawing! Do another drawing! We need more perspectives! We need to see the interior! We need to see this! We need to see that!"'[21]

When completed, his drawings for the large format paintings would go on to the team of painters for further development. In the period leading up to the exhibition, Wolfson remembers being sprawled across a table to complete larger drawings on tracing paper using Rotring ink pens. Final drawings had been traced from an amalgamation of layers of preliminary drawings below, using tools like shipwright's curves to draw the long sinuously curved lines of their imagery.[22] Even though a tall person, he laughingly recalled 'crawling over it'[23] when doing the drawing for the painting *Blue Slabs*. He also recalls the process of copying the finished drawing to already stretched final linen that had been taped onto plywood. Their final line work was achieved using A4 sheets of 'transfer' or graphite paper, applying pressure to original tracings using a ball-point stylus.[24] The result would be a fine grey line that was 'stable' when wet and did not react with the painting process.

Understanding that the height of these paintings was between two to three metres reveals the complexity and scale of this process. Painting was carried out 'on-the-flat', with many working around a table on the same image. Within this 'production', the relationship between drawings and paintings was never direct. For example, the drawing for *Blue Slabs* is notably smaller than the painting, and some details are less prominent.[25] Wolfson explained that there were often 'adjustments' made by Hadid herself, because of exhibition's requirement for impact.[26]

During the process of creating these complex final paintings, Boyarsky offered Hadid the use of a studio space within the school, enabling the team to expand.[27] Hadid's painters were led by Nan Lee, who continued to work with Hadid after preparations for the exhibition *Planetary Architecture*. Lee and Wendy Galway, both textile designers, took central roles in the painting process.[28] As well as painting, Lee oversaw mixing and keeping consistent the amounts required for each painting as it progressed.[29] Added to their expertise, Nicola Cousins and later David Gomersall joined the team. The acrylic paint is thin and applied in layers of translucent coats that would dry waterproof. Depth of pigment was achieved by adding second and third coats.[30] Cousins recalled, 'we had to do loads of coats! That's why we had a lot of people working.'[31] Gomersall's main contribution was working with Galway and Piers Smerin on *Confetti – Suprematist Snowstorm*. He explained:

> Zaha would arrive on occasions and talk through the projects on the table and how she saw them; [in the case of Hong Kong] how she saw that part of the city and how her building would work with, and contrast between things. And you would see her doodling and licking her brush and playing around with small paintings and sketches she would then discuss... Following this, Zaha would sometimes start painting, and she would be doing some areas and I'd be doing others and talking about the project as we painted. Through this, the process was a development in itself.[32]

Jonathan Dunn reiterated, 'the phenomenon of Zaha was she joined together a group of very talented people who could understand what she wanted and were well schooled in her [visual and descriptive] languages'.[33] Terms like 'whoosh', 'tic-tic' and 'potato chip' have been repeated by several as having distinctive applications. When seeing a 'potato chip' in one of the paintings while visiting a recent exhibition, Wolfson exclaimed, 'This is the potato chip. Boy, did we have arguments about that shape.'[34]

In his recall, Gomersall, who worked for Hadid for over 15 years, returned to highlight the importance of colour in Hadid's paintings:

With Zaha it was much more about feeling spatial qualities. The colours weren't necessarily just to do with red coming forward or blue going back, it's not really a mystery but just selecting colours through discussion and trial and error until the juxtapositions of shade and pigment started to suit the project. As work progressed each of us could see how the application of certain colours in specific locations starting to suit Zaha's thoughts about the project. This understanding developed new experimentation with the application of new colours. It was a process developed in constant discussion. It took time.[35]

Providing some hint at the way Hadid considered colour was the advertisement for a 'Colour Programme' taught at the AA with Madelon Vriesendorp and Zoe Zenghelis and described in the *Projects Review 1983–84*. Hadid explained, 'the aim of the "Colour Crash Course" was to provide a basis of colour and to apply it not as a decorative means but as a way of understanding architecture under different temperaments conceptually and climatically'.[36]

Hadid was recognised amongst all her assistants for her contributions to each painting. Referring to the painting *Exploded Isometric*, Nan Lee explained that Hadid completed the tonal gradations of the landscape setting.[37] This technique adopted the title 'whoosh', where tonal gradation across a plane added dynamism. The 'whoosh', in Hadid's mind, established a recognisable link to early 20th-century Russian Suprematism. It was Kazimir Malevich who had described this visual technique as a plane in dissolution, or equivalent to the after-effect on the eye's reception of a beam of light whose linear edge had been dragged across a surface.[38] In the viewer's mind the image had dissolved sequentially over time. Hadid's process for creating the 'whoosh' entailed mixing ink or acrylic pigment with water, baby oil and/or detergent, thus enabling drying to be slowed and gradation to remain consistent.[39]

Four of the large paintings for The Peak project are analysed in this chapter and have been given the secondary titles *Exploded Isometric*, *Blue Slabs*, *Confetti – Suprematist Snowstorm* and *Divers*.[40] These paintings were created for a unique audience, specifically Hadid's architectural peers, and students from the AA, with the imagery of each painting anticipating this visually sophisticated and intellectual environment. The four paintings are most effectively analysed in pairs. In this way, each pair takes part in a visual dialogue, where, acting in the manner of protagonists, their imagery alternated propositions. Across the paintings, these visual propositions meld to present Hadid's complex approach to architectural form, its spatial layering and architecture's role within a densely populated contemporary city.

These four paintings of The Peak reveal a complex network of ideas confirming her personal approach to architecture. While earlier projects display a range of explorations in her developing inquiry, it is The Peak project where these coalesce into an integrated approach.

### Spatial Metamorphosis:
*The Peak, Exploded Isometric* and *The Peak, Blue Slabs*

The first pair examined are *The Peak* paintings with the secondary titles *Exploded Isometric* and *Blue Slabs*. *Exploded Isometric* is horizontally formatted, having an image of The Peak Club set within a vast stylised representation of Hong Kong's natural landscape (fig.23). It contrasts with *Blue Slabs* whose vertical format focuses on Hong Kong's urban centre, the City of Victoria, with The Peak Leisure Club shown at the top of the image.[41]

24
Zaha Hadid Architects
(detail) *The Peak, Exploded Isometric*,
Hong Kong, China, 1983
Acrylic and watercolour on paper
Zaha Hadid Foundation

What characterises these two paintings is an imagery that uses both representational and abstract visual conventions. This relationship is explained by Hadid in an interview with Boyarsky in 1983:

> Certain drawings do tell a story. For instance, the exploded isometric of the Peak [*Exploded Isometric*] shows the evolution of the building, with the landscape as backdrop; the beams appear from nowhere and intersect the landscape, ending up with the finished object, which is the building itself. The same is true of the most recent painting, the *Slabs*, which shows the context of the entire Hong Kong scene, changed to suit our purpose. It implies a superimposition on that city. Though the site on the painting is quite small, it relates directly to the city... Every drawing has a scenario, implying a manipulation of the city fabric including how the programme relates to an urban condition as opposed to something which is far removed from any implications.[42]

The natural setting of *Exploded Isometric* portrays the scene looking over the site, west, toward the Pearl River Delta and mainland China. Its semi-representational form means that viewers of this painting with knowledge of Hong Kong would recognise the actual view. The silhouette of mountain topography, and the view of islands and bays of the distant mainland, is well recognised.

In the foreground, the landscape's natural forms are abstracted. Looking more like layers of torn paper than vegetation, each shape's crisply modulating edges and deepening shadow give the appearance of unstable fissures. Layered into this setting are the floor plates of the Leisure Club, drawn using isometric drawing conventions. However, rather than being depicted as a complete building, each floor plate is separated and only loosely relates to others.

Contrasting this visual complexity, the night sky is depicted as a flat dark expanse with the horizon line cutting the composition into two. It is here that an ambiguous scene takes form. A silhouetted halo surrounding the upper floors of the scheme gives the impression of an aircraft in descent, hovering over the natural setting (fig.24). When viewed from a distance this illusion dominates the sky. For those familiar with Hong Kong at the time, it registers as part of the psychology, drama and intensity of its setting. The 'whoosh'-like characteristics of the form align with memories of the terrifying approach aircraft took in landing at Hong Kong's old Kai Tak Airport.[43] As recounted by Nan Lee, 'Zaha was amused and amazed by landing in Hong Kong's unusual old airport. Even years later she spoke of this when we took her on a private flight over New York. She was like a kid on a Ferris Wheel.'[44]

This illusion loses its power when the viewer moves toward the painting and notes it is the depiction of the upper floor and roof of the Leisure Club. When close, each of the floor plates and their furnishings (considered as a floor-scape) become more obvious, staggered in their alignment across the expanse of the natural setting. In some places, the room divisions and furnishings have been separated again, vertically distinct and located above the floor's surface. Interior elements are coloured in intense pure hues, emphasising their individuality rather than cohesion.

On further inspection of the painting, the viewer will notice that selected elements are repeated across the foreground. They include a swimming pool, and other 'slabs' and 'beams' that are each depicted with shadows cast over the ground. They suggest a surreal imagery, as if, in the manner of film stills, elements were captured in their 'flight' across the mountain, bringing a kinetic to the architecture as they find their place. Hadid reiterated that the 'beams' came to land on the mountain forming the schema for the final building.[45]

Hadid's companion painting, *Blue Slabs*, uniquely focuses on the broader urban setting and the towers of Hong Kong (fig.25). It announces the city's 'portraiture' as opposed to the site's natural vastness. Hong Kong's urban setting is interpreted with a distinctive tilting of its forms at odds with the painting's edge. This tilt is combined with a sinuous linearity that directs the viewer's eye toward the Leisure Club – isolated at the top of the mountain – and away from the city. These fluid lines take cues from known features of Hong Kong, like the winding thread of mountainous roads such as Hill Road of the Western District, or Magazine Gap Road – each approaching Victoria Peak. Hill Road is most distinctive and pictorially recognisable as it is elevated and twists between buildings.

*Blue Slabs* introduces a further visual strategy, where a contrast is developed between the vast scale of the portraiture of the city, and the detail required to explain the new architecture now compositionally too distant for the viewer to see. Drawn in dramatically different architectural scales from those of the scene, are a series of interiors that have been seamlessly integrated, and 'grafted' onto the tops of existing towers of the city.[46] In their detail, it becomes apparent that their visual coincidence acts to blur the inconsistencies that might be expected within such a change of representational scales (fig.26).

Supporting this sense of spatial 'grafting', the abstracted floor surfaces of each plan for The Peak Club are coloured to retain the pale grey or dusty pink hues of the city's buildings. Across these plans brightly coloured elements are scattered. Because of their relative size, from a distance these details give the appearance of potential furnishings on the rooftops of buildings. From a mid-distance, their colouration acts to draw attention from the viewer – like visual noise, these elements prompt closer investigation. And yet, when close, there is no greater legibility achieved for the architecture they 'depict'; their coloured shapes remain enigmatic and without recognisable function. At certain points the architectural ambition of some elements is more explicit: a set of steps, a wall. However, their purpose remains unclear. Instead, their importance to the painting slips between representation and abstraction. These shapes integrate pictorially into a semi-abstracted scale of Hong Kong's urban fabric as much as they gesture toward the interiority of the scheme for The Peak Club. Rather than the furnishings recognised for their familiar purpose, their imagery remains inconclusive in the play of scales: the scale of the city montaged with the scale of the interiors. Viewers are encouraged to engage spatially with this painting as they respond to its complex visual cues (fig.27).

Questioning how these paintings communicate architectural ideas opens two levels of inquiry. Firstly, how they work as artworks, and then how they project architectural meaning. It is this relationship between drawing, painting and architecture that remained critical for Hadid. In her first published interview with Boyarsky in 1983, she pointedly reaffirmed the centrality of Suprematist painting to her early architectural development.[47] But not so clear is how her paintings respond to other theoretical discussions at the AA to further an understanding of purpose for each painting's imagery.[48] It was in the intellectual milieu of theoretical debate evident at the AA that Hadid was exposed to an eclectic range of images. At the AA the use of imagery was particularly acknowledged as distinctively informing for theoretical propositions on architecture.[49] Hadid's reliance on images, and her response to certain important images popular in the period, contributed to her unique characterisation of architecture.

Visual and theoretical references become useful indicators of this environment and inform how these two paintings for The Peak can be understood. Hadid's pairing of *Exploded Isometric* with *Blue Slabs* in discussion with Boyarsky is particularly telling, opening discussion within the context of intellectual debate at the AA.

25
**Zaha Hadid Architects**
*The Peak, Blue Slabs*, Hong Kong, China, 1983
Acrylic and watercolour on linen,
259.1 × 183 cm (102 × 72 in)
Zaha Hadid Foundation

26
**Zaha Hadid Architects**
(detail) *The Peak, Blue Slabs*,
Hong Kong, China, 1983
Acrylic and watercolour on linen
Zaha Hadid Foundation

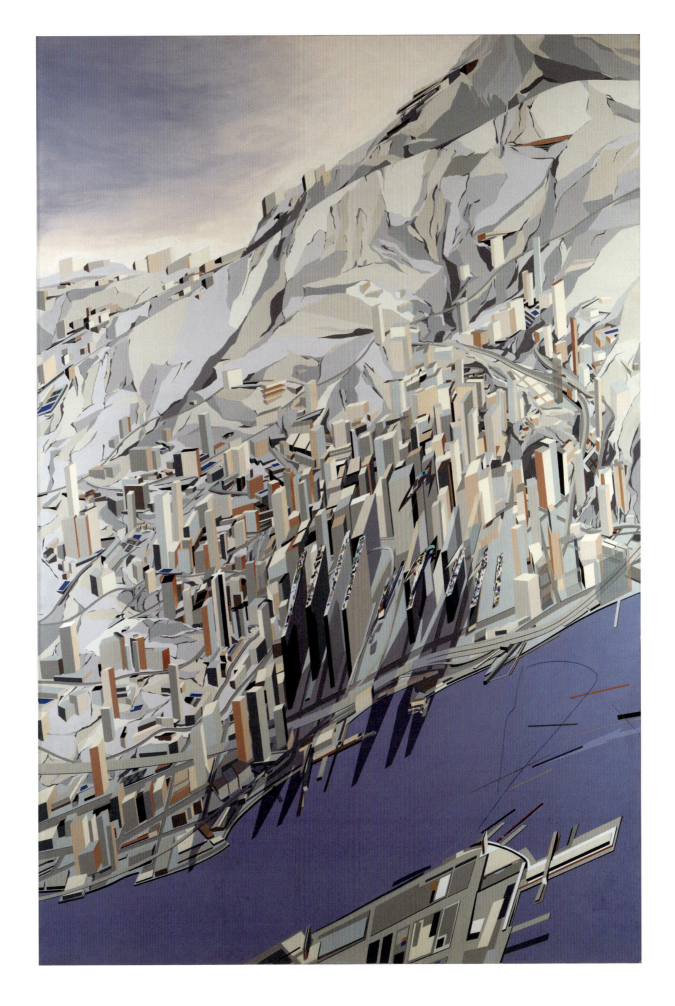

During early discussions of the Postmodern, a search for meaning in architecture had considered the classical Roman architect Vitruvius's *De architectura*, regarded as the oldest treatise on architecture, for a renewed relevance.[50] By the late 1970s, architectural historian and critic Joseph Rykwert had become a key figure in these debates at the AA.[51] His arguments were supported by illustrations sourced from historical commentary of Vitruvian ideas. Two illustrations used by Rykwert in his book *On Adam's House in Paradise: The Idea of the Primitive Hut in Architectural History* are pertinent to Hadid's pairing of *Exploded Isometric* with *Blue Slabs*.[52] The first of these to highlight, portrays the origins of fire and in doing so signifies the origins of the urban condition. Rykwert used the illustration from Cesare Cesariano's translation and commentary of Vitruvius from 1521 (fig.28).[53] He saw Cesariano's illustration as a way to interpret Vitruvius for contemporary audiences. Cesariano portrayed a community gathered around a fire and idealised this scene as the origins of the 'congress of men, and their counsel together and cohabitation'.[54] For Rykwert, urbanity reflected architecture's required sense of order and 'grace' within a spatial order, mirroring behaviours tempered through communal interactions and customs. The second illustration presents nature as the origin of order for architecture. Rykwert used the 1755 frontispiece of Marc-Antoine Laugier's *Essai sur l'architecture* (fig.29).[55] Interpreting this image of the primordial dwelling emerging from nature, Rykwert quoted Laugier, 'never has there been a principle more fruitful in its consequences; with it as a guide it is easy to distinguish those parts which are essential components of an order and those parts which are only introduced through necessity or added by caprice'.[56] Rykwert thereby reinforces the idea that in a material and tectonic sense, nature had imbued architecture with rational order and hierarchy.

Rykwert's use of images reflected the heroic themes that were inferred by Hadid's paintings *Exploded Isometric* and *Blue Slabs* but to very different effect. Viewers at Hadid's exhibition *Planetary Architecture Two* would have recognised the power of her critique and its reconfiguring of these heroic themes. Being considered as a pair, her paintings suggested a renewed consideration of architecture's relationship to its settings. For Hadid's interpretation of Hong Kong specifically, the precursors of nature and the city were equally felt but distinctive. Her paintings were not simply reiterations of Rykwert's reflections, but instead critiqued their normalisation in architecture as ancient 'truths' by adapting other sources to further refine her ideas.

One of these other sources included an influential image in contemporary AA debates. It is the photograph *Nine-Lens Photograph of New York City*, 1938, that had first been published in *Life* magazine in 1947 (fig.30).[57] In the context of the AA, this photograph had also been used by both Rem Koolhaas and Daniel Libeskind

27
Viewers at the exhibition *Zaha Hadid*, Palazzo Franchetti, Venice Biennale, 2016
Private Collection

28
Cesare Cesariano
*The Congress of Man*, from Vitruvius, *Di Lucio Vitruvio Pollione de architectura libri dece: traducti de latino in vulgare affigurati: comentati: & con mirando ordine insigniti*, trans., Cesare Cesariano, 1521, Book II, XXXI
Woodblock, 21 × 18 cm (8¼ × 7 in)
Centre Canadien d'Architecture /
Canadian Centre for Architecture

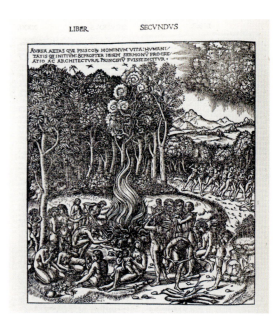

29
**Charles-Dominique-Joseph Eisen** (Engraver)
Frontispiece, Marc-Antoine Laugier, *Essai sur l'architecture*, second edition, 1755
21 × 14.7 cm (8¼ × 5⁵⁄₁₆ in)
Centre Canadien d'Architecture /
Canadian Centre for Architecture

to support their very different ideas about architecture. Libeskind reproduced it in his Jung-inspired teaching in the 1975/76 academic year.[58] Libeskind, like Jung, realigned the original photograph (as it has been in the *Life* image) to emphasise the orthogonality of the grid-like order of New York City and its 'rational command over nature'.[59]

Creating the opposite effect, Koolhaas included a detail from this photograph in his explanation of 'The Culture of Congestion' published in the *Architectural Design* (*AD*) special issue on OMA in 1977, where he stated: 'Manhattan represents the apotheosis of the ideal of density *per se*, both of population and of infrastructure; its architecture promotes a state of congestion on all possible levels and exploits this congestion to inspire and support particular forms of social intercourse that together form a unique culture of congestion.'[60] Significantly, Koolhaas had aligned the photograph by turning it anticlockwise, cropping it to focus on the section where the diagonal overlaying of skyscrapers emphasises a 'congested' urban intensity. This is a symbolism also referenced in Hadid's paintings.

These applications show how a single image could reinforce very different arguments. Hadid's interest in this image is confirmed in her acquisition of an equivalent survey photograph of Hong Kong (fig.31). The date is telling in this instance, as the image is dated after the completion of the competition and during the consideration of the paintings. The tilting of the city in both photographs became an opportunity to bring her interest in Suprematism and the city into more contemporary intellectual debates. It also provided recognition that unlike New York, because of its mountainous setting, the metropolis of Hong Kong was represented equally by its natural terrain and its dense urbanity. The offset angle of buildings in the New York City photograph – more clearly than in the one for Hong Kong – emphasises the height and density of the city, its composite visual layering and multitudinous social activities.[61]

This visual commentary had been useful to Koolhaas, and it was also useful to Hadid. Her painting *Blue Slabs* transforms the tilted offset geometry of the skyscrapers to reinforce the 'congested population of Hong Kong'.[62] Through conventions of isometric drawing, the added distortion of the incline destabilises any sense of spatial regularity. By adapting the visual complexity of the survey photographs, Hadid's painting references her response to Hong Kong's social and visual form, and her perception of its intense, distinctive and 'congested' culture.[63]

From her training at the AA, it would have been expected that Hadid engage

30
**Association of Commissioned Officers**
*Nine-Lens Photograph of New York City*,
U.S. Coast and Geodetic Survey, 1938
Photograph. As first published in *Life* magazine, 1 September 1947
Author's Collection

in a critique of this type of imagery, and the approach would situate her own propositions. However, the radicality of her approach developed not only from this critique, but more dramatically in her adaptation of Malevich's conception of pictorial space. Hadid explained its importance through comparison with Mondrian's De Stijl paintings. Mondrian's *Composition with Large Red Plane, Yellow, Black, Grey and Blue* from 1921, for example, shows a purposeful removal of depth and orientation, reducing pictorial space to the two-dimensional surface of the canvas (fig.32). Rather than this two-dimensional organisation, Hadid recognised in Malevich a distinctive dynamism that inferred three-dimensional spatial juxtaposition and implied movement between elements. She explained that both had implications for her architecture. Malevich's approach can be seen in his *House Under Construction* painting of 1915–16 (fig.33). Hadid claimed:

> If you compare De Stijl and Suprematism there is a kind of equilibrium in both, arrived at in the former through total control, while the latter was totally energetic – not unlike a photographic freeze frame. Mondrian could change his composition until in the end it was balanced and frozen. In the case of Malevich, the guiding forces seem not to be bound by earthly conditions. The implication is one of liberation. If flying objects in space land, they become grounded and there is a cessation of movement.[64]

While Russian artists like El Lissitzky and architects such as Ivan Leonidov had experimented with how Suprematist ideas transferred into architectural design, their work remained schematic and unrealised.[65] Interpreting Malevich's paintings, Hadid proposed an architectural equivalency to focus on the 'differences between linear space which is cellular and a linear space which is fluid'.[66] She recognised that in his paintings, when elements coalesced within the painting's sense of pictorial depth, an abstract and dynamic system of balance was introduced that for her had architectural implications.

For Hadid, Malevich's 'cessation of movement' recognised the balance achieved in abstract painting, when elements coalesce to resolve a unified, balanced, yet dynamic composition. The unique insight The Peak paintings propose is an adaptation of the abstract sensibilities of Malevich's dynamic and abstract spatiality within the more figurative and representational references necessary for architecture.

However, her amalgamation of abstraction and figurative representation was, in itself, problematic in terms of adapting Suprematism into architecture. Malevich had criticised realism in painting, claiming:

> Imitative art attempts to halt the changing pattern, to fix the fact in an immutable pose, to lead it to artistic condition, the condition outside of time, such a relationship is the essence of imitative art, but in reality, the artist understands this essence in a different way, and it is assumed to be a method of painting reality of depicting a phenomenon on canvas. But this attempt is vain, there is no reality.[67]

His aim for painting was, instead, to engage with intuition where 'intuition [was] the new reason, consciously creating forms'. Rather than reflect the world of objects, forms would be freed from 'the impression of the wholeness of objects', and an artist would respond to their sensation only through the 'essence' of their 'energy', its 'statics, speed, and dynamics'.[68] Expanding this claim, he argued that Cubism and Futurism had done little to resolve the problem of this quest.

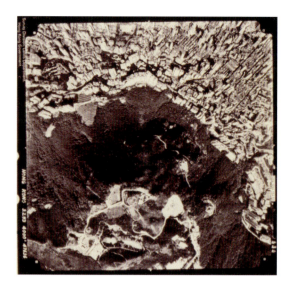

31
Survey Division Lands Department, Hong Kong Government
*Hong Kong 4000' 3.2.1983*
Zaha Hadid Architects

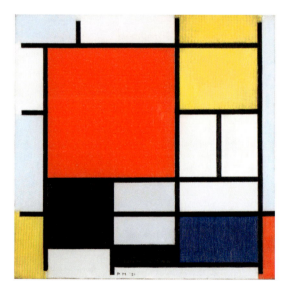

32
Piet Mondrian
*Composition with Large Red Plane, Yellow, Black, Grey and Blue*, 1921
Oil on canvas, 59.5 × 59.5 cm (23⁷⁄₁₆ × 23⁷⁄₁₆ in)
Kunstmuseum Den Haag, The Hague

33
Kazimir Malevich
*House Under Construction*, 1915–16
Oil on canvas, 97 × 44.5 cm (38 3/16 × 17 1/2 in),
National Gallery of Australia, Canberra

34
Kazimir Malevich
*Landscape with a Yellow House
(Winter Landscape)*, 1906
Oil and wax tempera on card,
19.2 × 29.5 cm (7 1/2 × 11 1/2 in)
Russian State Museum

For Cubists, he concluded, their aim had been akin to a fragmentation of views only to return to traditions of representation and a focus on the object when multiple views were superimposed, claiming 'in our era of Cubism the artist has destroyed objects together with meaning, essence and purpose'.[69] This argument he extended to Futurism, suggesting their portrayal of movement relied on multiple depictions of individual static views, albeit transformed and layered to create the impression of movement. He did, however, applaud their aim to deal with time's affect, and with the sensation of movement, but concluded 'they achieve only the dynamic of things'.[70] Their return to the representation of objects remained problematic.

A series of paintings and drawings from Malevich show the transformation from his early semi-representational imagery to this new 'intuitive response to sensation'. The progression is revealed in his art by comparing *Landscape with a Yellow House (Winter Landscape)* painted in 1906, with a drawing from the *Suprematism: 34 Drawings* collection of 1920 (figs 34 and 35).[71] Placed side by side these images have a similar structure, the first established through representation, the second abstract. In the drawing there is what appears to be an arching curve thrusting horizontally. Its arching linearity is combined with a series of vertical forms layered into the composition. These attributes spatially structure the imagery of both painting and drawing. However, while in *Landscape with a Yellow House* these gestures give the impression of trees located in front of a house, in the example from *34 Drawings* there is no inference of a 'picture', or the painted landscape's horizon or its spatial integration of foreground and background. Within the image from *34 Drawings* representation is avoided. Its spatial logic relies purely on the interdependencies of tonal relationships within a pictorial space. It defines what Malevich describes as an abstract logic of sensation while *Landscape with a Yellow House* remains closer to the impression of a scene and the making of a picture to represent that natural setting.

What is revealed by this comparison is the relationship considered between representation and abstraction in the work of Malevich. His sense of abstract spatiality emerged from sensation rather than pure geometry by removing the structuring determinism of perspectival realism. What becomes more compelling is when the image from *34 Drawings* is placed beside a sketch produced in the same year titled *Suprematist Construction No. 118* (fig.36).[72] The image as published is oriented horizontally over two pages, reinforcing its comparison with the landscape. The drawing is completed vertically. The writing at the base of the drawing suggests orientation may not have been an issue as both vertical and horizontal formats achieve a similar linear and spatial effect: a relationality only available in a pictorial space. It was in this publication that he stated,

> Suprematist form also represents, surely, the sign of a force that has been recognised – the acting force of utilitarian perfection in a coming concrete world. The form clearly indicates a state of dynamism and, as it were, is a distant pointer to the aeroplanes path in space . . . the harmonious introduction of form into natural action, by means of certain interrelation.[73]

Malevich further developed this approach in his use of colour where his understanding of sensation reconceptualises the depth value of 'pictorial space'. The painting titled *Suprematist Painting* of 1915 uses colour to provide what he recognised as a 'gravity' between forms: where each hue/tone implies depth based purely on their abstract value (fig.37). To explain this effect, he referred to the pictorial surface as equivalent to infinity, a 'receptacle without dimension' or, the 'white, free chasm, of infinity'.[74] Malevich's 1915 painting, arguably his first Suprematist painting, portrays an infinite number of space–form relationships, structured through the proximity of colour, shape, relative size and directionality.[75] There is a tension between shapes that infers an abstract relationality. Each visual attribute is recognised as having a conceptual 'weight', and each develops and affects others within the painting. There is an energy inferred that is not simply gravitational.[76] While some painters of this period equally experimented with abstract values in colour, shape and line, Malevich uniquely retained and argued for abstract painting's referencing of sensation as derived from natural observation. It is an approach that retained a pictorial spatiality and depth deriving equally from the networked dynamics of line, shape and colour to evoke sensations of movement, weight and depth.

As suggested earlier, Hadid's paintings for The Peak depict nature's tie to architecture in *Exploded Isometric*, and its connectivity to the human settings of the city in *Blue Slabs*. However, these ideas can now be juxtaposed conceptually with the integration of pictorial space, and the movement, weight and depth reinforced by colour and shape. It is an approach that mirrors the abstraction referenced in Malevich's paintings, but they also reference debates where pictorial sources worked as evidence for ideas. In Hadid's paintings, it is as if representations of architecture, nature and the city were bound as ideas within the same abstract spatial logic of Suprematism. Yet, because her paintings remain partially representational, their imagery reinforces the necessary double referencing required to prompt the desire in viewers for an architectural 'apprehension'.

It is through the abstract spatial influences from Suprematism that the narrative possibility of each painting is made more precise. There is a lack of gravity and 'ground' and an introduction of spatial tension and energy. In *Exploded Isometric*, 'nature' is presented not as the conceptual precondition of architecture as it had been in Rykwert's argument, but as fragmented and emergent. Hadid's 'nature' projects the idea that the terrain and its surface-effects reinforce the dynamic potential of the architectural event unfolding in the scene. Architecture 'explodes' into a juxtaposition of tectonic and programmatic elements, directing each viewer to understand their movement. For Hadid nature and architecture remain co-dependent, each signifying a semi-abstract state:

> The idea of The Peak really emerged through the carving of the rock under Hong Kong Island. Through carving of the rock, the landscape was replaced with a new geology... beginning to replace it with new kinds of geological players [earlier, she used terms like 'beams', 'voids', 'platforms', and 'suspended satellites' as these players] there emerged a new geology... Underpinned by new engineering, the idea of fluidity and a degree of freedom emerged within the building itself.[77]

Her 'nature' is explained as 'liberated' from its traditional role in architecture and is no longer to be considered as the constant or 'true' precondition of architectural form. Instead, through abstraction, in their new symbiotic relationship, nature and architecture remain in equal metamorphosis.

The painting *Blue Slabs* repeats this idea with its focus on the city. The imagery reclaims architecture's emergence as an urban form emphasising the complexity of the contemporary metropolis. The metropolis is understood through its congestion, confusion, constant change and complex layering. In Hadid's painting, this is visualised through the abstractions, tilts, and the layering that occurs within its composition. The superimposed plans on the rooftops of the city reinforce Hadid's new sense of pictorial space as one mirroring the impact of architecture's superimposition on that city. Her painting affirms that if cohesiveness exists in

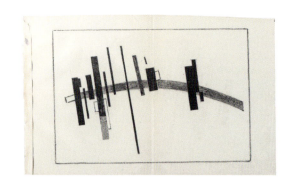

35
Kazimir Malevich
*Suprematism: 34 Drawings*, 1920
Print image, double page,
18 × 21.8 cm (7 1/16 × 8 9/16 in)
Museum of Modern Art, New York

36
Kazimir Malevich
*Suprematist Construction No. 118*, 1917–18
Drawing on paper,
27.2 × 18.2 cm (10 3/4 × 7 3/16 in)
Stedelijk Museum Amsterdam

37
Kazimir Malevich
*Suprematist Painting (with Black Trapezium and Red Square)*, 1915
Oil on canvas, 101.5 × 62 cm (39$^{15}/_{16}$ × 24$^{7}/_{16}$ in)
Stedelijk Museum Amsterdam

38
Anon.
Zaha Hadid, Michael Wolfson (*left*) and Alistair Standing, with *Confetti* (*right*), opening of *Planetary Architecture Two*, 1983
The Architectural Association Archive, London

cultures, it is evidenced within the fluidity of the changing metropolis as it adapts to new formations and lifestyles. Having the floor-scapes grafted onto the city's forms in *Blue Slabs* prompts the idea that architecture and the city rely equally on this sense of abstracted space–form connectivity, mirroring the differing scales of urban experience; each infers transformation of the other. *Blue Slabs* implies the network of dependencies formed between opposites: urban scale and domesticity; new and old; detail to whole; and colour variations and spatial intensity.

Hadid had spoken of valuing Malevich's understanding of the term diagram as something spatially complex, one that reflected the connectivity she implied within these two paintings. Two statements explain her idea of painting's diagrammatic affect and its importance for architecture. Initially, she explained: 'I had looked at Malevich and realised that architecture is not only on the level of the tectonic but on the level of the diagrams and that these [diagrams are] also meant to be a segment of architecture.'[78]

Hadid's subsequent statement further clarifies the spatial implications as one of the abstract diagrammatic effects: 'If you use the term space, like a public space, it is an overall condition, like air. You can never perceive of the whole, unless it is an open space and not on the ground. Our interest is the connection between certain conditions which together form a space, or [how] a series of spaces ... create a certain condition.'[79]

Both *Exploded Isometric* and *Blue Slabs* visually present an understanding of this diagrammatic and spatial complexity within her perception of Hong Kong. Examining these paintings together reinforces that this new spatial logic is presented as a visual dialogue that recognises how architecture could be considered as spatially affective. Without both the narrative possibilities of representation and the abstraction informed by Malevich's conceptualisation of pictorial space, their message could not have been delivered. This complex series of dialogues takes a specific direction in a second pair of paintings: *The Peak, Confetti – Suprematist Snowstorm*[80] and *The Peak, Divers*. These paintings extend an idea tied to Malevich's proposition for painting where imagery is related to differing sensations of time. Hadid's focus was to question how the idea of time had implications for an understanding of space and form in architecture. Both these paintings respond to the visual abstraction of Suprematist art, and the visual perception of movement, time and sensation.

### Defying Gravity:
### *The Peak, Confetti – Suprematist Snowstorm* and *The Peak, Divers*

In the sequencing of production of the paintings for the *Planetary Architecture Two* exhibition, *Confetti* was quite possibly the last painting completed prior to the opening in mid-November of 1983 (fig.39). Although not included in the catalogue, it can be seen prominently displayed in photographs of the occasion (fig.38). David Gomersall recalled its imagery was 'developed through cutting, tearing and layering a series of preliminary drawings', then recomposing them. He concluded 'it was all the pieces blown apart, blown up, or coming together'.[81]

From a distance, *Confetti* is an abstract painting, where polygons are suspended within an abstract visual field. The polygons signify little other than their juxtaposition, an attribute that more directly references Malevich's discussion of gravity within pictorial space, where spacing, directionality, shape and colour imply a relativity and tension between elements. In the painting, there is no 'ground', or sense of representation. What distinguishes *Confetti*, however, is its inclusion of small isometric views of floor surfaces, portraying what appears to be furnishings and walls. On closer inspection these floor-scapes reveal they are the same as those first depicted in *Blue Slabs*.

In *Confetti*, rather than being 'grafted' onto the rooftops of towers in the city, they are suspended within the painting's abstract composition. Because they can be recognised as architectural, they act to restore a narrative focus to this painting. Being architecturally 'explicit', some elements depict recognisable programs: the entry drive and forecourt to the Leisure Club, the pool, diving board, staircases and walls. However, while they are larger in scale than those depicted in *Blue Slabs*, and viewer expectation would be that this greater size would increase their legibility, this is not always the case. Items that suggest furnishings and functionality remain elusively 'fuzzy', opening questions of how their inclusion furthers a communication of architectural ideas (fig.40).

In opposition to *Confetti*'s dynamic yet abstract spatial complexity, *Divers* freezes time differently (fig.41 and page 2). It uses realistic representation to portray a specific point in the act of diving, where two men are frozen in time between two worlds. While they are spatially located above a pool with one diver partly immersed in water, there is no clear architectural referencing of the 'material space' surrounding them. Its geometries remain abstract.

Including depictions of the human body was unusual for Hadid. The realism of these divers draws attention to the late-Suprematist photography of Alexander Rodchenko, particularly *The Diver* (fig.42). His photographs document the scene when a diver is airborne at the midpoint after being propelled from the platform. Rodchenko's notion of 'photo stills' responded to Malevich's idea of 'the logic of sensation', and both were bound within concepts of time and space.[82] What was of interest to Rodchenko was the relationships that the image implies, its complex interweaving of time, movement and sensation – rather than photography's interest in picturing a scene. Hadid later referred specifically to Rodchenko's photographs as inspirational for their sense of defying gravity, of a suspension of the body in space.[83] However, the framing of bodies in the act of diving in Hadid's painting is different from Rodchenko's. These divers are in the precise act of entering the water, causing the surroundings to blur, and the speed of their act removes the clarity of visual references that might define their architectural setting.

The representational value of *Divers* clearly identifies an idealisation of this absence of both time's duration and gravity in relation to a physical action, but it also emphasises the realism reminiscent of these photographs. Viewers could ask whether the focus on men's bodies was used to simply illustrate the activity of people engaged in hedonistic pursuits. Hadid had, after all, explained the program of the building as relating to the concept of leisure: 'Seen from Hong Kong, the mountain cliff forms a backdrop to both leisure and intellectual activities which are suspended in the air. The architecture is a condenser of luxurious and "high" living, intense in its programme.'[84]

In one sense her painting depicts two men in the act of sensory and mental pleasure.[85] However, it is the hedonism of leisure that Hadid considered had a specific speed, as timeless and suspended in relation to life in the city, supporting the new lifestyle of the metropolis. This is clarified when she further explains the differing speeds of life in Hong Kong:

> In a metropolis, people oscillate between very calm activity and that of very hyper, and, to people who take part in that, they are both very important . . . I think, in a metropolis, you oscillate between these two conditions; that's why we like it . . . I think what we are trying to do is to really elaborate that living condition.[86]

39
Zaha Hadid Architects
*The Peak, Confetti – Suprematist Snowstorm*,
Hong Kong, China, 1983
Acrylic and watercolour on paper,
275 × 91 cm (108¼ × 35¹³⁄₁₆ in)
Zaha Hadid Foundation

40
Zaha Hadid Architects
(detail) *The Peak, Confetti – Suprematist Snowstorm*
Acrylic and watercolour on paper
Zaha Hadid Foundation

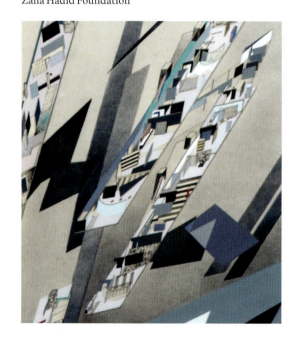

These ideas are more directly referenced for their architectural implications in Hadid's interview with Boyarsky prior to the exhibition in 1983:

> I didn't see it as a gentleman's club to be used only by old Establishment, but as something to be used by all the different age groups and groupings … I wanted something condensing all the things that actually occur in very specific and limited areas. I think what is interesting about the Hong Kong project for me is the notion of floating elements within a given space.[87]

In *Confetti* and *Divers*, the static time of the instance of being caught between two 'worlds' identifies the importance Hadid devised for 'sensation' and 'zero gravity' in architecture.[88] Reinforcing this approach is a small painting, *The Peak, Elements of Void*, completed at the close of the competition and published at the time in *Vision, Architecture + Design*.[89] *Elements of Void* and its published detail, titled *Approach to Residences by Ramp*, portray the layered spatial sensations of a visitor moving at speed toward The Peak (figs 43 and 44). There is an ephemeral quality retained within the architecture, where transparency of form has enabled superimposition in response to a viewer's changing approach. The result, however, may not have achieved the abstract clarity that Hadid desired to construe.

By contrast, *Confetti*'s abstract formulation of polygons and floor-scapes suspended within a non-gravitational space reminds the viewer of the energy and tension implicit within Malevich's notion of pictorial space.[90] Its equivalence in architecture implies a spatiality that is informed by the abstract fragmentation of sensation. *Divers* is more specific – as well as the scale of human form, it portrays an instance in time, a point when a body's unconstrained, geometrically formulated movement references the earth's gravitational pull, yet appears to defy it. It is a temporality that projects the sublime. Within *Confetti* the symbols of architecture are suspended by an invisible energy where connections are relative to the experiencing gaze of the viewer. In *Divers*, the imagery portrays this energy as if held within a body's implicit relativity. Here, the surrounding architectural form is limited to shards of colour, as pure sensation becomes dominant. Both paintings present similar inferences for architecture, of time as implicit within its spatial constructs and their material containment. Evidenced in their imagery is the proposition that architectural form prompts sensations of this complex spatiality, and that rather than space being a by-product of hierarchies of material forms it is sensation that defines architecture's spatiality.

By the early 1980s, when the architect-educators from the AA were being recognised for their success in architectural competitions, it was their distinctive approaches to space and form in architecture that supported their critical acclaim. Bernard Tschumi's winning scheme for the Parc de la Villette had transformed his interest, suggesting architecture could be considered in terms of its compilation of differing spatial 'events' (objects/points, movements/lines and spaces/surfaces), where juxtaposition of architectural elements and programs enhanced the programmatic dynamism of this park.[91] For Tschumi, architecture and its programs were the result of superimposition of these differing individual spatial events.

Koolhaas and Zenghelis had also devised specific conceptions of space in architecture, where intensity and congestion of programmatic complexity were emphasised. Their scheme for the Parc de la Villette competition coincidently used the term 'confetti' to support this idea, with Koolhaas writing: 'Confetti: small-scale elements (refreshment kiosks, children's playgrounds, picnic areas, etc.) which occur throughout the site are distributed according to mathematically derived grid points. Since the park is divided into bands, these elements occur

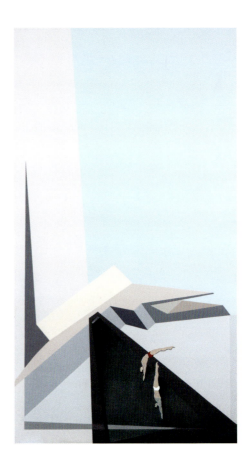

41
Zaha Hadid Architects
*The Peak, Divers*, Hong Kong, China, 1983
Acrylic and watercolour on paper,
180.3 × 104 cm (71 × 41 in)
Zaha Hadid Foundation

42
Alexander Rodchenko
*Zambullida* (*The Diver*), 1934
Photograph, gelatin silver print,
30 × 24 cm (11 13/16 × 9 7/16 in)
Museum of Fine Arts, Boston

43
**Zaha Hadid Architects**
*The Peak, Elements of Void*,
Hong Kong, China, 1983
Acrylic and watercolour on paper,
38.1 × 55.88 cm (15 × 22 in)
Zaha Hadid Foundation

each time in different zones, thereby influencing the character of the "host" zone. Their projection over the entire site creates a unity through fragmentation.'[92]

Their 'confetti' was small-scale built elements, providing an increased spatial complexity in architecture, and as a consequence onto the spatial intensity of experiencing the city. It was an approach structured through overlaying systems that were recognised as having similar formal attributes to that of Tschumi.

Hadid's contribution uniquely focused on the idea of space in architecture considered through the logic of sensation. Like Tschumi, she had been dismayed that space had been considered as 'an overall condition, like air'.[93] However, the consequences she brought to this proposition were vastly different. Her conceptualisation was explained as part of an interview with the magazine *Transition*, where she was asked to comment on her approach to The Peak.[94] She opened by comparing the spatial logic of Malevich's paintings with a development in architectural forms that she recognised in the work of British architect Cedric Price.[95] Hadid's previous project for 59 Eaton Place, and a design for a house by Price, were exhibited together at the AA in June 1982, possibly prompting the comparison.[96]

For Hadid, recognition that Price's interiors were comprised of a series of ordering strategies that were layered and superimposed, opening volumes to visual/spatial interpenetration, became fundamental to her developing approach. His strategy had added intensity to the programs that could be achieved within architectural spaces. She recognised how spatial layering, and its multiplicity of programs, could be extended to architectural form: 'I think that his work, which I find very exciting, is programmatic, but in this case, he would never match that excitement in terms of... the image of the building. What he always ended up with was a shed... But we felt that at this moment, all these things ought to really merge together.'[97]

In the paintings for The Peak, she takes this further. The combination of the possibilities provided by Malevich's notion of pictorial space, and Price's programmatic layering, had suggested to Hadid a new spatiality for architecture and its forms. She focused on architectural form not as enclosure but as fragmented containment where spatial layering is privileged. The ideas were first made evident in her description of the scheme in The Peak Competition Report where she described it as 'Suprematist Geology':

> The site area... is excavated, the rock is blasted out, its highest point levelled to the lowest point of the site. That rock is then taken, polished and added at different degrees to various parts of the site to form the man-made polished granite mountain. Set into the hill it is to incompose all the Club's hedonistic activities. The new polished granite cliffs are erected to meet the top of the site... The architecture appears like a knife cutting through butter devastating all the traditional principles and establishing new ones. Defying nature but not destroying it... The building is layered horizontally, architectural beams superimposed upon each other, constituting a series of different programmes... The void becomes a new architectural landscape within it are suspended all the Club elements hovering over the deck like spaceships at differing heights.[98]

Spatially, her architecture retains the qualities of connectivity, first recognised in Price's interiors but now considered as an architectural landscape: creating a new 'nature', new programmatic relativity and new formal juxtapositions. Reinforcing this as radical, her use of terms – like 'a knife cutting', it 'defies nature', its 'elements hover like spaceships' – to describe architecture works to

44
Zaha Hadid Architects
(detail) *The Peak, Elements of Void*,
Hong Kong, China, 1983
Acrylic and watercolour on paper
Zaha Hadid Foundation

fragment traditional claims of cohesiveness in the 'hierarchy' of architecture's forms. Instead, they reflect the 'hovering' shapes of *Confetti* and the bodies of *Divers*.

This complex realignment of architectural thinking is reinforced through Hadid's use of terms like 'incompose'. It is edited out in later publications, but in context, the term is fundamental rather than a naïve misspelling in an explanation of her paintings' affect.[99] 'Incompose' suggests a purposeful incompleteness or undoing of the architectural object that remains. It introduces the power of non-gravitational understandings of space/object relationships and the superimposition of programs and void spaces in architecture as an idea of transparency and spatial interdependence. Under the logic of 'incompose', space and form can only be partially known, and their relationship is without the contestation of hierarchical order. For paintings like *Confetti* and *Divers*, terms like 'incompose' reinforce an understanding where sensation is outside of time's duration and spatial constraints, and now structured to defy traditional architectural values of order and hierarchy. In an architecture of 'incomposed' space and form, ancient origins of ordered habitation so evidently critiqued in *Exploded Isometric* and *Blue Slabs* are exposed as static and, in their completeness, now irrelevant to contemporary lifestyles of the metropolis. When Hadid stated that the city of Hong Kong 'was changed to suit our purposes', she portrayed a reimagined city of interpenetrating programs, where each experience changed perceptions of the whole.[100]

45
**Zaha Hadid Architects**
*Grand Buildings, Trafalgar Square,
View of Site with London Skyline*,
London, United Kingdom, 1985
Acrylic on paper, 42 × 59.4 cm (16½ × 23⅜ in)
Zaha Hadid Foundation

# 3 Politicising the Urban Character of London: Grand Buildings

Zaha Hadid had a distinctive affection for the city of London. Because she arrived during her early adulthood, London as a city mixed the involvement of her studies with being immersed in the free-roaming social and cultural offerings of galleries, nightclubs and punk counterculture of the 1970s. Central London, with its urban complexity and historic building stock, was still recovering from the aftermath of the Second World War bombing, exacerbated by the blight of both post-war ill-conceived public building initiatives and developer exploitation. The late 1970s in Britain was a time of widespread industrial action coupled with a renewed recognition of social inequality. Derelict buildings, mounting uncollected rubbish and squatters were interwoven with out-of-date and decaying urban infrastructure. Despite the vibrant lifestyle for a young architecture student the idea of 'the city' – as an intense commercial, residential, social and cultural interchange, with a distinctive character that was immediately understood as 'London' – was yet to be realised.

The architectural competition for the project known as Grand Buildings became a focus for arguments about how to proceed with the renewal of the heritage centre of the city. The architectural competition was launched in 1985 to redevelop the historic Grand Hotel, built in 1879, which was located directly opposite Trafalgar Square.[1] Hadid's approach to the competition was partly influenced by the academic environment of London's Architectural Association (AA), where she was teaching at the time. In its School of Architecture, students were taught to see Central London and its spaces as a laboratory of architectural knowledge, or as a type of complex artefact requiring intellectual and physical engagement. Because of its contemporary decline, the city had become understood not as a benign entity, a background to life, or a vessel waiting to be inhabited by new architectural schema, but as a series of unique spaces that were politically meaningful, and open to a contestation of contemporary ideas embedded within the process of urban renewal.

Following her recent success in The Peak international competition in the first half of the 1980s, Hadid had entered the intellectual inner circle of AA educators. Other young members of this circle were also successfully establishing their careers as significant architects. Rem Koolhaas's book *Delirious New York* had been released, and the work of his office, OMA, had been exhibited at the Solomon R. Guggenheim Museum in New York and at the first Venice Architecture Biennale of 1980.[2] One of OMA's earliest projects, commissioned in 1981, was for The Netherlands Dance Theatre in The Hague.[3] Léon Krier's book *Rational Architecture Rationelle: The Reconstruction of the European City* was gaining recognition internationally, and influencing debates about historical city centres.[4] In London, Krier became instrumental in the re-evaluation of the recent scheme for the expansion of The National Gallery, ultimately being appointed the leading architectural advisor to HRH The Prince of Wales.[5] Bernard Tschumi had been involved in the Paris Biennale of 1980, completing a series of publications culminating in the book *The Manhattan Transcripts: Theoretical Projects* published in 1981, and by early 1983 had been announced winner of the 'Parc de la Villette' architectural competition in Paris, which in its realisation over the following years established his professional standing.⁶ While continuing to teach at the AA, Zaha Hadid, who was a generation behind her colleagues, extended her architectural reputation internationally through exhibitions and small commissions.⁷

The early 1980s also saw contemporary French philosophy having a growing importance for architectural discussions at the AA. New propositions on architecture were broadly influenced by the writings of contemporary philosophers and sociologists including Jacques Derrida, Michel de Certeau, Henri Lefebvre, Guy Debord, Roland Barthes and Michel Foucault.⁸ Discussions informed by their philosophical discourses became tied into the broader intellectual settings of critique at the AA. They became more direct when Tschumi developed a close association with Derrida in the resolution of his 1982 Parc de la Villette competition.⁹ Similarly, North American architect and educator Peter Eisenman, through his growing interactions with Derrida, expanded his involvement at the AA, where he lectured and discussed contemporary understandings of power and language in relation to architecture. Hadid's interest in philosophy was more oblique and broad ranging. As discussed in earlier chapters, her interests lay more in the domain of experience and sensation in architecture. It was an idea that first emerged from her interest in Suprematism, particularly in the writings of Kazimir Malevich, but in a coincidence of inquiry, it developed synergies with contemporary philosophical approaches.

In this context, ideas from contemporary philosophy were not studied at the schools for their integrity, but more often discussed within a critique of architectural propositions already in play. Interactions were not based on one discipline following another, but philosophy and architecture were both reconfiguring ideas within their own intellectual processes, often expressing the complex nature of these ideas by borrowing terminology and methods from across disciplinary boundaries. The synergy between the disciplines relied on explicit and common interests used to revitalise experimentation. The introduction of contemporary philosophy to the debates within the AA enabled architecture's complex considerations to be vocalised in new ways.¹⁰ These approaches informed debates on the city that had previously relied, in the architectural press, on more disciplinary specific texts such as Colin Rowe and Fred Koetter's *Collage City* and Aldo Rossi's *The Architecture of the City*.¹¹ Rowe, from Cornell University, had been a respected visitor at the AA since the mid-1970s, and Rossi's writing, originally in Italian, had been interpreted for English audiences especially at the AA by Léon Krier.¹²

Rather than resolve the complex nature of ideas within these debates into a singular 'School' approach, AA Chairman Alvin Boyarsky's intention was for a 'smorgasbord' of ideas and propositions.¹³ However, the core attribute of unity in this smorgasbord was the introduction of certain conceptual associations between the idea of the contemporary city and the critique of its social and regulatory planning frameworks.

Hadid's approach to London's future architectural development is contextualised in part by these occurrences. They are first made evident in her teaching.¹⁴ Her teaching Unit descriptions in the *Architectural Association Prospectus* from the 1982/83 and 1983/84 academic years provide evidence of an understanding of the city that is conceived as a vehicle for architectural activism. While not explicitly naming her influences, the student projects that she led moved away from the usual site-specific interests of architectural pedagogy to engage more with issues of power-relations within the city. Her interest was for students to become active agents in London's future:

> The damage done to London after the war and more recently is devastating. Architects, critics, and historians are somewhat removed, they resigned

themselves to believing that it is out of their hands. The day of their awakening will be when it is too late, and their fault outweighs that of the developers. Where is the debate? We will have to initiate it.[15]

This rallying cry for students to challenge London's conservativism was referenced in her own work through opposition to two political environments within which architects worked. The first was the approach to the city undertaken by urban planners. Hadid critiqued the 'somnambulance' of London's planning approaches.[16] The second was the architectural conservativism directed toward the future of Central London. Her critique here was epitomised by the public furore surrounding the 1982 architectural competition to extend The National Gallery. For her, the role of the architect was to 'invent and create appropriate programmes at appropriate points in the metropolis' and not to have a 'noddyland suburban development even at the heart of the metropolis'.[17]

It is this more specific architectural context that needs some explanation. The competition for the Grand Buildings required a mixed-use redevelopment. The Grand Hotel was acknowledged as a rundown building, but because of the site's significant heritage location facing Trafalgar Square, planning requirements for the final scheme demanded a single facade of 'Bath stone' for the Strand and Northumberland Avenue frontages. As noted in the architectural press, the significance of this site could not be underestimated.[18] The owners – Land Securities – had attempted its redevelopment several times over the previous decade, and just prior to the launch of the competition, achieved conditional approval to demolish the rundown building *only if* the competition successfully led to a commission that would fulfil the brief's strict requirements.[19]

The Grand Buildings competition coincided with the aftermath of an ill-fated architectural competition aimed to extend London's National Gallery. The success of the winning scheme had been compromised when HRH The Prince of Wales, when addressing the Royal Institute of British Architects (RIBA) in late May 1984, delivered a damning criticism, claiming it as a 'monstrous carbuncle on the face of a much-loved and elegant friend'.[20] This winning scheme by the architects Ahrends, Burton and Koralek (ABK), an undeniably sophisticated and modern solution to the competition brief, was finally denied planning permission in late 1984.[21] Subsequently, Léon Krier was appointed to scope the possibility of a more classically explicit masterplan for the Gallery and the precinct abutting Trafalgar Square.[22] In the same speech to the RIBA, HRH The Prince of Wales then directed his attention to the Grand Buildings competition:

> As if the National Gallery extension wasn't enough, they are now apparently planning to redevelop the large, oval-bellied 19th century building, known as the Grand Hotel . . . As with the National Gallery, I believe the plan is to put this redevelopment out to competition, in which case we can only criticise the judges and not the architects, for I suspect there will be some entries representative of the present-day school of Romantic Pragmatism, which could at least provide an alternative . . . Goethe once said, 'there is nothing more dreadful than imagination without taste'.[23]

The entry of HRH The Prince of Wales into London's urban politics added to an already predominantly conservative attitude to the urban redevelopment of the Grand Buildings site.[24] The competition entrants would have been aware of the possibility of royal critique and its influence on the competition and their careers. At its conclusion, the announcement of Sidell Gibson's scheme as the winner confirmed this caution – with their proposal based on the strict retention of the historical pattern and material forms of streetscapes surrounding Trafalgar Square, and a building that conformed with a Victorian-inspired perimeter-walled classical historicism.[25]

Entries for the first round of the competition closed early in March 1985, and included a submission from the partnership of Zaha Hadid and her AA colleague Elia Zenghelis. Zenghelis's name was included most likely to overcome Hadid's lack of the required UK professional and residential status – a pattern of association evident since 1979 when she entered the competition for the Irish Prime Minister's Residence.[26]

In later conversations with Alvin Boyarsky, Hadid dismissed the competition's 'dull brief', its lack of intellectual ambition and its requirement for a perimeter-walled enclosure. She foretold the resulting outcome saying that 'everybody would design a well-mannered building, following the boundaries of the site, made of stone and Victorian references'.[27] Her conclusion was that, 'We knew we could not win because of the atmosphere surrounding the competition – Leo Krier [sic] and all that ... but it was important to make a counter statement.'[28] Her ambition for the site was for a distinctively new type of public domain – intellectually and physically opening Trafalgar Square to influences of the surrounding urban environment. Her scheme was politically provocative and ignored past architectural typologies typified by the area's perimeter-walled blocks, classical porticoes and axial alignment to monuments.

Developing strategies from The Peak project, Hadid explained her approach:

The idea behind The Peak was that by cutting off the ground and replacing it with beams, each with a specific program of use, then the public domain would be captured within the resulting void. In the case of Trafalgar Square – a completely different context – we formed a slab to act as a backdrop to the slender towers, thus avoiding anything of the sheer bulk and declared the site a public space ...

With The Peak we carved the site out to layer it horizontally. With The Grand Building we thought it was necessary to attach the base of the site to the underground station so that it becomes a Grand Lobby for the underpass to the square and the nearby railway station at Charing Cross. It creates a public level which is below ground and has cinemas and shopping on a 24-hour basis. The public level doesn't remain underground, it goes up the ramp and becomes the horizontal lobby of the slab building with connections to the towers which are also public.[29]

It was as if the architectural diagram from The Peak was to be turned at 90 degrees and aligned vertically as towers on to the new site.[30] Her scheme introduced a single long slab-building toward the rear of the site as a backdrop to a series of thin towers placed on a multi-levelled public plaza opening through an underpass toward Trafalgar Square and Charing Cross Station. By opening the space to public view and access, and separating floor space over several building types, what seemed like a simple intellectual realignment of the conceptual apparatus of Hong Kong now became a bold counter proposition to London's existing neoclassical urban context. Hadid's scheme challenged the requirement for London's formal division between public, institutional and private spaces by introducing spatial porosity.

Hadid's black and white drawings submitted for the competition were published in the *Architects' Journal* magazine editorial 'Grand Exits', in August 1985.[31] The subsequent paintings for the scheme, developed after the closure of the First Stage, were in response to an invitation to mount a retrospective of her paintings at the GA Gallery in Tokyo, opening later that year.[32] The Tokyo exhibition became the subject of the publication by *Global Architecture* in the following year.[33] Her paintings for the Grand Buildings were important in this context as they had not been exhibited before, enabling Hadid to introduce her now 'politicised' vision of urban renewal for London to international audiences.

For these paintings, Hadid chose ways of imagining her scheme using visual strategies that would support her criticism of the conservativism of the competition brief and its outcomes. When Boyarsky questioned why she continued to investigate this scheme, she responded:

> I always advise students that they should never go back and finish an old project, unless something can be learnt from it . . . I see the additional work as a kind of research and the drawings we are now doing on Trafalgar Square show the relationship of the building to the site and the city, from the air, from below and even sideways. It's one last statement about a program for Central London. It's also because of one's frustration with London.[34]

Even before the exhibition in Tokyo, the paintings were taken up by the architectural press. As early as September 1985, in an article titled 'Grand Tour', the journal *Building Design* reproduced two that they titled *Worm's Eye View with Ramp and Towers*, and an early rendition of *Back Elevation Toward Trafalgar Square (Night View)*.[35] It was in *Building Design* that the personnel of the complete team were named: Zaha Hadid, Michael Wolfson, Brian Ma Siy, Piers Smerin, Kar-Hwa Ho, Gareth Pierce and Madelaine Palme.[36] Elia Zenghelis's name had been dropped from the list, reinforcing that his earlier inclusion had been the result of necessity in competition registration requirements, rather than actual involvement. By December 1985, when Hadid's scheme appeared for a second time, in a more fulsome coverage in *L'Architecture d'Aujourd'hui*, the list of assistants extended.[37] In this publication, Hadid's scheme was treated independently under the title 'Dynamiser L'Urbain, Concours pour Trafalgar Square, Londres', losing any connection with the competition.[38] This repeated interest from the architectural media for her approach to London's historic centre reinforced the idea that Hadid's paintings were by then being recognised as powerful forms of communication, informing architectural debate at an international level. The growing interest from the French architectural press may coincidentally have been in response to Hadid's inclusion in the exhibition *Les Immatériaux* held at the Centre Pompidou in Paris, curated by Jean-François Lyotard and Thierry Chaput.[39] It is when the imagery of her Grand Buildings paintings is viewed in this context that certain affinities develop between approaches absorbed from Suprematism and overlaid with ideas central to contemporary philosophical debates opened by Lyotard.

Like The Peak, each final painting for the Grand Buildings scheme had passed through many hands in the process of completion, with assistants delivering what had been recognised as their personal expertise. It was through their individual and collective negotiation with Hadid, about the structuring of each drawing, the implications and selection of colour and tone, and the speed of the processes of creating a composition, that certain elements were exaggerated. Brian Ma Siy remembers creating some of the original drawn sketches and preliminary paintings. He explained that final compositions often 'combined [his] preliminary drawings, later redrawn by Michael Wolfson before being further interpreted through drawing prior to painting'.[40] As with earlier schemes, the assistants who drew these images rarely mixed colours or painted. However, each of the team remembered that it was Madelaine Palme whose technique of painting the sky, emphasising a certain weight and density not seen before in Hadid's work, had changed the relationship of drawing to painting in this instance. Palme's involvement in the painting of *View of Site with London Skyline* especially, reflected a new pictorial sensibility.

For discussion in this chapter, analysis will focus on the paintings as a collective. Included are those with the secondary titles *View of Site with London Skyline*, *End Elevation Towards Trafalgar Square*, *View from Trafalgar Square*, *Worm's Eye View with Ramp and Towers*, *Inside Podium: Lobbies and Towers* and *Interior of Office Scape in the Slab-tower, Floor Planes*.[41] When initially compared with the paintings of her earlier schemes, what is unique is the small size of each painting. When displayed in a gallery setting, they would demand a viewer's close attention. This becomes significant when placed beside paintings of The Peak, for example, as their imagery worked differently. For the paintings of Grand Buildings, exploration would be intimate and close, with the viewer engaged across the range of different paintings displayed as a group. Rather than adopt the method of inquiry used for The Peak paintings, for this analysis each painting for Grand Buildings will be explored for its pictorial affect prior to opening an interpretation of how their images work as paintings, and then questioning how these paintings coalesce as an idea politicising the conservativism underpinning development in London.

### Fragmentation versus Totality in the Politics of the View: Paintings for Grand Buildings

The paintings *View of Site with London Skyline*, *End Elevation Towards Trafalgar Square* and *View from Trafalgar Square* form a set of small, distorted perspectives viewed from above. In *View of Site with London Skyline* a densely textured sky dominates the top half of the composition (fig.45). Roofscapes of the city sit below a consistent gentle curve of the horizon, which in turn accepts the spatial weight produced by the sky's textured tonality. At points, the recognisable spires of the tower of St Martin-in-the-Fields, and the lantern and cross of the dome of St Paul's, prick through the solidity of this division. Reaching just higher than the collection of new office buildings defining the background, the spires have little effect other than subtly reminding the architecturally informed viewer of the consistent height limits that reinforce the 'Protected View Corridors' of London's planning policies.[42] These restrictions were created by the 'Greater London Development Plan' in the 1970s, and subsequently introduced into law, and remain a development requirement. Trafalgar Square lay on one of these 'view corridors', where coincidentally the painting's viewer now hovers looking eastward. The corridor, connecting Trafalgar Square with Parliament Hill and the Palace of Westminster (the Houses of Parliament), remains the control implicit in this painting. These 'view corridors' projected from both the Palace of Westminster and St Paul's Cathedral control height limits and other development restrictions for new buildings in Central London.

Hadid's Grand Buildings scheme, portrayed at the bottom right of the composition, accepts the height restrictions of its location, set within the heritage triangle of the city implied by these containment lines. In the painting's compositional emphases, the scheme appears to conform with planning restrictions, but it breaches one edge of the painting's perimeter. It is as though, in the placement of the scheme onto a site in Central London, certain elements will 'escape' its architectural constraints and their governance – even while accepting others. This imagery subtly reinforces the message that Hadid openly questioned the limits being placed on architectural innovation.

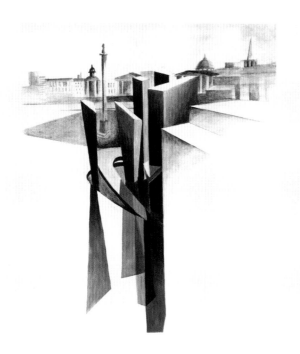 

above left:
46
Zaha Hadid Architects
*Grand Buildings, Trafalgar Square, End Elevation Towards Trafalgar Square*,
London, United Kingdom, 1985
Acrylic on paper, 61 × 63 cm (24 × 24 13/16 in)
GA Photographs

above right:
47
Zaha Hadid Architects
*Grand Buildings, Trafalgar Square, View from Trafalgar Square*,
London, United Kingdom, 1985
Acrylic on paper, 61 × 63 cm (24 × 24 13/16 in)
Zaha Hadid Foundation

Adding to this narrative, the other paintings, *End Elevation Towards Trafalgar Square* and *View from Trafalgar Square*, form a pair that are distinctively partial glimpses, each taken from differing viewing points (figs 46 and 47). Rather than be deferential to the monumental setting close by – of Trafalgar Square and adjoining buildings – their subject is Hadid's schema for the Grand Buildings: elongated and distorted as a series of semi-abstracted vertical forms, isolated from neighbouring buildings and the street level.

In *End Elevation Towards Trafalgar Square* the spire of St Martin-in-the-Fields is in the top right of the composition, and the inclusion of Nelson's Column and the classical portico and dome of The National Gallery helps signify its historic urban context. The National Gallery facade is elongated and fragmented as if transformed as a false panorama, enabling its end cupola to be imagined stretched to appear south of Nelson's Column. In *View from Trafalgar Square*, a similar exaggeration of the scheme becomes the focus of a scene looking toward the south, where South Bank, the old Charing Cross Railway Station and Hungerford Bridge can be seen in the distance. In both these views, Hadid's scheme is presented as the visual focus. The imagery avoids peripheral contexts that might be considered as extraneous fillers or contextualising prompts for an architectural order or formal deference. What is also avoided is the hierarchy of urban spaces expected in architectural presentation drawings, where the view would be 'constrained' by the dominating presence of London's historic monuments.

Two further paintings reverse this type of distant view by focusing within the scheme's urban spaces. *Worm's Eye View with Ramp and Towers* and *Inside Podium: Lobbies and Towers* create a distorted scenography where the viewer, internal to the painting's imagery, is located below street level (figs 48 and 49). There is a purposeful ambiguity developed in these paintings where the ground plane seems the most ill-defined aspect of the composition, with the architectural form remaining semi-abstract and ephemeral. Hadid had designated this space as a vast 'urban lobby', acting as a forecourt to Trafalgar Square as much as it was a pedestrian link to Charing Cross Station. The scene in both paintings encapsulates the view toward the Grand Buildings site and denies any dominance given to the street level of the Strand. Where the street level is implied, it is only revealed through a change in tonal values.

48
Zaha Hadid Architects
*Grand Buildings, Trafalgar Square, Worm's Eye View with Ramp and Towers*,
London, United Kingdom, 1985
Acrylic on paper,
42 × 59.4 cm (16½ × 23⅜ in)
Zaha Hadid Foundation

49
Zaha Hadid Architects
*Grand Buildings, Trafalgar Square, Inside Podium: Lobbies and Towers*,
London, United Kingdom, 1985
Acrylic on paper,
42 × 84 cm (16½ × 33 in)
GA Photographs

Defined only through shades of pigment, the architectural forms depicted in these two paintings negotiate the functions of the site without any sense of exclusion or exclusivity between what is public and what private. Spatial containment and division remain suggestive and ill-defined. Even the walls of the towers are ephemerally portrayed as shadowed tone, encouraging the viewer to look through their transparency and imagine spaces and towers, beyond their surfaces. In *Inside Podium: Lobbies and Towers* small brightly coloured elements are seen deep within this spatial layering and suggest a second 'centre' or architectural point of interest. In *Worm's Eye View with Ramp and Towers* the right side of the painting includes a further series of drawings, layered over the scene. They depict the plans and three-dimensional forms of the scheme from different angles, as if the viewer is circumnavigating the site.

The last painting considered in this group, *Interior of Office Scape in the Slab-tower, Floor Planes*, comprises only horizontal and vertical planes distributed across a background (fig.50). If it were not for the recognisable fluid shape of the Thames River coloured bright blue in the background, this painting's relation to others would have remained elusive. Within its composition there is a vertical division separating left from right, with two seemingly unrelated parts: the left dominated by vertical planes and the right by horizontal ones. Viewers are left to ponder what relationships are suggested by this juxtaposition. Its collection of elements opens questions of what defines substance in architecture. If the requirement for the competition was a perimeter-walled building in stone, this image questions the 'power' given to a wall's spatial division. Here the wall remains absent, present only as a division, its architectural meaning stripped to the essentiality of abstract planes.

When considered together, these six paintings display an abstracted and distorted depiction of architecture, each differentiated in their techniques when compared with traditional conventions of drawing in architecture.[43] What unifies them is the techniques they adapt from painting: their soft tonality, their juxtaposition of ephemeral forms, and their complex layered spatiality. As a collective these paintings define neither the scheme nor its surrounds within any sense of 'calculated standards' that might be expected from perspectival drawing in architectural practices. They evoke an architecture through the emotive and expressive sensibilities of painting.

As discussed in Chapter 1, within architecture's geometrically aligned construct of perspective with its origins in Leon Battista Alberti's writing during the early Renaissance, there is an avoidance of 'deceptive appearances' that could be construed as expressive and central to the artistry of painting.[44] Hadid presents an alternative proposition, where the idea of appearances and their deceptions are purposefully embraced. At the level of the image, these paintings initiate an inquiry specifically prompted by architectural concerns. However, where detail occurs in the imagery of her paintings, it often increases the ambiguity of the scene rather than clarifying its architectural or material precision. In architectural practice prior to Modernism (and importantly re-emerging during the Postmodern era), the use of the perspective drawing was favoured to illustrate the contextual fit of new architectural forms, where buildings were represented within the precisely drawn details of their urban settings.[45] Within the construct of perspectival geometry there is an alignment between the 'eye' of the viewer, the scene's spatial and formal qualities, and its vanishing point(s).[46] By the early 20th century, historian Erwin Panofsky concluded that perspective techniques were so pervasive in Western art and architecture that perspective could be considered a 'symbolic form'.[47] He argued, 'in a sense, perspective transforms psychophysical space into mathematical space'.[48] For Panofsky, the perspective notion of geometric accuracy and verifiable

50
Zaha Hadid Architects
*Grand Buildings, Trafalgar Square, Interior of Office Scape in the Slab-tower, Floor Planes*,
London, United Kingdom, 1985
Acrylic on paper,
57 × 84 cm (22½ × 33 in)
Zaha Hadid Foundation

scenography had changed the very construct of how the world was understood. Within the structure of perspectival depictions in architecture is an implied sense of formal order, spatial distancing, gravity and ground.[49] The subject content of the image becomes a mirror, locating the viewer's understanding of themselves in the context of what they observe and consider as rational order. As a technique, perspectival geometries develop an agreed logic of distortion, to present a consistent and measurable spatial depth diminishing from the picture plane toward infinity.[50] So, the question arises, what was Hadid doing in the representation of her Grand Buildings scheme?

The key to understanding her paintings is in their difference from these principles. It takes on a purposefulness when she critiqued the politics behind the architectural renewal of Central London, and her evaluation of 'Leo Krier [*sic*] and all that'.[51] Within this critique, Hadid drew attention to how, through architectural drawings and particularly through their conformity with perspective techniques, Krier had swayed public and architectural opinion whilst concealing the extent of the change proposed. Central to her concern were the drawings that Krier, or an acolyte, had submitted in support of the Skidmore, Owings & Merrill (SOM) proposal for the extension to the National Gallery competition in 1982 (fig.51).[52]

It was a distinctive style and technique that Krier had applied for some years. It included a fine-lined perspective picturing that relied on a base photographic image that was then over-drawn. In his approach, a consistency of line reinforced the totality of the view, in one sense repeating the 'realism' of the photograph, but implicitly signifying a 'cleansing' of the chronology and corporeality of the change proposed by the addition of a new scheme. In this type of drawing, there is no differentiation of the new with reference to the old. While there was some debate at the time amongst trustees of The National Gallery in support of SOM's scheme, as an alternative to the eventual competition winner, it remained runner-up.[53]

The fine linearity of Krier's rendering style was well known amongst architects and students at the AA, and given Hadid's outcry to Boyarsky, it likely prompted her further damning criticism: 'The most superficial aspect of that architecture, its graphics and the strength of its formalism is always the most dangerously

51
Skidmore, Owings & Merrill
*Unexecuted competition design for the National Gallery Extension project, Hampton site, Trafalgar Square, London: perspective view of Trafalgar Square, including the church of St Martin-in-the-Fields and Nelson's Column, from the proposed extension, London*, 1982
Print, 59.4 × 84.1 cm (23 ⅜ × 33 ⅛ in)
Royal Institute of British Architects Archive, London

appealing. We cannot stop that. We are not censors ... we have to believe that we the authors of architecture, can change circumstance.'[54]

The frequent use of perspective representations in architectural practice had by the 1980s become a topic of interest in contemporary debate on society and the city. French sociologist and philosopher Michel de Certeau, whose interests were in experiences of the everyday, critiqued the Krier-like approach to perspective drawing in architecture. De Certeau had specifically criticised the utopianism of this type of aerial perspective. In its desire for 'seeing the whole' he claimed perspective views, like that completed by SOM, had proposed architecture as 'a theoretical simulacrum, in short a picture' rather than providing an understanding of the city or of architectural reality.[55] De Certeau argued that this type of view only considered the city as a two-dimensional picture that 'haunts users of architectural productions by materialising today the utopia that yesterday was only painted'.[56] Through Krier's drawing style, the city as lived could only fail to materialise the utopia of its depictions.

Like de Certeau, Hadid was concerned about this type of utopian scenography, one that she considered 'remained dangerously appealing'. By comparison with Krier's manner of drawing, her paintings for Grand Buildings introduce a different understanding of 'the view', by using painterly techniques to avert or distort the potential 'utopian picturing'. One source that might explain Hadid's direction was obliquely referred to in an interview she had with the critic Hans Ulrich Obrist in 2010. Obrist leadingly asks Hadid to respond to the comment that she exploited the ambiguities of Suprematism including 'the ways in which its forms can be read as horizontal or vertical and its spaces recessive or flat at the same time'.[57] Hadid responded: 'Yes, that was influenced by the Russians, but not the drawings – by photography like Alexander Rodchenko's.'[58] What is argued here is that it is Rodchenko's distinctive approach to photography during the late 1920s and early 1930s that has parallels with Hadid's avoidance of the pictorial completeness usually found in perspectival renderings.[59]

It is useful here to explain some attributes of Rodchenko's approach, as his photographs reference a distinctive way of 'seeing' that invites links with

52
Alexander Rodchenko
(cover) *Novyi LEF*, no.9, 1928
Print, back and front cover,
two pages × 23 × 15.2 cm (9 1/16 × 6 in)
Museum of Modern Art, New York

53
Alexander Rodchenko
*'Experiment 28', Myasnitskaya Street balconies*,
Moscow, 1925
Photograph, gelatin silver print,
15.7 × 23.9 cm (6³⁄₁₆ × 9⁷⁄₁₆ in)
Rodchenko family collection

philosophic discussions on the city during the mid-1980s. Rodchenko's photographs imply an alternate understanding of perspective and how the 'realism' of a scene can be interpreted. By the mid-1920s, the subject matter of his photographs focused on his personal surrounds. Often experimenting with unique orientations of each view, placement of the camera's gaze, and cropping, he signalled a subjective rather than objective relationship between the photographic 'eye' and the scene captured by the camera. Through experimentation with linear and angular contrasts, where orientation of these scenes was difficult for viewers to discern, Rodchenko's interest was that the viewer needed to more actively engage with what they were attempting to interpret. To make this logic explicit, when he presented photographs in the graphic context of his periodical *Novyi LEF: Journal of the Left Front of the Arts* images were often compiled or montaged to exaggerate different orientations (fig.52).[60] Examples of this are also seen in the magazine *Pioneer* (fig.54).[61] The final compilation was often disorienting, where through the camera's close proximity and dynamic angle of view, the perspectival construct of each image was distorted. When published, these individual views were collaged where negatives are sometimes reversed for effect, as seen when comparing figures 53 and 54. Rodchenko called these images 'perspectives', but clearly attributed their difference from those focused on 'scene making'. His perspectives presented viewers with a puzzle to solve, and he claimed that through activating viewer engagement, these images constituted a new way of seeing. His use of the term *foto-kadry* (photo still or snapshot) to explain his work rather than *foto-katriny* (photo-picture) was to avoid any claim of their resemblance to the 'picturesque' totality of scenic views.[62]

There is a political imperative to Rodchenko's photographs. Examples included here are photographs of where he lived on Myasnitskaya Street in Moscow. The street is lined with wealthy 18th-century classical buildings and remains one of the most recognised historic merchant streets of the city. Rather than the monumentality of the historic street facade, he focused on his own dwelling, the artists' apartment building in its rear courtyard. The modernity of this imagery is in stark contrast with the monumentality of the historic facade. As seen in figure 53, attention is on the building's modernity, the linearity of the composition and the separation of the subject from its background. Rodchenko claimed that his aim was to find a 'new (have no fear) aesthetics, impulse, and pathos for expressing our new socialist facts through photography'.[63] At the time, this new approach

54
Alexander Rodchenko
*'Foto-vopros'*, Пионер (*Pioneer*), no.13, July 1933,
p.4
Photographic collage, collection unknown

to photography was criticised by the group ROPF (the Revolutionary Society of Proletarian Photographers) as aestheticising the image where form became more important that content.[64] Discounting this claim, Rodchenko's emphasis was on essential fragments of life, where an object's form was reinforced by the dynamism of outlines and spatial contrasts idiosyncratically framing that life, and where the subject of the view symbolised the 'facts' of lived experience.

Rodchenko's interests in the spatiality of the image led him to argue that this approach to photography and photomontage better recorded the 'modernity' of contemporary Soviet Russian society as experienced.[65] His aim was to describe this new culture as distinct from Western traditions, especially in painting where perspective was understood as ubiquitous and utopian. His proposition was that for an understanding of the contemporaneity of the Russian situation there must be a way to 'see' experience without replicating the traditions of Western art. Commenting on this attribute in Rodchenko's art, French philosopher Jean-François Lyotard noted its alignment with a new type of 'seeing' that implied a bodily engagement: 'Our body, upset in its natural balance of viewing and reading, must shift, find new positions from which reading once again becomes legible: the seeing seen.'[66]

The question arises: was Rodchenko's politicisation of the perspectival image a prompt for Hadid in relation to her Grand Buildings scheme? It is an idea necessary to test. Establishing correspondences between Hadid's paintings for Grand Buildings and Rodchenko's photographs provides an understanding of the power of images to project ideas that have architectural implications. Such comparisons would also invite consideration of the ideas of the philosophers like de Certeau or Lyotard for their potential influence on her architectural thought.

For Hadid's paintings, a reference to Rodchenko's photographs in the light of comments by de Certeau or Lyotard reinforces her interest in the sensation of a world as experienced, where each fleeting ambiguity of a glimpse remains powerfully partial. And that in the multiplicity of sensations there is a reconsideration of the purpose of representation. By adapting Rodchenko-like compositional strategies, Hadid's selection of views for Grand Buildings begins to 'frame' a new spatiality, one she proposed was required in architecture to show the potential of London's contemporary sense of urbanity. Certain pictorial strategies become a prompt for viewers to consider: the broad and expressively dominant sky; the view across sites of monumental dominance rather than along their urban axes; and of an architecture remaining ephemerally ambiguous rather than clearly integrated as contextual form.

### The Transformation of *Foto-Kadry* to Visualise Architecture's Spatial Role in the City

In her descriptions of the Grand Buildings scheme, Hadid spoke of the necessity to make a 'counter statement' directed to the competition's constraining briefing documents and the political interference over the extension of London's National Gallery. For her, the briefing requirements of the competition to recreate a perimeter-walled facade symbolised an exclusivity in Central London that she felt was no longer viable – an unwelcoming and threatening sense of privileged interiority. She also recognised that in this understanding, a pedestrian's experience of London's urban spaces would continue to be confined to the networks of narrow footpaths and by the social controls that 'privilege' commands. This type of spatial division had been emphasised in SOM's scheme for the extension to The

National Gallery, where perspectives show new streets created to further formalise the institutional structuring and monumentality of urban spaces like Trafalgar Square. Hadid's paintings for Grand Buildings present an alternative; politicising their imagery by using Rodchenko's understanding of *foto-kadry*, they present a London in which the utopianism implied by traditions of the perspectival view in architecture is not reinforced. Because she focused on points of transition and an experiential transparency in the architecture's network of public domain types, her London envisaged the complex nature of contemporary lifestyles and their refusal to be reduced to ancient structures of order and status.

From Hadid's previous projects like The Peak, architecture and the city were considered as embedded within a notion of the 'metropolis'. The concept of the 'metropolis' accepted the city as spatially layered, with competing programs held within a state of continuing metamorphosis – an environment that cannot be known in any totality, nor controlled by the utopian distinctiveness of historical time frames.[67] Her paintings of Grand Buildings represent the importance of the micro-scale of individual experiences rather than the macro-scale of the mass and social order. Each of Hadid's paintings has an idiosyncratic focus as they negotiate the new in relation to the old, the subjective in relation to the collective. The paintings present the idea that within their reformulation of architectural and spatial forms, London's monumental spaces are recalled in the minds of individuals for their referencing of subjective time, rather than their role in regulatory spatial and objective order. They form a juxtaposition between old and new that reminds the viewer of the powerful analogy that juxtaposition suggests – that the metropolis is a living organism.

Her paintings invite an inquiry of how these ideas might register within considerations of urbanity and the city during the mid-1980s. Contemporary architectural discussions on the idea of the city referenced two books that had expanding readerships: the new English translation of Rossi's *The Architecture of the City* published in 1982 was now critiqued in the context of Colin Rowe and Fred Koetter's *Collage City* of 1978.[68] Additionally, and important for its centrality to debates on London's historic centre, was Léon Krier's ongoing interpretation of Rossi's ideas in his own *Rational Architecture Rationelle: The Reconstruction of the European City*.[69] To question how Hadid's paintings reflected or critiqued their ideas broadens an understanding of the approach she presented on the issues raised by the historical city, and more specifically by London. When these are seen in the light of her statements on Rodchenko, and her response to more immediate events, there is a context for understanding the approach taken in the paintings and architecture of Grand Buildings.

Rowe and Koetter's *Collage City* had presented the complexity of historic cities as an urban collage having both spatial and chronological significance. Explaining their use of the term collage through the practices of Synthetic Cubism in the fine arts, their imperative was to recognise 'a combination of dissimilar images'.[70] From Synthetic Cubism they realised that, while the final art object or image of this group's work gave the impression of a unified thing, each component part in itself could engage viewers in an inquiry of its former use or value. In the context of architectural debates, the notion of this type of collage helped explain a city's complex assembly of new and old forms, now recognised within a compounded, yet apparently singular, 'bricolage' of architectural and spatial characteristics that may have emerged in different periods.[71] The 'city as collaged' acknowledged the idiosyncratic temporality and presentness of everyday experiences of habitation, as well as the chronology of each city's origins and its overlay of multiple spatial and political structures.

Hadid's schema accepted this notion of accretion of forms within a city, and with this came the acceptance of new with old. But further, the experience of individual sensations of urban form was recognised as idiosyncratic and not able to be attributed essentially to rational sources. The imagery of each of her paintings was enriched by other – politicised – understandings of urbanity, where she was more directly critical of contemporary values. Within this context, her critique of Krier's interpretation of Rossi's text is more direct. Fundamentally aligned to understanding historic cities, Rossi focused on meaning in the city, claiming there was 'something more intrinsic to the nature of the city, almost a typological characteristic, of undefinable order', whereby 'very deep layers of urban life . . . are largely to be found in monuments, which possess the individuality of urban artefacts'.[72] His desire for questioning meaning recognised the importance of urban settings in the psyche of a city's residents. Rossi had noted:

> The soul of the city becomes the city's history . . . One can say that the city itself is the collective memory of its people, and like memory it is associated with objects and places. The city is the locus of the collective memory. This relationship between the locus and the citizenry then becomes the city's predominant image, both of architecture and of landscape, and as certain artefacts become part of its memory, new ones emerge. In this entirely positive sense great ideas flow through the history of the city and give shape to it . . . Thus, the union between the past and the future exists in the very idea of the city.[73]

However, when Krier absorbed Rossi's ideas of 'soul', 'memory' and 'monument' into his own notion of status and value, he transformed these into rules for architectural development within historic precincts. Krier claimed: 'The street and the square represent the only and necessary model for the reconstruction of a PUBLIC REALM. In this context, we also stress the necessary dialectical relationship of BUILDING TYPOLOGY and MORPHOLOGY OF URBAN SPACE and inside that dialectic, THE CORRECT RELATIONSHIP OF MONUMENTS (public buildings) AND THE MORE ANONYMOUS URBAN FABRIC (buildings for private use).'[74]

Within Krier's emphatic capitalisation of strident terms like 'correct relationship' and 'anonymous urban fabric', there is a transformation of Rossi's more nuanced interpretation of the temporality of the city, now seen as rules to be followed for architectural design without regard for the idiosyncrasies of urban distinctiveness. In Krier's interpretation, the deep values and subtlety of urban settings that Rossi had recognised in the accretive make-up of European cities, were now redefined as if stemming from ahistorical 'truths' – ones that could be applied to new developments, and ones also evidenced in the underpinning directives of the briefing documents for the Grand Buildings competition. By the time of the earlier competition for the extension to The National Gallery in London, Krier had already transformed elements of Rossi's inquiry into a design method.

For Hadid, there is a direct critique of Krier's approach in the light of Rossi and Rowe evidenced when she spoke with Alvin Boyarsky in 1986, and there is also a level of frustration with Krier's narrow understanding of London's prevailing spatial governance. Underlying this conversation is a more guarded critique of Rossi. Coincidentally, Hadid's stance on the city is consistent with her reading of Rodchenko's *foto-kadry*, or politicised 'snapshot', as a way to visually frame that critique within the imagery in her paintings for Grand Buildings. However, it does not explain the paintings' use of muted and layered tonality, nor their refusal for clarity within their depictions of the architecture. The complex ethereal imagery

55 and 56
Jean-François Lyotard and Thierry Chaput
*Les Immatériaux*, exhibition at Centre Pompidou, Grande Galerie, Paris, 28 March 1985 to 15 July 1985, photographs
Centre Pompidou, Paris

of these paintings builds a visual response to urban space that is suggestive of an individual's subjective gaze, but when grouped, they provide an impression of a London where new and old coalesce without hierarchy and where the politics of privileged space is upended. This type of visual referencing prompts further inquiry of Hadid's intellectual milieu, to pinpoint where ideas can be recognised for their possible synergy of approach.

This requires a further link to be explored. Late in 1984, Hadid, Rem Koolhaas and Peter Eisenman were each invited to take part in the exhibition titled *Les Immatériaux* at the Centre Pompidou in Paris (figs 55 and 56).[75] For Koolhaas it was this exhibition that had been fundamental in the shift away from mainstream architectural debates. Historian and theorist Léa-Catherine Szacka more recently interviewed Koolhaas, questioning the influence from this exhibition over his later manifesto *S,M,L,XL* published in 1995. He claimed the exhibition's value was that 'it was not connected to an architectural movement: it proposed a kind of thinking through a condition . . . It had nothing to do with matter or substance – it was concerned with thought.'[76]

*Les Immatériaux* had also coincided with Peter Eisenman's exhibition *Fin d'Ou T Hou S* opening at the AA where, after the opening in Paris, he presented talks and interviews at the London school.[77] An anonymous editorial in the magazine *Building Design* brought the events together, citing discussions surrounding Eisenman's launch at the AA where an introduction by architectural theorist Jeffrey Kipnis had drawn attention to the importance of Lyotard's exhibition.[78] The coincidence of dates between the exhibitions and Hadid's submission for the Grand Buildings competition, and the period following where the series of paintings for its central ideas were created, provides a link in the precise context of her thinking.[79] Reflecting on the ideas and discussions prompted by Lyotard and Chaput's exhibition in Paris, her responses were immediate and visual. They provided a way to encapsulate differences between Rodchenko's photographs and Hadid's approach for Grand Buildings. Within the imagery of the paintings for Grand Buildings there is a search for how to consider the 'immaterial', in a critique of the city that is echoed within her more strident criticisms of Krier, coupled with the comments by HRH The Prince of Wales, in his attempt to maintain hierarchical order in the historicising of Central London.

An introduction to Lyotard's aims for *Les Immatériaux* pinpoints the directness of Hadid's visual inquiry and supports understanding of some of the comments made by Koolhaas in his response to Szacka. Lyotard's direction for the exhibition was tied to questioning the 'condition' of the individual in contemporary society. His interest in an understanding of 'the self' as embedded in a Postmodern society had identified that individuals now lived in a state of 'confused adaptation' as they negotiated new types of social interfaces and the sensations that contemporary urbanity presented.[80] He recognised a society complicated by information, whether it was experienced spatially through text or graphic sources derived from urban signage, or non-spatially from digital origins, including the televisual or data. He claimed that for the contemporary individual, the complex level of input absorbed was now so overlayed that the value of any one item had become indeterminant.[81]

As distinct from 'Postmodernism' in architecture, Lyotard's 'Postmodern condition' reinforced his exhibition's curatorial aim to spatially realise the complexity of contemporary life.[82] The exhibition's viewers were placed within an immersive environment where a juxtaposition of image, sound, text and computer data delivered visual and auditory discord.[83] There was no clear passage to guide a response. Each participant-viewer was left to negotiate the collection of sounds and visual effects. Lyotard had claimed that this type of spatial and experiential discord was similar to that predominating within the city, because of the continuing liminal and subliminal interference of media and/or data types. Within the gallery space, all attributes remained present to all senses – cluttered and demanding the attention of viewers in much the same way as the city presented visual, auditory and psychological spatial complexity. His aim for the exhibition was to replicate this 'immaterial' affect as 'events' continuously changing in their juxtaposition within the experiences of the individual.[84]

For *Les Immatériaux* Hadid had included a painting from the 59 Eaton Place project. However, it is in the paintings for Grand Buildings that there are distinctive visual explorations of the exhibition's key propositions mixed within her contemporaneous interest in Rodchenko's approach to *foto-kadry* in photography. By referencing Rodchenko's approach to photography, its close focus, and ideas of a politicised 'gaze', Hadid presented a notion of subjective time into her paintings for Grand Buildings. Their imagery emphasises the way 'the gaze', and an individual's experience of city spaces inherently politicises the normalcy of the objective, rational 'view' of the city, and its representation. Within the paintings for Grand Buildings, the city is presented as ideologically, spatially and historically muted. Extending this complex layering is an introduced impression of immaterial affect symbolised in the indeterminacy and tonal over-exposure of each urban setting. Her propositions, although visual, when considered within the more architectural contexts of debates and contemporary writing on the city made an important contribution.

The 'views' in her paintings were selected with precision, exposing the trajectory of meaning that remains politically potent across their collective. In each of the final paintings, forms remain fragmented, distorted and illusionistic. A viewer, now attuned to the visual propositions within Hadid's paintings, would realise that the city is inherently politicised. Her paintings project the idea of a contemporary London where recognition of its history is a part of the collective memory of its inhabitants, but in the paintings those monumental fragments from the past remain partial and amongst other more immaterial influences. In Hadid's London, their monumentalism is no longer dominating the structures of its city's future, nor the everyday practices of its populations. Her contribution to the debate was a recognition of how the relational nature of urban spaces could be informed, but not controlled, by historical monuments and the city's landmarks. In her fine-grained understanding of everyday responses to the city, and in accepting the complex situation of London's historic centre, there would be no requirement in architecture for a nostalgic return to 18th- and 19th-century classical facadism, or any equally nostalgic return to imperialism.

Two attributes become important to Hadid's London. The first openly criticises the naïve architectural propositions perpetuating London's traditional architectural forms, of transferring their implicit ideologies into new developments. Hadid stood against any return to an architectural mimicry of past architectural forms and the formal and spatial expressions that reinforced those desires. The second presented the idea that architects had been unknowingly reinforcing the normalcy of this type of conservativism through the very act of how they represented their projects. Her paintings visualised the city differently by changing the scope of architectural representation. For her the act of painting had shown how traditional representational techniques like perspective were implicitly politicised and how they could be recognised for their restrictive ideological force.

# 4 Body, Sensation and the Immaterial in Architecture: Office Building on Kurfürstendamm 70, Berlin

Zaha Hadid's paintings of the mid-1980s explored her growing interest in the spatial effect of architecture as experienced. Her developing visual inquiry for Grand Buildings had coincided with her involvement in the architectural exhibition *Les Immatériaux* at the Centre Pompidou in Paris, and it was their synergy of ideas that can be observed in the way she considered and depicted architecture from that time.[1]

As discussed in the previous chapter, *Les Immatériaux* curators Jean-François Lyotard and Thierry Chaput proposed a distinctive understanding of how individuals engaged with the context of their urban life. Lyotard claimed that within contemporary society the judgement of what is real, logical or rational was no longer easily ascertained or observed. To explore this dissonance, his curatorial aim for the exhibition was to activate discord in how viewers resolve the multiple sensory triggers associated with exhibits. The viewer was no longer conceived as passively standing in awe before a masterpiece but had to negotiate a labyrinthine space where chronology, origins or other forms of ordering were avoided. In each viewer's passage through the exhibition, visual and auditory intrusions influenced their capacity to focus on individual objects.[2] This approach intensified viewer engagement, introducing a sense of uncertainty, as experiences could not be predicted, duplicated or assured.[3]

These ideas had parallels with sentiments being expressed by Koolhaas and Hadid who had both participated in the exhibition.[4] Each proposed an idea of the city as a metropolis outlined in their teaching Units. The metropolis was considered as an intense and unknowable organism – a culture of congestion – and both architects had considered the Paris exhibition as fundamental to understanding the contemporary urban condition.[5] In Lyotard's talks prior to and during the exhibition he explained his approach had, in part, come about because of two articles he had recently read.[6] The first of these was by architectural theorist Paul Virilio and the second by the Italian architect Giairo Daghini. Lyotard had seen both articles when they were published in French in the first edition of the magazine *Change International*.[7] Virilio's essay was to have a lasting impact on his exhibition and subsequently for architectural discussions during the mid-1980s. Interest grew partly from Lyotard's identification of Virilio's concept of the 'overexposed city' as a way to explain the unease embedded within contemporary society.[8] He had contextualised Virilio's essay by raising the question of the relationship between the 'old' metropolis, that of buildings and their monumental spatial programs, and the new 'informatic metropolis'. He recognised that Virilio had identified the intrusion of differing forms of information from techno-cultural and digital media, or the 'immaterials' of contemporary society, as affecting how the city could be comprehended.

In many ways Hadid's paintings for the project Office Building on Kurfürstendamm 70 respond to these interests. The project resulted from an invitation to take part in a limited architectural competition held in mid-1986, promoted by the developers Euwo Holdings.[9] The brief was for a commercial building on a very thin slice of land in West Berlin at a critical point on Kurfürstendamm where the exclusivity of its shopping strip transforms into apartments and suburban retail. Six architectural companies had been invited to participate, with Zaha Hadid being one of the two international inclusions.[10] The judging panel included architectural historian Heinrich Klotz and architect Rem Koolhaas.[11] The 'Summer edition' of the magazine *AA Files* was the first in London to announce Hadid's success in winning the competition accompanied by a description of the scheme with a series of illustrations, including the submitted drawings and some additional preliminary paintings.[12] The description focused on the scheme's architectural innovation, where site constraints had led to a vertical 'sandwich' building enabling a significant cantilever. Through negotiation with regulatory authorities Hadid had extended floors above ground level, increasing the width of development by cantilevering over the pedestrian footpath of the city's street. It was an innovation enabling greater floor space, making the building viable as offices.

However, this descriptive clarity did not explain how or why the paintings developed as they did over coming months when the architectural resolution was still underway. They return to the architectural potency of ideas delivered by Lyotard and Virilio. It was during this time after the competition that additional paintings were completed for an exhibition at the Aedes Galerie in Berlin, opening on 23 September that year.[13] This heightened productivity suggested an inquiry that was ongoing and did not modify in approach despite the changing priorities of design development. By the time of a following exhibition at the Max Protetch Gallery in New York in June 1987, the number of paintings for the project had increased significantly.[14] In a review of the Protetch Gallery exhibition, Deborah Dietsch from the magazine *Architectural Record* asked Hadid to defend her use of painting and drawing in the context of professional critique.[15] Dietsch recounted: 'Countering the often-made claim that she is a "paper architect," Zaha Hadid says, "I wouldn't go through all the trouble it takes to do the drawings if I didn't fundamentally believe my proposals could be built".'[16] In the context of the architectural profession there was a precariousness to Hadid's interest in the exploratory nature of painting.[17] Her response to Dietsch highlights her frustration at having to continually validate her commitment to architecture, and that painting's visual purpose was tied essentially to the realisation of architecture, rather than be considered only as artistic expressionism.[18] The rationale was specific for Hadid; painting enabled an exploration of architecture's spatiality that was not fettered by the constraints of technical architectural drawing, nor the cautiousness of consultants, clients and regulatory authorities. For her, spatial relationships in architecture could be considered outside those confines. Defined distinctively through the painted surface, architecture was framed as an inquiry having different conceptual layers.

In 1985 Hadid's office had moved from her small mews house to take residence in its new address at Unit 9, 10 Bowling Green Lane.[19] Her studio team for Kurfürstendamm 70 included Michael Wolfson, Brett Steele, Piers Smerin, Charles Crawford, Nicola Cousins and David Gomersall.[20] Wolfson still has in his collections a series of perspectival studies that he had drawn and coloured for the project prior to submission for the competition.[21] A selection of these were included in the article in *AA Files*.[22] Painting of the final large compositions was the primary domain of both Cousins and Gomersall. Although Smerin recalls being involved with both the drawings and painting for *Movement Sequence*,[23] Wolfson's technique is evident in its final drawing and in *View from Kurfürstendamm*.[24] Hadid, herself, painted this small original for its inclusion in the competition set, and it was this image that was used in the poster for the Aedes Galerie exhibition later that year.[25] Gomersall recalls then painting an enlarged version of this image that was used for exhibition, completing the 'whoosh' in Teppachi watercolour used for Japanese painting. It was a technique that he claimed Hadid had taught him.[26] It was this painting that was reproduced using lithographic techniques and is included in this chapter. Gomersall explained he used these same Teppachi techniques for the painting of *Section/Perspective with Curtain Wall Detail* that had been drawn by Steele. Even though mentioned earlier in this book Gomersall's recollections are again pertinent here with the selection of colours for this project: 'With Zaha it was much more about feeling spatial qualities. The colours weren't necessarily just to do with red coming forward or blue going back, it's not really a mystery but just selecting colours through discussion and trial and error until the juxtapositions of shade and pigment started to suit the project.'[27]

For the large composite painting titled *Movement Sequence* Smerin explained:

There are two paintings, one white and the other black. The second, was set up on black paper using white transfer paper to create a white line drawing on black background, that was then partially painted in watercolour and acrylic paint. It was called 'Rotation' or 'Movement Sequence' and shows views of the building from a shifting series of standpoints as the viewer walks past the building on Kurfürstendamm, merged like overlaid stills from a movie sequence or as Alvin Boyarsky (then chair of the AA) remarked, like a latter-day version of Duchamp's *Nude Descending a Staircase*. Again, this way of exploring how a building would look from differing vantage points is now commonplace in all 3D CAD modelling software but back in 1986 existed only in the imagination.[28]

Investigating this project and its paintings reveals their awkward connection to arguments about deconstruction in architecture, developed from their being included in 1988 in the symposium at the Tate Gallery, London, called *Deconstruction in Art and Architecture*.[29] The Tate symposium was a precursor to Philip Johnson and Mark Wigley's later exhibition *Deconstructivist Architecture*, held at MOMA in New York.[30] At the Tate symposium, paintings and drawings from the Office Building on Kurfürstendamm 70 project were introduced as Hadid's most recent work, and lauded under the banner of 'Deconstruction'. In an interview looking back at this event Hadid questioned this connection, explaining: 'People have not observed the work develop over the past five years . . . It was never really about deconstruction. What changed dramatically was the move from the plan to the volume – to making spaces. It really occurred with Kurfürstendamm 70 . . . because the space was so tight, it really required tremendous precision in the placement of the element.'[31]

Hadid's approach to painting's inquiry continued a reflection on the broader issues and theoretical concerns underpinning architecture's space–form priorities for the city. This approach was reinforced as central to concerns of disciplinary debate, when by May 1986, Virilio's essay, which had been influential for Lyotard, had been translated into English for architectural audiences in the publication *Zone 1:2, City*.[32] Hadid must have been aware of this essay and its key propositions, given her experiences with Lyotard's exhibition, and that its publication in *Zone* was alongside other articles by Rem Koolhaas and Peter Eisenman, each of whom became central to the continuing discussions at the Architectural Association (AA).[33] Virilio's essay moved the debate away from considering the city as a series of built monuments and urban infill. Its focus instead was the Postmodern condition emanating from an urbanity considered as an information metropolis, where society had been dislocated permanently from the ordering structures of monuments that previously delivered meaning.[34]

Hadid's paintings layered this way of thinking within her growing understanding of the conceptual aims of the Suprematist movement. Her exposure to Suprematist imagery and ideas had broadened since she was a student, following her personal engagement with the artworks.[35] For her, Suprematism was conceived not just as an art movement defined within the 'Western tradition', but one whose meaning derived from a visual experimentation that aimed to represent the unique qualities of post-revolutionary Russia.[36] This politicisation of art had stimulated Hadid's perception of change in contemporary society and mirrored her response to ideas discussed by Lyotard and Virilio. To consider the confluence of their ideas with Suprematism, Hadid described a new spatial engagement between architecture and painting, criticising the singularity of approach in Western painting, claiming, 'I think there was an idea that there's one rationale, which is a kind of Western rationale. And there was no other logics.'[37] This is then countered as an approach in an explanation of her work: 'That's why there is the idea of the explosion or a chaos. But of course, [in painting] chaos is under equilibrium because it's in a canvas, so to speak. [In architecture] it's not like that, and we can't make these things floating in space. But certain kinds of techniques, painterly techniques ... I use, are to show [the potential] of the real building.'[38]

It is within statements like this that Hadid makes distinct the purpose of painting for her architectural inquiry. The combination of ideas and visual prompts from Suprematist sources continued to infuse her questioning of the contemporary city and the place of architecture within that construct. However, through their juxtaposition with discussions centring on the ideas of Virilio and Lyotard, the paintings for Kurfürstendamm 70 record an inquiry more precisely nuanced and aligned using her own 'take' on the importance of sensations and 'immaterial' influences on the individual's experience of urban societies.

The paintings to be investigated in this chapter include two images from those first published in *AA Files* at a time very close to the competition. They are known by the secondary titles *View from Kurfürstendamm*[39] and *Section/Perspective with Curtain Wall Detail*.[40] A further two examples with secondary titles *Red Painting* and *Movement Sequence*, were completed for exhibition at the Aedes Galerie.[41] As a group, these four paintings present Hadid's response to a series of differing ideas in architecture, bringing bodily sensation and intellectual engagement together with architecture's space–form characteristics. Their imagery responds to the juxtaposition of three speeds of sensation – the instantaneous, the idealised or conceptually static, and the sequentially variable. Each painting raises questions regarding the relationship between the experiences of a viewer's subjective engagement with the city, and the level of their intellectual focus as they reference the architecture's objective material and tectonic assemblage. They invite questioning the meaning of architecture within contemporary urban environments.

### The Temporality of Sensation:
*Office Building on Kurfürstendamm 70, View from Kurfürstendamm*

The painting *View from Kurfürstendamm* was completed for the competition's submission and its final form develops a distinctive narrative when compared with another perspective drawing included. By comparison, the drawing *Office Building on Kurfürstendamm 70, The Major Facade* is a traditional perspective of a similar view seemingly drawn with a technical audience in mind (fig.57). Focusing on the prominent corner, this technical drawing incorporates information – from a photograph of the site – that had been included within briefing documents. The depiction of urbanity, with its bric-a-brac of surrounding buildings and urban walls, provides a viewer with what they assume is an important context for the scheme and how it is montaged into the urbanity of the city.

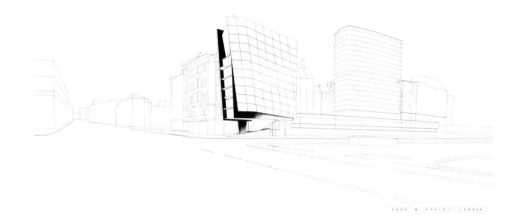

57
Zaha Hadid Architects
*Office Building on Kurfürstendamm 70, The Major Facade*, Berlin, Germany, 1986
Ink on Mylar®, 43 × 61 cm (16¹⁵⁄₁₆ × 24 in)
Zaha Hadid Foundation

The painting *View from Kurfürstendamm* changes that narrative intent, distorting the view and shading the facade whilst removing the urban context and any reference to transparency in the facade (fig.58). The image of the building is now isolated in a pictorial 'ether' without any grounding other than the urban wall of the office complex to the rear, now equally isolated from its tower and abstracted. Implicit within the 'view' of Hadid's scheme in this painting is the underside of the first floor, revealed as a surface with the ramping and structural elements of the entry abutting its solidity. Colour is applied to small details using acrylics: the green of the lift lobby at ground level, red used to define the extension of the entry ramp leading to the lobby, and an intense yellow darkening to orange of the side boundary wall. Other details clearly remaining black include the rear structural wall, the ramp and the heavy 'piloti' separating the ground from the upper levels of the proposed building. The vast screen of the facade above them relies only on the black tonal Teppachi watercolour wash, varying in intensity as it 'whooshes' the surface and the remnant wall behind.[42]

The juxtaposition of colours, blackened surfaces and the 'whoosh' registers the importance of the scheme's 'curtain wall' facade, an urban element envisaged as a ballooning volume without the implications of gravitational weight. However, confounding this lightness is the similarity of spatial modelling applied to the remnant wall of the adjoining building. Its embrace into the scheme imagines the effect of a particular sensation, rather than registering material differences. When commenting on the evocative quality of this image, architect Lebbeus Woods pronounced: 'Now her building glows mysteriously in an urban landscape devoid of life, last survivor of an apocalyptic *fin-de-siecle*, or harbinger of a more hopeful world – hopeful only because angst is sublimated finally into artistic form.'[43]

Many years later Hadid was to recognise the underlying importance of her 'whoosh' technique to consideration of urban form. It referenced the speed of an instantaneous glimmer rather than architectural materiality that would describe an object. In *Tate Talks* 2014, she recalled:

Certain kinds of techniques, painterly techniques... I use, to show certain [attributes] of the real building. I used to do these whooshes in white on a black drawing... and honestly, I was once [on location] it was pitch black... Because there's no other building next door, the whole [visual] field was black. But because it was moonlight, one of the surfaces which was curved, caught the light, and became like a whoosh. So that was exciting because suddenly, reality becomes like the drawing.⁴⁴

Her emphasis on sensation was an idea held between an effect of knowing that architecture is made of materials countered with each viewer's reception of stimuli at distinctive times and situations. Through the graphic technique of the 'whoosh', this glimmer of light on the facade and the wall in this painting implied a sense of subjective temporality, of a visual sensation of dissipating light gained when a viewer is distracted and temporarily diverts their attention toward a scene. As she recalled, it is an effect gained if travelling at speed past a building, the sheen of light hitting a glazed surface, with the adjoining wall, having the same visual effect. Materiality is not the issue here, and neither is architectural fenestration. Each viewer's response is to an instance in time where the absence of duration ties architecture to atmospheric impressions.

58
Zaha Hadid Architects
*Office Building on Kurfürstendamm 70, View from Kurfürstendamm*, Berlin, Germany, 1986
Colour photo-offset lithograph of original (original in Teppachi watercolour with acrylic on paper), 48.9 × 65.7 cm (19¼ × 25 ⅞ in)
Alvin Boyarsky Archive, London

59
Kazimir Malevich
*Yellow Plane in Dissolution*, 1917–18
Oil on canvas, 109 × 73.5 cm (42⅞ × 28¹⁵⁄₁₆ in)
Stedelijk Museum Amsterdam

60
Alexander Rodchenko
*Composition – Flying Shape*, 1918–19, catalogue cover for the exhibition *Alexander Rodtschenko und Warwara Stepanowa*
Original, oil on canvas, 92 × 59 cm (36⅛ × 23¼ in)
Alvin Boyarsky Archive, London

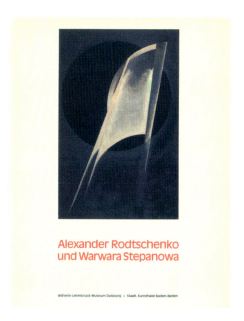

The technique of the 'whoosh' had been central to Hadid's representations, mentioned by all assistants as her personal signature.[45] However, not all 'whooshes' are used in the same way as that on the facade of the painting *View from Kurfürstendamm*. Hadid's interview clarifies an aspect of the technique as having precise meaning in this painting, where in an emphasis on the immateriality of sensation there is an equivalence between very different material surfaces as they are viewed. The effect cannot be guaranteed to reoccur. The 'whoosh' suggests in this case that materiality and meaning in the realised architecture is tied, therefore, to a viewer's precise situation, reflecting their responsiveness to the passage of the sun, or the night's idiosyncratic lighting effects. Meaning in architecture is not necessarily perceived in the mind, only as the fabric determining construction, such as bricks, concrete, metals and glass, or their volumetric disposition.

For Hadid, the importance given to sensation in architecture emerged from two distinct avenues of inquiry: the first was from painterly techniques with their sources in Suprematism, while the second was more theoretically derived architectural inquiry. Kazimir Malevich's series of Suprematist paintings known as *Dissolution of a Plane*, painted between 1917 and 1918, and Alexander Rodchenko's *Composition – Flying Shape* of 1918–19 reference the notion of time and its relation to sensation. When interviewed in 2014 by the *Royal Academy of the Arts Magazine*, Hadid explained:

> Malevich's *Dissolution of a Plane* (1917) represents an important moment. His geometric forms began a conceptual development beyond the planar, becoming forces and energies, leading to ideas about how space itself might be distorted to increase dynamism and complexity without losing continuity. My work explored these ideas ... The ideas of lightness, floating and fluidity in my work all come from this research.[46]

Hadid had included the Malevich red painting *Dissolution of a Plane* in the exhibition *Zaha Hadid and Suprematism* at Galerie Gmurzynska in 2010, where it was given significance by being positioned at the entry.[47] Malevich's *Yellow Plane in Dissolution*, shown here, similarly portrays the impression of movement of a plane across a field, as if dissolving as it travels (fig.59).[48] Rodchenko's *Composition – Flying Shape*, while less publicised, in its use of white on black ground emphasises a similar response to the notion of surface and atmospherics. His painting had been included in Andrei Nakov's book *Avant-Garde Russe* released in English in 1986,[49] and it was also used for a catalogue cover for the exhibition *Alexander Rodtschenko und Warwara Stepanowa*, held in Duisburg in 1982–83 (fig.60).[50] Importantly, while it remains unclear whether Hadid attended this exhibition, Alvin Boyarsky, chairman of the AA, saw it, and bought the catalogue – understanding the importance of its imagery for Hadid.[51]

What becomes central to the discussion of Hadid's *View from Kurfürstendamm*, in the context of the Malevich and Rodchenko paintings, is her interest in their perception of the dissolution of a plane as having the implications of a spatial force. Rather than movement being the focus, their idea of dissolution references the memory of something already past, or force itself. In these paintings there is no referent or object, only the memory of a specifically visual sensation.

In the catalogue of the exhibition of Hadid's own work at Galerie Gmurzynska, in 2010, historian Charlotte Douglas explained the importance of the theoretical setting of Malevich's painting. During this period, Malevich had developed a close working relationship with the Austrian physicist and philosopher Ernst Mach, who 'maintained that sensations are the only things that we truly know, and that based on them we construct the rest of the world'.⁵² It is an idea central to Malevich and to Hadid as each negotiated how the world can be known. But these ideas also have synergies with Lyotard's interest in the expectation that sensation's affect is more psychological.⁵³ The connection directs attention to the architectural debates of the period. Sensation had now been implicated within a societal 'condition' emanating within a metropolis where information and data were ubiquitous, and the city was no longer framed within notions of monumental meaning and order. Bringing these ideas together references the second avenue of inquiry where Hadid's painting *View from Kurfürstendamm* shows a consideration of sensations in architecture as if theoretically important to contemporary discussions. The referencing of immaterial affect in this painting develops synergies that are fundamentally embedded within the theoretical propositions emerging from Lyotard's exhibition and Virilio's growing influence in architectural debates during 1985 and 1986.

In his article 'The Overexposed City', Virilio considered how individual cities might be understood as a physical 'reality' that embedded meaning. His argument critiqued the approach presented by Robert Venturi, Denise Scott-Brown and Steven Izenour in *Learning from Las Vegas*, claiming that their book had missed the point of understanding the contemporary city.⁵⁴ Venturi, Scott-Brown and Izenour defended the idea that it was the highway billboard and signage in Las Vegas that 'through their sculptural form or their pictorial silhouettes ... identified and unified the megatexture [of the city]'.⁵⁵ They claimed that meaning could thus be recognised, having a structural and material effect within a city's forms. Virilio's counter position claimed that the city was now no longer understood through such mechanisms and constructs but only by something more subliminal and sensate. Such physical objects or urban monuments like the contemporary billboard had little impact. He argued that it was 'the incessant multiplication of special effects which, along with the consciousness of time and of distance', would 'affect the perception of the environment'.⁵⁶

Hadid's imagery for the painting *View from Kurfürstendamm* portrays synergies with Virilio's argument – where the surface represented as 'architectural' negotiates the material/immaterial uncertainty of an environment that is no longer tangible through its physical boundaries. In Hadid's painting, rather than being conceived as a billboard, monument or urban infill, surfaces are described by their ephemerality, perceived only through the negotiated reception of a sporadically engaged viewer. The painting challenges 'material stability' in architecture by bringing Malevich's staging of the 'memory of sensation' into an understanding of the effects of techno-cultures within contemporary society. For Hadid, Malevich had clarified how architectural 'space itself might be distorted' and intensified as a source of meaning. Within this sensory response, architecture, now being void of its context and solidity, floats as a memory in an 'electronic ether', a remnant of a city never evident in any material or monumental sense.

Mirroring Virilio as well as Malevich, Hadid's ideas juxtapose a network of visual references indicating alternative formations of knowing and understanding architecture. The painting *View from Kurfürstendamm* navigates two explicit states. The first is a visual sensation of architecture's 'material' form, captured not as a solid or grounded object, but within the instantaneity of its dissolution. The second is the acceptance of speed's presence in this 'sensation', recognising from the Suprematist painters that sensation was a unique attribute of space–form–time correlations.

## Questioning the 'Primacy' of Architectural Drawing: *Office Building on Kurfürstendamm 70, Red Painting* and *Office Building on Kurfürstendamm 70, Section/Perspective with Curtain Wall Detail*

The two paintings – *Red Painting* and *Section/Perspective with Curtain Wall Detail* – expand on these complex ideas by considering the implications of architectural materiality and the representation expected from the prescribed processes of technical drawing. The imagery of *Red Painting* portrays three two-dimensional elevations of the scheme with the most prominent elevation on Lewishamstrasse centrally located. Countering this orthogonal clarity, *Section/Perspective with Curtain Wall Detail* focuses on materials and their assembly, where alternative visual strategies use perspectival conventions to portray the structure supporting a curtain-wall facade.[57] The images form a pair, both emulating the idealistic precision of technical architectural knowledge, while at the same time juxtaposing an expressive undoing of the realisation of this proposition as authentic.

Moving beyond technical knowledge to achieve an artistic sensibility, these paintings direct viewers to consider the complex logic underpinning the relationship between a realised building and architecture's spatial affect.[58] Introduced through their application of colour and tone is a visual incongruence whereby painting contributes a resolution of ideas that lie between architectural drawing's instrumentality, painting's expressiveness and the realised building. While the techniques of architectural drawing remain clear in both paintings, it is in their application of colour and spatial layering that new emphases arise.

*Red Painting* can best be seen as a response to *Section/Perspective with Curtain Wall Detail* where the intensity of its 'red' colouration frames a comparison with the cool blue logic and rationality of the detail evident within the curtain wall drawing. *Red Painting* continues Hadid's interest for layering colour across the surface of a painting (fig.61). The painting 'screams' red as an important attribute. There is little referencing of spatial depth, as colours form juxtapositions of contrasting hue rather than representing a reality. The elevations of the scheme utilise distinctive colour palettes where the left elevation is predominantly yellow with highlights of blues, beige and black. It portrays the view abutting Kurfürstendamm. The central elevation is of Lewishamstrasse, predominantly coloured in shades of blue representing the curtain wall with highlights of near-whites and near-blacks defining specific attributes like the ramp, entry void and rear firewall. Here again the dominating form of the rear office building is reduced by ghosting its edge. The most dominant element, the variegated rendering of the glass curve of the facade, is depicted using highlights of differing blue tones. The right rear elevation is again rendered using a series of darker hues with dark blue and black predominating. Each elevation is unified by the continuity of the darkened brown facades of adjoining buildings.

Viewers who are architecturally informed will attempt to focus on the orthogonal 'truth' of imagery defining this to be an image of architecture. However, the intensity of the red background fights any potential apprehension of its architectural detail. The assurances that orthographic projections implicitly provide architects is lost. Instead, it is the complex relationship developed between colour and technical drawing that introduces a strange distancing effect to the architectural knowledge presumed. This painting repels! Its red hue, perhaps reflecting Malevich's colour in the painting *The Red Square (Painterly Realism of a Peasant Woman in Two Dimensions)*, develops a distinctive visual resonance where the eye strains to focus on other attributes.[59] Art historian Andrei Nakov recognises the use of red by Malevich, claiming it to be a registration of the 'quintessence of (pictorial) emotion'

61
**Zaha Hadid Architects**
*Office Building on Kurfürstendamm 70,
Red Painting*, Berlin, Germany, 1986
Acrylic on paper, 80.5 × 126 cm (31 11/16 × 49 5/8 in)
Zaha Hadid Foundation

seen to enhance the ideality of 'pure' painting.[60] He relates the story that El Lissitzky had made a children's 'comic' about the *Red Square*. The story had used a red square on its cover with the number '2', 'notifying children, that it was about a tale of two squares, of which only the red one, considered to be the victor against the "Old World"… made it onto the cover'.[61] In Hadid's use of 'red' there is an equivalent claim about the 'old world' in relation to objectivity in architecture and its drawings.

For Hadid it is the purity and emotional power of this colour that presents this painting as sensation rather than a return to the objectification of architecture through its conventions of technical drawing. Here sensation avoids temporality. When compared to the painting *Section/Perspective with Curtain Wall Detail*, commonalities of approach are revealed even though the focus within the drawing of this image is purportedly the pure rationality of building construction and the detailed resolution of connecting materials (fig.62). Its imagery's pale blue tones reinforce the terms of Nakov's explanation; as opposed to the emotion of 'red' the depiction here becomes a narrative about rationality that invokes irony. Using perspectival techniques, this painting introduces shade and shadow to indicate depth variations within the suppressed cool tonality. However, while these attributes are traditionally used in architectural renderings to 'stabilise' representation within a single projection of the sun's rays, in this painting their application contradicts those conventions.[62] The representation of the surface of the facade retains a tonal dominance over the structural operations depicted, and a more whimsical application of colour dominates the supposed technical verity of the drawing. In this interplay between two architectural systems of drawing and painting, there is an emphasis on sensation, and the intangible spatiality that can only be made possible through the non-representational logic of painterly abstraction.

To explore this effect it is necessary first to think through the implications of the transformation of orthographic drawing into perspectival projection.[63] What is apparent under close examination is that in the act of extending into a three-dimensional perspective, the base drawing in this case has been supplemented with additional lines, creating a drawing that is beyond the technical requirements for realising the building.[64] These lines appear to confuse the clarity required in the context of an architectural technical drawing. They invite a different engagement from viewers.

The visualisation of the architecture in this drawing and its adapted techniques from painting, respond more to a series of theoretical propositions in the discipline. The first is focused on how structuring and assembly of materials in architecture could be understood as ordered through the analogy of the human body. At the AA at the time, such discussions would have been led by the historian and theorist Joseph Rykwert. His writing on early modern architecture and the Enlightenment had referenced the importance given to human anatomy as a way of explaining concepts of architectural beauty and rationality.[65] He referred to the analogy between architecture and the body's skeleton giving support to the vascular systems, musculature and skin. Imagery used by Rykwert and others most often derived from early anatomical books, often modelled on Renaissance anatomist Andreas Vesalius's *De humani corporis fabrica libri septem* (*On the Fabric of the Human Body in Seven Books*) (fig.63).[66] In architectural discussions, the common understanding of the relationship between the architectural 'skin' and its structural 'bones' and their interdependencies prevailed as a clear way of describing the important hierarchies of rational thought.[67]

Hadid's drawing for *Section/Perspective with Curtain Wall Detail* visualises the complex inner 'anatomy' of architecture but also adds a superfluity of colour and line that undoes the clarity of the 'rational beauty' that Rykwert was keen to establish as a principle. It is in Hadid's painting that the pseudo-technical nature of the line drawing moves beyond accuracy to introduce a distinctive abstract planarity, and it is through the addition of colour and tone that the relationship between 'skin and structure' is critiqued. Rather than remove the skin from the body and drape it aside as the Vesalius engraving had shown, Hadid's perspective in both drawing and painting has retained a small section of the exterior facade in situ. This small component of the facade has been painted with a different hue of lighter blue and includes a single protruding linear spandrel isolated in red. Consistent with this 'remnant' surface, the implications of its perimeter are continued, depicted as dotted lines that are difficult to perceive unless close. When painted, the inscribed form left by these dotted lines implies a 'surface', their tone 'bleaching out' elements behind, as if ghosting over the depth of the facade's inner structure. Its effect can be seen when a viewer closely examines the image, where darker contrasting tones of the sectional cut through the floors and walls can be 'seen' from below. On occasions this spatial layering works against understanding the technical clarity of the architectural drawing, with depth relations usual in perspective now 'blurred' or inverted. It is only at the very top apex of this facade's perimeter, when the tone applied to its pointed edge becomes very dark, that viewers will realise the implication of this surface is both spatial and hierarchical.

The use of a range of cool blue/grey tones in *Section/Perspective with Curtain Wall Detail* and the stark redness of *Red Painting* challenge the implications of materiality as an architectural value. By using the technical conventions of the orthogonal elevation, sectional and perspectival projections, the material systems of architecture project rationality yet are sublimated to colour's affect. However, the opposing of red with blue has a psychological and emotional impact that, like technical architectural drawings, is atemporal. The use of colour now suggests that the delivery of meaning in architecture has more complicated origins.

In part, this idea returns discussion to how Lyotard exhibited Hadid's and Koolhaas's differing schemes in the exhibition *Les Immatériaux* in Paris in 1985. In a position countering Walter Benjamin's claim discussed in Chapter 1, Lyotard suggests that the visual extension of contemporary architectural drawing through artistic references makes the resulting graphic the potent attribute of the architectural project.[68] His explanation of Koolhaas and OMA's *Isometrische Ubersicht der Gesamtanlage, Triptychon*[69] now known as *Boompjes Tower Slab* (fig.64), expressed a distinctive understanding of the architectural drawing:

> The tryptic, Axonometric for Rotterdam, is the real place of architecture. The built realisation will only be [its] representation through materials that will disappear as such, the reproduction fatally inadequate and perhaps not even necessary. Taking the form of a painting, the architectural drawing imposes its presence as a thing which is the negation of [its] value as representation.[70]

Lyotard's claim was for the painting to be considered the 'real place of architecture', the location where the 'architectural' occurs. In this sense, the resulting building becomes a copy, 'its representation', one that is 'fatally inadequate'. In this move from drawing to realised building, Lyotard's claim is that architecture disappears. The final sentence of Lyotard's statement above takes the idea further. Here, the issue of figurative painting arises, where Lyotard questions whether realised architecture has the capacity to communicate. By doing so, he opens a consideration of painting in architectural practice as being distinct from that of figurative art. For him, Koolhaas's and Hadid's use of artistic conventions enabled distinctive and meaningful associations to become evident.

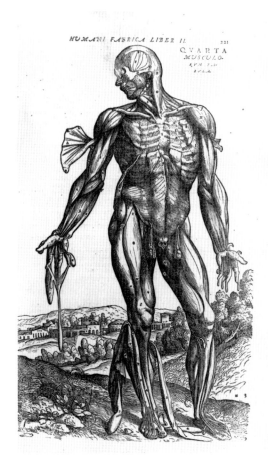

62
**John Stephen Calcar** (Sculptor)
Andreas Vesalius, *De humani corporis fabrica*, 1555
Woodcut, 38.7 × 26 cm (15¼ × 10¼ in)
Metropolitan Museum, New York

63
**Zaha Hadid Architects**
*Office Building on Kurfürstendamm 70, Section/Perspective with Curtain Wall Detail*, Berlin, Germany, 1986
Teppachi watercolour with acrylic on paper, 133 × 84 cm (52⅓ × 33 in)
*Architectural Record*

64
OMA, Rem Koolhaas and Madelon Vriesendorp,
Bernard Ruygrok (Silkscreener)
*Boompjes Tower Slab*, triptych, 1982
Silkscreen print,
71.6 × 121.6 cm (28 3/16 × 47 7/8 in)
Drawing Matter Collections, Somerset

Of Hadid's submission for the exhibition, where the painting *Three Towers: the Flamboyant, the Suprematist, the Clinical* from the project 59 Eaton Place was included, Lyotard's caption reads: 'The basis of the graphic does not innovate by its technique but more so in instituting an agreement, between the architect and his judges, to give this kind of representation the status of a project, these "graphic interludes" indicating yet again the lack of interest for architecture as a finished object or product.'[71]

This caption continues Lyotard's observation that the relationship developed between architectural drawing/painting and realised building had fundamentally changed. Like Koolhaas's triptych, Hadid's painting as displayed in the Paris exhibition would not have been isolated but placed within the context of other images and layers of information introduced through sound and digital media. The key intention of curatorial interest in relation to Hadid's image was a recognition that such architectural representation be given the status of a project, that is, the place where architectural ideas are evidenced.

It is in this context that Hadid's paintings *Red Painting* and *Section/Perspective with Curtain Wall Detail* should be considered. Their colours were not simply used to aestheticise a technical drawing but to raise questions of the stability of architectural meaning for contemporary society. The compositional complexity of these paintings bridges the boundary between architectural drawing's expected atemporal instrumentality and its centrality as emanating from art's affect. Within the AA, along with discussions led by Rykwert on the analogy of the body being a reflection of the stability of meaning in architecture, it is the implications for architectural drawings raised in an essay by theorist Robin Evans, teaching at the AA, that seem to respond to Lyotard's ideas. Evans provides a way to consider Hadid's architectural painting.

Evans's 1986 essay, titled 'Translations from Drawing to Building', was first published in the same issue of *AA Files* as Hadid's Kurfürstendamm scheme and seems to consider many of the ideas underpinning the complex logic of her paintings in the light of Lyotard's claims.[72] In 1983, Alvin Boyarsky, then director of the AA, had affirmed the centrality of architectural drawing to its aims as an institution: 'We create a very rich compost for students to develop and grow from and we fight the battle with the drawing on the wall. We're in pursuit of architecture, we discuss it boldly, we draw it as well as we can, and we exhibit it. We are one of the few institutions left in the world that keeps its spirits alive.'[73]

65
Jean-François Lyotard and Thierry Chaput
*Les Immatériaux*, exhibition at Centre
Pompidou, Grande Galerie, Paris, 28 March 1985
to 15 July 1985, photograph
Centre Pompidou, Paris

Because of the AA's interest in the impact of a particular type of architectural drawing and by extension painting, their topicality would have been a vibrant context for such debates. Evans's essay provides a way of unpacking the implications of Lyotard's as well as Benjamin's understandings of architectural drawing, and the way Hadid's paintings disrupted the logic of the assumed purpose traditionally given to architectural drawing.

Evans presents the idea that contemporary architectural representation could be considered either as 'artistically pretentious' or as 'purely instrumental' and used for the realisation of building.[74] He appears to counter Lyotard, arguing that the representational conventions of architectural practice were contiguous across output, each embedding a continuity of thought from the artistic and conceptual to the instrumentality required for architecture to be realised. In architectural debates, what made Evans's approach unique was his return to representation and its centrality within architectural practices. Like Lyotard, he reasoned drawing's capacity to project ideas, but as well, he understood architectural drawing's direct purpose to facilitate the realisation of ideas into building. To develop his argument Evans initially recognised the ambiguous relationship of contemporary architectural drawing to realised building where many of these drawings had become consumable artistic objects, able to be exhibited and sold, rather than used only for the realisation of building. This new status had become an important indicator of the changing value of architectural drawings within the profession. By reference to historical examples, Evans made the claim for contemporary architectural drawing's greater affect. For him it was through the abstraction enabled by new drawing techniques that the discipline of architecture supported experimentation and developed new and potent forms:

> This, then was architectural drawing in a new mode, more abstract in appearance, more penetrating in effect, capable of a more unsettling, less predictable interaction with the conventional inventory of forms of which monumental buildings are normally composed, destructive also of metric proportionality, the foundation of classical architecture, and suggestive of a perverse epistemology in which ideas are not put in things by art, but released from them. Accordingly, to fabricate would be to make thought possible, not to delimit it by making things represent their own origin.[75]

Like Lyotard, his argument considered architectural drawing to be at the forefront of disciplinary inquiry and experimentation, one not limited by essential correlations with the realised building. But rather than define contemporary architectural drawing only through an equivalency with art, he concluded: 'The drawing would be considered not so much a work of art or a truck for pushing ideas from place to place, but as the locale of subterfuges and evasions that one way or another get round the enormous weight of convention that has always been architecture's greatest security and at the same time its greatest liability.'[76]

When read in parallel with Hadid's paintings *Red Painting* and *Section/Perspective with Curtain Wall Detail*, these nuances suggest further understanding. In 1988 she returned to Lyotard's assertion for architectural drawing to reiterate: 'The projection of the architecture becomes the architecture itself.'[77] Siding with Lyotard, her paintings accept art's role as theoretically potent, while balancing a negotiation of the implications of technical drawing's anticipated purpose. Within the imagery of the paintings for Kurfürstendamm 70, there is a hint of the material, the tectonic and the statically scaled dependencies that conventions of drawing bring to a recognition of architecture's systems and assembly, but this is

66a
**Zaha Hadid Architects**
*Office Building on Kurfürstendamm 70, Movement Sequence*, Berlin, Germany, 1986
Acrylic on paper, 97 × 200 cm (38 3/16 × 78 3/4 in)
Deutsches Architekturmuseum, Frankfurt

nonetheless expressed within painting's capacity to affect, to counter elements of atemporal instrumentality by appealing to the subjective. These paintings violate the rationality of architectural drawing, making Hadid's contribution to theoretical discourses embedded within the complex agenda of Evans' arguments.

### Sensation's Speed:
*Office Building on Kurfürstendamm 70, Movement Sequence*

These ideas are extended again within the imagery of the last painting to be considered, *Movement Sequence* (fig.66a). Across the long horizontality of its composition is a series of individual views that through juxtaposition and layering suggest a narrative. The drawn linearity repeating the scheme's forms contrasts with the painting's black background, where a consistent 'ground line' and low-level viewing point introduce drama. Within each component image, distortion is used to exaggerate perspectival diminution skyward. The chalky white lines, pale 'whooshes' and restricted use of red highlights across each changing view support the idea of movement through sequenced repetition. Like the flip of stills used in early 'flipbook' animation techniques, the sensation of viewing this painting is one of intermittent engagement with the scheme, without introducing any sense of the smooth continuity of filmic speed. This painting explores the expressive qualities implied when a viewer is moving past the scheme, as if their view is registered through the differing speeds of each footfall and gaze.

Important in recognition of this intermittent reception is a comment made by Hadid in 2014: 'It took me twenty years to convince people to draw everything in three dimensions, with an army of people trying to draw the most difficult perspectives. Now everyone does 3D on the computer, but I think we have lost some transparency in the process. Through painting and drawing, we can discover so much more than anticipated.'[78] As recalled by her architectural assistant Piers Smerin in his reference to Marcel Duchamp, it is the multiplicity of collaged sequential views that reinforces Hadid's emphasis on sensation and affect.

Because of the horizontality of the composition, the sequence of views may be read from left to right or right to left, the emphasis being that this image is to be negotiated through bodily movement in a gallery space, aligned with the viewer's own temporal engagement as they move. However, resolving speed within this painting's structure is difficult as the composition combines three distinctive references to speed in how a viewer might consider what they see. What becomes significant in terms of architecture is each viewer's reception of what they see, and the artist's conscious reassembly of architectural references – as if incorporating each fragment into a more studied set of experiential impressions. Structuring this effect, *Movement Sequence* includes two independent collections of collaged sequences, interspersed between three orthogonally aligned views. The first of these is the elevation from Lewishamstrasse, located on the left, portraying the scheme's most dominant facade. While partly concealed by the main structure of movement sequences, this image is resolved easily by association with other paintings. The second is located close to the centre of the painting. It depicts the thin knife-like facade on Kurfürstendamm. The third is at the right extremity of the composition and depicts the elevation of the back facade, where the scheme's boundary wall projects beyond its neighbouring apartment buildings.

Between this tripartite structure are two distinctively layered sequences, reflecting different types of movement by a viewer. On the left is a repetition of facade images that overlap in an irregular fashion (fig.66b). Their misalignment

66b
Zaha Hadid Architects
(detail) *Office Building on Kurfürstendamm 70, Movement Sequence*, Berlin, Germany, 1986
Acrylic on paper
Deutsches Architekturmuseum, Frankfurt

becomes key to an understanding of the complete composition, as it avoids interpretation that any forced single observational speed and distance has been maintained. Each misalignment and displacement suggests that speed and engagement are varied, and the implied observation has the quality of an intermittent reception, as a viewer on the street might move closer or recede, not always focused on the scene before them. On the right of the composition's fulcrum are two views suggesting the return gaze, as if having passed the Kurfürstendamm facade, a viewer returns their gaze at slow speed looking back on the scene.

The emphasis in this painting is on the idiosyncrasies of retinal, bodily and cognitive inquiry. The composition responds to the city's pedestrians at an individual level, where architecture is recognised only through a disengaged bodily reception of environments within the city. Speed as depicted in this painting is layered, idiosyncratic and varied, attached to an intellect that privileges impulse rather than focused inquiry. Through the staccato juxtaposition of outlines and colours, the painting's narrative is not an essay in special effects derived from film, nor is it about the accuracy of an instrumental observation, but it implies a return to the impulsive reception of a semi-engaged viewer, who is only partly conscious of the objects they encounter.[79]

To understand this compositional complexity, it is useful to be reminded of Virilio's proposition on speed's effect, where 'Speed ... abolishes the notion of physical dimension.'[80] In this construct he argues that rather than the grand narratives of societies and their privileging of symbolic objects and monuments, the apprehension of architecture now defers to new micro narratives where 'the emergence of forms and volume ... has been replaced by images whose only duration is one of retinal persistence'.[81]

The importance of Virilio's comments for Hadid's *Movement Sequence* is that they enable a consideration of the multiple and layered imagery of the painting as being beyond Futurism's or Cubism's attempt to document moving bodies. It would be a mistake to judge the imagery of Hadid's painting as reminiscent of their attempt to portray the eye's reception of a moving figure, where a static observer documents the mechanisms of a subject's movement, such as can be seen in Giacomo Balla's *Dynamism of a Dog on a Leash* (fig.67) or even in Duchamp's *Nude Descending a Staircase*. Hadid's painting purposefully reverses the conceptual construct of the relationship between object and viewer, and in doing so also reverses its narrative power. While for Malevich, Futurism's ambitions to portray the impact of speed on society failed as they reverted to simple repetitions of static images, Hadid's spatial sequencing in *Movement Sequence* complicates Malevich's critique.[82] Through references to the ephemeral nature of viewer engagement with architecture, the painting draws attention to a complex phenomenon of its reception at differing speeds and the attention of each gaze from viewers. This painting's repetitions were not an attempt at empiricism, as Futurism had been, but quite the opposite. Rather than depict speed as a representational construct, Hadid's painting considers a core issue for architecture, the disengaged reception and distractions implicit within visual sensations of the everyday – and she questions their implications. The painting explores a new type of seeing that implied the effect of the 'immaterials' on the city's inhabitants.

67
Giacomo Balla
*Dinamismo di un cane al guinzaglio* (*Dynamism of a Dog on a Leash*), 1912
Oil on canvas, 89.8 × 109.8 cm (35⅜ × 43¼ in)
Buffalo AKG Art Museum, Buffalo, New York

Becoming central to Hadid's painting, this proposition had special significance for architecture as a theoretical practice. Through Virilio, Lyotard had recognised that for the contemporary occupant of a city, the environment was now perceived as if equivalent to other forms of media. Virilio's broader concern saw the impact of this as a new structure for the city, where geopolitical boundaries embedded within its monuments no longer defined anything more than a montage of visual emissions. In both their understandings, media remained just one of a number of visual distractions overpowering the monumentality of architecture. Lyotard had pointedly situated the projects of Hadid and Koolhaas in close proximity with a model of Malevich's *Arkhitekton*, stressing the immateriality of each of their representational 'states', and their distinctiveness from the material and utilitarian concerns of realised building. Extending this through Virilio's understanding of the televisual, Lyotard focused not only on representation in architecture but also architecture's shifting meaning and the bodily engagement required to find legibility. While both these propositions would implicate Malevich in a distinctive way, for Hadid they opened a level of critique for architectural drawing in the broader context of the AA, where she remained critically engaged in the education of architects.[83]

Together, the paintings for Kurfürstendamm 70 form a spectrum of differing conceptions of an inquiry of architectural space–form–time: from the subjective temporality of an instant defined by lighting conditions to the fragmented sensation of movement in a gaze toward the building, to the rational hierarchies of 'anatomical' interdependencies in architecture's 'skin' and 'bones'. Each framed a distinctive requirement for architectural representation that remained an open inquiry. Her paintings each consider differing aspects of the material/immaterial relationships held within architecture. Their images refer to a distinctive notion of time's influence on architecture: from the instantaneity of a glance to the idealised and temporal/atemporal logic of its surfaces and structures, to the sensation of experience in movement. For Hadid, what remained important was the bodily and intellectual reception of architectural affect, coexisting as layers – but not determined by its status as object.

# 5 Spatial Force – Architecture as Urban Impact: Vitra Fire Station

In 1988, after Zaha Hadid's paintings, drawings and models for The Peak, Hong Kong, had been included in the *Deconstructivist Architecture* exhibition at the Museum of Modern Art (MoMA) in New York, there was an assumption that her approach to architecture could be considered a form of 'deconstruction'.[1] The consensus of responses in the architectural press to the exhibition's complex and often conflicting propositions forms the context for the exploration of Hadid's Vitra Fire Station. It was commissioned late in 1988[2] – just months after deconstruction's philosophical tenets entered architectural debates across two continents.[3] What becomes most evident from those debates was that although deconstruction was a complex philosophical concept introduced by philosopher Jacques Derrida, it provided architects with a way for reconsidering architecture's potency within the city.[4] The architectural historicism or contextualism evident in Postmodern debates on the city held prior to 1980 no longer held power over architecture's impetus for urban form.

The curators of the *Deconstructivist Architecture* exhibition were architects Philip Johnson and Mark Wigley; the proposed exhibition was considered by the museum as a bookend to Johnson's curatorial career. Establishing this symmetry, the exhibition reflected some of the curatorial aims of Johnson and Henry-Russell Hitchcock's declaration of the 'International Style' in Johnson's first exhibition, *Modern Architecture: International Exhibition* at MoMA in 1932.[5] It was the framing of the *Deconstructivist Architecture* exhibition through the concept of style that exposed its intellectual underpinnings to criticism, becoming one of the main topics of debate at a symposium held at the Tate in London just prior to its opening. The London symposium was given the title *Deconstruction in Art and Architecture* and incorporated as speakers many of the architects who would be part of the MoMA exhibition.[6] Making the events more entwined was the inclusion of Mark Wigley in London, who used the opportunity to present his curatorial aims for MoMA's exhibition as distinct from Johnson's.[7] While both symposium and exhibition brought together a similar collection of architects, each venue differed in their manner of considering the term 'deconstruction' and its application to architecture.[8]

The Tate symposium had questioned deconstruction's role across art and architecture. It began with theorist Christopher Norris interviewing Derrida who, being unable to attend, had recorded his responses in English, making his propositions and logic more immediately accessible to the audience.[9] The interview became the focus of further discussion with philosophers, and art and architectural theorists including Stephen Bann, Andrew Benjamin, Geoff Bennington, Christopher Norris, Charles Jencks and Michael Podro structuring debate alongside architectural presentations.[10]

Norris's questions of Derrida, and the subsequent live discussion, highlighted the gap between philosophy and its application in architecture. Derrida had opened his interview by prompting the question of deconstruction's transferability to architecture:

> Can there be such a thing as Deconstructivist architecture?... At first, I thought no, it was a 'displaced discourse'. Later I concluded that the most efficient way of

putting through deconstructivist discourse was through art and architecture . . . Deconstruction doesn't mean that we have to stay within those metaphors – it is a way of questioning the architectural model itself – the metaphysics of foundation, architectonics etc. It means putting into question architecture itself.[11]

Here, Derrida accepts the intellectual complexity of the proposition that a philosophical approach could be used to question the very basis of architectural norms: 'I think that Deconstruction comes about . . . when you have deconstructed some architectural philosophy, some architectural assumptions – for instance, the hegemony of the aesthetic, of beauty, the hegemony of usefulness, of functionality, of living, of dwelling. But then you have to reinscribe these motifs within the work.'[12]

In the act of reinscribing a critique of aesthetics, beauty, usefulness and function into new architecture, rather than becoming an acceptance of 'contradiction' or 'complexity' as had been seen in Postmodernism, for deconstruction it was a reflection of the impossibility of unity rather than the appearance in architecture of simple oppositions.

While describing the forms of selected projects as deconstructivist for the exhibition at MoMA, Johnson and Wigley avoided any engagement with the question of how each project 'worked' as an after-effect of deconstructive processes of thought. It must be remembered that Hadid may have criticised such an inquiry. She had previously defended the individuality of her own approach to architecture in discussions with Alvin Boyarsky, saying: 'the show suggests that the architects on display read some Derrida and then invented a wholly new style of architecture. Not only is this wrong, but it trivialises Derrida.'[13] For her, there was no direct authority between philosophy and architecture.

However, the MoMA exhibition had provided a series of settings whereby each architect was compelled to defend their association with deconstruction and its theories without undermining the tenets of their own work. The tensions of this approach became most evidenced in interviews in the film *Deconstructivist Architects* (1989), which followed the exhibition.[14] As each architect was interviewed, the alignment between Derrida's philosophical approaches and the explanations of projects exhibited was one of filmic juxtaposition and a collage of ideas rather than a focused explanation. In the film, Hadid continued to describe her approach as being consistent from the time of The Peak project.[15] Her central interest had been a reconsideration of the tenets of early 20th-century Modernism. She explained that through an exploration of selected works from Suprematism and the Russian avant-garde, she perceived a distinctive way for considering the term 'program' in architecture, where program was not limited to an understanding of its function or functionality. For Hadid, program became operative without being tied within the 'hegemony of aesthetics' that might be considered in statements well known in architecture like 'form follows function'.[16] Program derived its potency from a layering of spatial responses to the networks and ties between what Hadid described as the 'players' in that program. Its 'players' were not simply the client and their processes, but also within its remit were the internal and external complexities of the architectural space, and the temporal reception of forms and their material surrounds: to the site, the landscape, and the culture and pattern of urbanity within a city. These were all 'players' informing the architectural programs.

When interviewed by curator Peter Noever, artistic director of the Austrian Museum of Applied Arts / Contemporary Art (MAK), Vienna, in 1990, Hadid was asked to respond to the claim of her work being considered as a form of deconstruction. She remarked:

Labels are always problematic, they quickly become obsolete. I've also always had difficulties with the word Deconstructivism, it's a combination of two words that have a real connection, or not. However, the connection between the participants in the exhibition seems to me to be of far more fundamental importance. [For others involved] the constructivist concept doesn't really make sense, I think. Rather, what is decisive is that in each individual exhibit was a concern with statements about contemporary architecture instead of depicting irregular buildings. Nevertheless, Peter Eisenman has his roots in Deconstruction, perhaps so does Bernard Tschumi.[17]

It is in this immediate context that the paintings for the Vitra Fire Station display Hadid's distinctive response to the issues facing contemporary architecture. The Vitra paintings stage a series of visual explorations of the project's emergence. Within their visual structure, architecture takes part in the assembly and layering of many differing programmatic cues, each having linear and volumetric consequences, kinetically resolving over time into a material form. While their resolution could infer in part a deconstructive act, this was importantly never stated as a claim.[18] Central to their structuring is her use of painting's capacity for implied spatial networks, based on ideas of linearity, collage, montage and juxtaposition, used to present the radicality of the scheme's emerging 'programs'.[19] Painting provided Hadid with a method for imaging the spatial energy and material processes of the form's resolution into architecture.

Of interest to investigating the paintings of Hadid's design for Vitra Fire Station, however, one presentation at the Tate symposium by philosopher and architectural theorist Andrew Benjamin drew reference from Derrida's arguments by citing an excerpt from René Descartes. These references become fruitful to the interpretation of Hadid's paintings. Benjamin retold an aside, where Descartes claimed that like architecture, a city required a single vision to be considered as beautiful. Descartes commented further saying, 'ancient cities which have gradually grown up from mere villages into large towns are usually ill proportioned, compared with those orderly towns which planners lay out as they fancy on level ground . . . [For ancient cities] you would say it is chance rather than the will of men using reason, that placed them so'.[20] Benjamin then expanded on the consequences of Descartes's logic:

> The lack of order in the ancient city is marked by – as well as being the mark of – the lack of reason. It has the consequence that not only is the city in some sense 'mad', it can also be thought within the totalising purview of reason, except of course as mad. Therefore, when taken to its logical extreme the architectural metaphor indicates both the possibility of a unified totality – to be provided by the application of reason – as well as that which stands opposed to this possibility, namely madness; presented here as the untotalisable plurality of the ancient city . . . The triumph of reason over madness, Descartes is insisting, is the path to be followed by the philosopher as architect and architect as philosopher.[21]

For Benjamin, embedded within Descartes's idea of the new city was the necessity for erasure of the old, and the triumph of the new as complete and reasoned. Benjamin's repurposing of this aside from Descartes opened consideration of Derrida's claim that such oppositions were a fiction. For Derrida the deconstruction of such fictions of ordered resolution had become central to recognising the possibility of architectural experimentation in the city. Within Hadid's complex layering of ideas for architecture and the city in her paintings for Vitra Fire Station, there is a consideration of the schism Benjamin raised between 'reason' and 'chance' in recognising the 'madness' in the lack of order in the ancient city. To begin to investigate this synergy of ideas, it is important to know a little of the context for Hadid's architectural project, and to examine how the paintings develop their compositional power.

Vitra is a company well known for its distinctive design and manufacturing of mid-20th-century and contemporary chairs. At the time of Hadid's commission Vitra manufactured and distributed the designs of Charles and Ray Eames, George Nelson, Verner Panton, Alexander Girard and Jean Prouvé. Although originally only in partnership with the American furniture manufacturer Herman Miller – producing their licenced products for the European market – by the mid-1980s Vitra discontinued the exclusivity of this arrangement and licenced directly with designers.

The Vitra Group's facility is located in the semi-rural industrial town of Weil am Rhein in Germany, on the borders of Switzerland and France, with the Swiss city of Basel its closest urban centre. It lies between the vineyards and 'long-run' agricultural lands of Tüllinger Mountain, which define its north-eastern boundary and railway marshalling yards located below a cutting to its west, creating a barrier between its campus and the city of Basel. Defining the conceptual aspirations for the site had been a central concern for Rolf Fehlbaum, the president of the Vitra Group, as he considered how to rebuild the factory and showroom after fire destroyed its plant in 1981. In 2010 in an interview with Enrico Molteni for the Italian magazine *Casabella*, he recounted the complex relationship Vitra had with the city of Basel. Molteni asked whether the concept for the factory complex was closer to the idea of a collection, a city or a campus. Fehlbaum considered the poor fit of each descriptor, and in doing so raised the importance of Basel as a frame of reference for the factory precinct.[22] He continued the explanation noting that initially, after the fire, he had commissioned architect Nicholas Grimshaw to develop a masterplan to 'program growth in a more orderly way than in the past'.[23] However, he explained his vision for the precinct radically changed following the completion of a sculpture by Claes Oldenburg, which he claimed had altered the 'chemistry of the place'.[24] It was Oldenburg's friend Frank Gehry who at the time introduced Fehlbaum to a broader concept of how the site might be enriched spatially. This, Fehlbaum claimed, had internationalised the culture of Vitra, typologically inscribing it within a vision of urbanity that was closer to that of a city.

Fehlbaum had first been introduced to the work of Hadid through her furniture design.[25] Hadid recalled that her interior for the Cathcart Road apartment (1985–86) had been published in the Italian magazine *Casa Vogue* and that Fehlbaum had contacted her to design a piece of furniture for Vitra to develop and manufacture.[26] This association faltered, but in Hadid's subsequent commission for the Fire Station Fehlbaum reiterated that, unlike furniture and sculpture, the brief for developing architecture for the precinct required 'a concrete purpose for a building'.[27]

The Vitra Fire Station was to house the company's own fire trucks and services, as the city had not been able to adequately provide for the scope of its fire-safety requirements.[28] As the project progressed, Fehlbaum's brief expanded and requested Hadid to propose ways of rethinking the boundary and edges of the factory's complex. He wanted her to explore the potential of interstitial or 'left spaces' that could increase the public amenity for the Vitra complex as it grew. Hadid later described these spaces as an 'open air room or carved-out space . . . [where] the walls of the buildings become like furniture'.[29] It was an idea that drew links from the landscape to the sense of 'interior urbanism', required by Fehlbaum, creating a new spatial complexity for the facility, an idea that challenged the dominance of the grid-like organisation of the Grimshaw master plan.

Completing the project saw an expansion of the office now taking the name Zaha Hadid Architects. There were now also distinctive project groups in the office, each led by one of Hadid's senior associates. Other major projects of the period included the Internationale Bauausstellung, Berlin (IBA), urban studies for London, Berlin and Barcelona, and several architectural competitions and exhibitions of paintings. For the Vitra Fire Station, Patrik Schumacher and Kar-Hwa Ho took leading roles in the initial design, with the full project team increasing to nearly 20 people.[30] Like all architectural projects, the Vitra project had the added complexity of input from engineering, project management and construction documentation teams with knowledge of local regulatory authorities.

Two paintings are important in examining how the design for the project evolved. The first, titled *Vitra Fire Station, Plan and Aerial Perspective of Overall Scheme*, can be dated by its publication in 1991.[31] This painting remained one of the main inclusions for the exhibition at the Aedes Galerie opening in May of 1992, titled *Zaha Hadid: Vitra Fire Station*.[32] Amongst those staff members listed in the Aedes exhibition catalogue were David Gomersall and Nicola Cousins who produced the paintings. They had both joined Hadid's studio in 1983 during completion of the paintings for the *Planetary Architecture Two* exhibition in London, and had become trusted members, each transforming ideas from drawings into paintings. The second painting has been titled *Vitra Fire Station, Aerial Painting* in the publication *Hadid: Complete Works 1979–2009*.[33] Brian Ma Siy completed the underlying line drawing which was then painted by Gomersall for inclusion in an exhibition at the MAK, opening in 1993.[34] It is further included in the *GA Document Extra 03* publication of 1995, but without any caption.[35] Ma Siy made the comment that in the process of moving between the acts of drawing and painting, certain attributes of the composition had changed. In an observation that becomes suggestive of how paintings developed in the process of their completion, he explained:

> David would have the printers enlarge my A3 drawings to whatever size he required; usually dictated by the width of the roll of cartridge paper he was working on. At the right size, he would transfer the drawing (a little like using carbon paper) onto the final paper. He would then adjust some of the lines and make some amendments to the drawing or add more detail. The problem of my drawing at A3 size was that some of the detail would be missing... During the painting process, David and I would have a couple of short discussions about some of the details and intersections, but it was largely left up to him to continue.[36]

The two paintings form a pair framing the trajectory phases of the design process in the realisation of the final building of the Vitra Fire Station. Each painting, therefore, addresses the differing aspects of the design's conceptual approaches as they developed over a number of years.

## The Conceptual 'Ground' of Painting:
### *Vitra Fire Station, Plan and Aerial Perspective of Overall Scheme*

At a distance, the first impressions of the painting *Plan and Aerial Perspective of Overall Scheme* are of the application of a single dominating background colour (fig.68). Nicola Cousins remembers this painting, explaining that in the process of considering its final form they had been 'very into chartreuse green and I had made quite a batch'.[37] While this choice of colour may seem whimsical, in its application it importantly confirms that colour, even for this background, was applied through the painting processes of layering numerous transparent washes vertically and horizontally across the surface until the final effect of flat luminescent colour was achieved.[38] It brings a powerful force to the composition – supporting its semi-abstraction rather than referencing a scene's reality.

However, in this semi-abstract state there are distinctively recognisable attributes. The pictorial 'ground' is defined partly by the presence of an arcing line separating the upper and lower parts of the composition. It becomes an important element in the impact of the painting, making some reference to the curvature of the earth's horizon and holding the perspectival vanishing point that defines the painting's dynamism. It is a device Hadid's studio had used previously, harking back to the painting *The World, The Eighty-nine Degrees* completed in 1983 for the exhibition *Planetary Architecture Two*.[39] For the Vitra painting *Plan and Aerial Perspective of Overall Scheme*, the earth's surface is portrayed as if disappearing beyond a viewer's visual perception and over the horizon.

Within the composition, architectural form is described by a group of seemingly random shard-like elements coloured in pale tones of blue, ochre and white, and where black and red are introduced as highlights to infer the edges of planes. These shards seem to hover over the ground casting a series of shadows, and where on its surface, the lines of technical drawings add faint traces of architectural references. Despite being composed from the combination of many study drawings, this painting is dominated by the implied velocity of these fragments. The idea of movement in the architecture, imagined as an intellectual process, had long been a theme in Hadid's paintings. An example can be seen in *Exploded Isometric* for The Peak, where beams had been depicted 'moving' across the foreground toward their resolution as the building, and again in the paintings for the Irish Prime Minister's Residence of 1979, where elements were shown to violently intersect – changing the resolution of spaces in their path, an action which Hadid had described as an 'explosion'.

Within the imagery of *Plan and Aerial Perspective of Overall Scheme*, the top half of the composition repeats elements from the line drawing *Vitra Fire Station, Landscape Study*, continuing its effect by adding a large complex elongated shadow over the 'ground' in the lower sections of the painting (fig.69). However, this shadow does not have an immediate referent object that would cast its shape. Its purpose seems compositional, providing a dynamic relationship with the lines of technical drawings lightly referenced across the surface of the painting. Added within this lower section is a series of layered shards, oblongs, dots, dashes and wavy lines. Each shape sits above the complexity of technical lines projecting from what appear to be orthogonal architectural drawings. Selected shapes become more prominent through colour or 'whoosh' reductions of their tone. As painted, these elements bring a two-dimensional quality of abstraction to the composition, reinforced by colouration in red, blue and yellow, as well as tones of black and white. Many of the shapes in this lower section of the painting have synergy with elements from the

68
**Zaha Hadid Architects**
*Vitra Fire Station, Plan and Aerial Perspective of Overall Scheme*, Weil am Rhein, Germany, 1990
Acrylic on paper, 129.6 × 98.4 cm (51 × 38¾ in)
Taschen

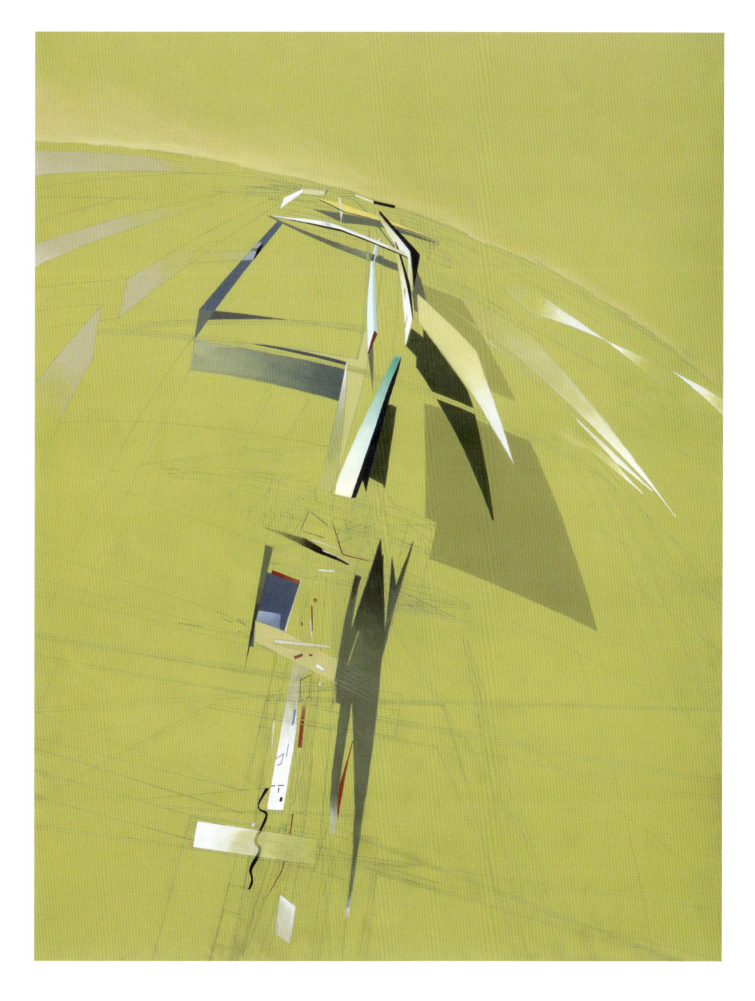

scheme's architectural landscaping, but these too resist being fixed in a final location or material form.

The complex layering of this section of the composition can be seen in a detail, where a 'whoosh' of white grading across a rectangular shape spans over a black wavy line without obstructing its forms (fig.70). Both elements overlay the lines below, and while their 'meaning' and architectural impact can be retrieved from other drawings, in this instance they have a different function. They respond to a painterly reference to the synergy of Hadid's painting with the paintings of Kazimir Malevich. Within the main grouping of shapes in this area, an elongated grey triangular shard abuts three overlaid trapezoidal shapes coloured in blues, green and red (fig.71). The resulting imagery is juxtaposed with a series of rectangles in yellow and with a 'whoosh' of varying white tones. The strength of their compositional abstraction is enhanced by a scattering of small rectangles in white and red, each intersecting with the principal shapes to create a dynamic balance between their forms.

Focusing on this group of elements, their importance for the painting can be seen in the context of a lecture that Hadid had given at the architecture school SCI-Arc in Los Angeles early in 1985, where she showed two Malevich paintings. One, Malevich's *Suprematist Composition (with Yellow, Orange and Green Rectangle)*, 1915–16, was used to explore correspondences between Suprematist imagery and its implications for architecture (fig.72). In this painting, Malevich layers differing coloured shapes, implying a spatiality between them. Hadid explains:

> The whole interest in Malevich was not again because of the kind of paintings but the implication that in some cases, the injection of Suprematism into architecture and the whole notion of this ... liberation from gravity ... and in every possible way that you break away from all the ties, that tie you down in terms of architecture.[40]

Still with this image in view, Hadid's lecture then focused on the transfer of the implications of this idea into architecture, which she suggested could be seen in part in the work of the Suprematist El Lissitzky, but more fundamentally in the work of Ivan Leonidov. It was in this context she explained how, in Malevich's painting, the 'liberation from gravity' and 'all that ties you down in terms of architecture' is resolved into architecture as an 'evolution of the kind of the new programs evident in Russia', one that had redefined its expression of culture after the Revolution.[41] Confirming this as an attribute she admired, in an interview with curator Peter Noever in 1993, Hadid reiterated: 'All these statements about the idea of liberation, liberation from gravity. That doesn't mean that the buildings are floating somewhere in the air, it simply means that one is completely free from learned, imposed rules, and once this threshold has been crossed, many perspectives open up.'[42]

Hadid was directing attention to the complexities introduced by spatial layering in architecture, where competing elements became essentially embedded within a new abstract level of responsiveness to culture and society and to their political renewal. These rather important ideas are embedded within the spatial relationships of her paintings for Vitra and its architectural programmes.

In *Plan and Aerial Perspective of Overall Scheme* there is a presentation of the complex layering of architecture's spatial and formal responses to the city, the site, the landscape, and the cultural and social markers of that place. But within the painting's imagery these programmatic concerns and their architectural resolution remain an open question. The design had not been finalised into material form and elements had not yet coalesced into architecture. Each spatial influence in the

70
Zaha Hadid Architects
(detail) *Vitra Fire Station, Plan and Aerial Perspective of Overall Scheme*, Weil am Rhein, Germany, 1990
Acrylic on paper
Taschen

69
Zaha Hadid Architects
*Vitra Fire Station, Landscape Study*,
Weil am Rhein, Germany, 1990
Ink on Mylar®, 42 × 83 cm (16½ × 32¹¹⁄₁₆ in)
Zaha Hadid Foundation

painting's structure brings a programmatic effect in an aspiration for a new urbanity within and beyond the Vitra complex, one where the hegemony of aesthetics and usefulness in architecture could be raised as a question. The introduction of Suprematism-like layers into this painting thus sits clearly within the architectural concerns of its programmatic definition.

The final component within the painting's complex composition is a series of pseudo-technical drawings faintly layered within the chartreuse green background. It is only when closely examining the painting that their delicacy as forms becomes obvious. Their subtle linear effect importantly tempers the abstract quality of the painting's dominant shapes and colours. Although, the lines are precise, each component seems to depict fragments that might have resulted from selections made from overlaid preliminary technical drawings, perhaps randomly collected on a desk. They suggest a questioning of meaning in the very act of technical architectural drawing. There is a series of parallel lines at angles that might define wall alignments, others depicted by dotted and solid straight lines that cross the whole pictorial field. Some lines coincide in vertices that appear like those used in the set-up of a two-point perspective projected from a vanishing point, but nothing is recognisable in the sense of an architectural detail or image. Unlike the plans included in The Peak paintings, here there are no visual 'symbols' such as stairs, or ramps or rooms that can be functionally aligned. To understand their intention, or the randomness of their angles and repetition, would require insider knowledge of the architectural project from other sources. For the viewer of this painting, apprehension of an architecture in terms of Walter Benjamin's claims for architectural drawing remains elusive, and the sense of rational determinism in architecture's traditional relation to the city is avoided.[43]

71
Zaha Hadid Architects
(detail) *Vitra Fire Station, Plan and Aerial Perspective of Overall Scheme*, Weil am Rhein, Germany, 1990
Acrylic on paper
Taschen

Through a compilation of layered elements – the merging of one sketch with others – the painting's final composition evokes a network of 'coincidences'. It is as though architecture's form is caught in the process of metamorphosis, with its 'programs', forms and spatial juxtapositions still uncertain while holding a suggestion of the importance of inscribing lines on the 'ground'. The architecture for now remains in a state of negotiated inquiry, an architecture gestured toward, rather than defined by any representational completeness. The painting posits a series of speculative questions as if considering a way forward in the architecture's resolution. Hadid describes this process as responding to:

> . . . a very extensive study very early as to how a site like this could first expand our pocket on the side . . . this kind of corridor . . . becomes a space that could be

carved out, could be a public space . . . you begin to kind of generate a program of civic function within the factory ground. We looked at the composition of all these elements separately. We began to look at the roof. The roof began to change . . . to deal with the energy of the site.⁴⁴

From the topography and geometry of the Vitra precinct it becomes clear that the painting negotiates a series of not always resolvable relationships – between the long narrow corridor of space defining the perimeter of the Fire Station, the landscape and industrial contexts, the urban and suburban fringes and city beyond, the aspirations and needs of the client, and the building's regulatory frameworks. The painting's fragmentation and layering present a need to escape such concerns 'that tie you down'.⁴⁵ When describing the process of design for the building, Hadid inferred a relationship between the importance of its siting in relation to the city and the propositions evident in the painting. She said:

72
Kazimir Malevich
*Suprematist Composition (with Yellow, Orange and Green Rectangle)*, 1915–16
Oil on canvas,
47 × 38 cm (18½ × 15 in)
Stedelijk Museum Amsterdam

There were two or three moments when there was a change that radically changed the diagram. It's not noticeable but it was an important change at the time. [Vitra] was designed in a roundabout way because we didn't start with the building, we designed this building looking at this whole site, then placing it, and then designing it . . . The building kind of expands and retracts in both ways. Physically in some ways and visually in others . . . The idea of the landscape also came very early; the idea of what these lines could mean on the site. It was really like land art. We still have this belt – this kind of corridor we called the urban space. We tried to . . . urbanise the site because the site is on the edge of the city, it's a kind of agricultural area. It's through making architecture that you urbanise the factory ground.⁴⁶

The imagery of the painting *Plan and Aerial Perspective of Overall Scheme* locates the potential of this state of inquiry and visualises how a projection of shard-like architectonic shapes and lines could provide the genesis of spatial energy, a force that would explore the 'civic function' of the Vitra complex.⁴⁷

By taking an aerial position architectural forms appear to emerge within an action, a process of negotiating how an urbanity might be considered and transformed. If the viewer attempted to locate the imagery of this painting within the realised building, they will find that the relationship is unclear. However, each element indicates a potential visual and conceptual purpose within Hadid's architectural thinking, each a partial reminder that the rational gridded logic of the existing masterplan is not the final organising principle of the Vitra precinct.

When asked by Noever, 'But isn't that an illusion? Your architecture is dynamic architecture, perhaps you could say dynamic architecture that doesn't move?', Hadid responded, 'No, but nobody says that it should.' She continued:

It was the idea of gradually moving towards a fundamental freedom in the way things are experienced and perceived, such as how players are manipulated. The projections became a tool to discover the architecture. The intention was to find a new perspective, a more easily changeable plan that allows people to move around in it and that also creates a new kind of space.⁴⁸

In the narrative force of the layers of imagery, *Plan and Aerial Perspective of Overall Scheme* becomes a representation as well as a process of working in the production of architecture. It represents the strategies of visual thinking. Its task was not just to mirror a technical drawing's purpose. Of importance to Hadid was how the configuration of colour, line and diagramming within a painting tied her understanding of Suprematism's sense of pictorial space that is politicised into the spatial complexity of differing programs in architecture, thereby dislodging the primacy usually attributed to technical drawings.

In this painting the juxtaposition between the differing layers of abstract and technical imagery becomes spatially suggestive. There is an implied depth, as if the viewer is flying above a scene where it is unclear whether the objects, or the viewer, are moving at greater speed. The notion of speed and energy brings a tension to the image, implying a relationship between the viewer and what is seen. With a strange synergy recognising the differences of approach to the aerial view of Michel de Certeau's understanding of ideality and that of Paul Virilio (both discussed in previous chapters), Hadid's aerial view of Vitra Fire Station can be seen to negotiate a new exploration of architectural spatiality.[49]

While de Certeau had criticised the aerial view as utopian, Virilio had considered it more as the implication of viewing into a computer screen's internal geometries, and the geometric relationship developed between object and operator or viewer:

> 'Video doesn't mean I see; it means I fly,' according to Nam June Paik. With this technology, the 'over-view' [or aerial view] is no longer a question of theoretical altitudes, of scale designs [as claimed by de Certeau] but has become an opto-electronic interface operating in real-time, with all that this implies for a redefinition of the image. If aviation, which began the same year as cinematography, instigated a revision of point of view, a radical change of the perception of the world, infographic techniques will instigate, in their turn, a revision of reality and its representations.[50]

The painting *Plan and Aerial Perspective of Overall Scheme* engages with such a change of perceptions. Hadid's painting anticipates the changing idea of the image where the computer screen was beginning to become a dominant visualising tool in architecture. However, for Hadid the impenetrable geometry of this spatiality is again considered through painting's affect. Each detail of the painting brings a negotiation of differing spatial apparatus: between the painted image, architecture's technical representation, pictorial abstraction, and the ether-like depth of a computer screen. The question of what these shards of colour represent becomes compellingly an architectural one.

As an inquiry into architecture, the imagery of this painting proposes a series of prompts defining an experimental force that is ongoing rather than complete. The schema of the architecture emerges kinetically. Architecture has not yet found its material form either intellectually or physically in this painting. The role of visual prompts within its composition signifies the apprehension of an architecture possible only through juxtaposition, layering and diagrammatic connectivity – each remnant force remains within the implicitly gestural formations of the painting. However, without the second *Vitra Fire Station, Aerial Painting* there is little referencing of deconstruction, or Descartes, or Benjamin's consideration of the city that is immediately obvious.

## Architecture's Urban Impact: *Vitra Fire Station, Aerial Painting*

It is only when the second painting, *Aerial Painting*, is examined that the implications and narrative force of the earlier painting, *Plan and Aerial Perspective of Overall Scheme*, develop a more direct connection with Hadid's changing approach to architecture. *Aerial Painting* was completed in late 1992 (fig.73).[51] It was drawn by Brian Ma Siy and painted by David Gomersall. Ma Siy remembers: 'It was drawn and painted quickly for the MAK. In other words, it was not a piece which pushed the design or investigated a new way to depict the project.'[52]

In this sense the motivation of this painting is one of reflection, visually emphasising the prompts that had been fundamental to the process of resolving the architecture. The construction phase of the building would have been underway when this painting was conceived. Its imagery responds to memories of the process of resolution from the more experimental drawings and paintings into the realised architecture. Through techniques adapted from the arts, there is a focus on the linear, planar and spatial networks within this painting's compositional strategies, used to assign a visual structuring of the extended program of the Vitra Fire Station. Fundamental to the image is the dynamic force and fragmentation of this 'scene's' linear thrust. Many years later Hadid was to reminisce on these attributes: 'If you look at the Fire Station in Weil am Rhein in Germany, it was all based, on movement, but I really wanted a space that was very calm. My intention may be to deal with speed, but the actual experience can be quite different.'[53]

The imagery of *Aerial Painting* builds from a muted tonal range of natural colours: of warm silvers, blue and pinkish-greys with ochre hints. Rather than focus its gaze toward the distant city of Basel, as had been the case in the earlier painting, the composition of *Aerial Painting* forces the viewer's attention back toward the Vitra precinct, and to the 'long-run' agricultural lands and vineyards of Tüllinger Mountain.[54] The long linear forms of its ploughed fields visually reference the pattern of the ancient traditions of farming in this part of Europe. Hadid considered them as 'land art' and their influence reinforces the scheme's arrowhead in the painting, thrusting toward the interface between the Vitra precinct and these fields. Just as in the painting *Plan and Aerial Perspective of Overall Scheme*, this dynamism is halted by an arcing horizon line where the dark sky beyond becomes void-like.

Within *Aerial Painting*'s composition, a second horizontal break is introduced at the intersection between the agricultural lands and the factory site, suggesting an important focus within the imagery. This division takes the form of a visual pause in the temporality of the painting's expressiveness. It introduces a second geometric thrust of collaged perspectival images, directed horizontally across the composition. At the point of intersection of these horizontally aligned representations and the dynamically thrusting vertical view of the Fire Station roof forms lies a small perspective of the entry portal to Hadid's scheme – its diminutive scale almost lost in the vastness of the painting. This cruciform of linear forces within the composition presents a clear statement of transformation: an act that brings together referents – from the landscape, the urbanity of the setting, and the other box-like structures of the adjacent factory buildings at Vitra – to portray how the Fire Station was to be architecturally considered.

In the lower sections of the composition, a series of dark, warm silver-grey tones take the form of roofs of factory buildings, repeating them across the industrial landscape of the nearby rail lines. Their patterning is now skewed away from the dominance of the grid to deflect its rigid geometries. In sections, the linear saw-toothed patterns of the factory roofs are defined, their implied chevron directing the attention of the viewer upward and toward the small entry portal perspective.

73
Zaha Hadid Architects
*Vitra Fire Station, Aerial Painting*,
Weil am Rhein, Germany, 1990
Acrylic on paper, 260 × 120 cm (102⅜ × 47¼ in)
MAK – Museum of Applied Arts, Vienna

Subsumed within these roofs are the lines of the railway marshalling yards – their power now integrated within the project's linear affect.

In the painting, the dominance of the rail lines has been defused; however, in three early study drawings included in the Aedes catalogue of 1992, it is these lines and the agricultural patterns that were graphically dominant.[55] In these study drawings each is displayed as an important prompt for rethinking the organisation of the Vitra campus. But what changes over this process is the play between attributes, either becoming spatially 'negative' and inactive, or becoming 'positive' in supporting the architecture. When the three sketches are seen together there is a notable progression of sequential thinking informing the design. The linear patterns of the Tüllinger Mountain fields are first considered as dark figures on a ground, emphasising through their 'blackened' representation their visual dominance over the rail lines, establishing the importance of their changing orientation around the factory footprint. In the second sketch, these fields are seen for their inferred dominant lines and the introduction of their possible impact by the cutting of the rail lines. In the third, each conceptual force has been given the status of lines, reinstated within the 'urban corridors' defined by the grid of factory buildings, reinforcing the consideration of the Vitra Fire Station site as embedded within a series of linear spatial forces (figs 74a, b and c). The importance of this layering of ideas has some synergy with the ideas that Benjamin raised about Descartes's claim for 'reason' being required to achieve beauty within the city. However, the complex layering of each form counters any approach to beauty as being one resolved within a single geometric logic. It instead presents a network of geometries.

These sketches provide an understanding of the compositional sources of *Aerial Painting*. Wanting to emphasise the geometric patterning of the agricultural lands, Hadid argued that the 'field geometry precedes the city geometry', thus becoming more important.[56] Their lines emphasise a counter to the rationality of the grid where layered patterning introduces a new divergence within the geometry of the scheme's spatial programs. Hadid claimed this created a 500-metre-long spatial 'corridor' within the Vitra precinct, saying: 'The artificial landscape within these corridors [is] inspired by the linear rhythm of the agricultural landscape outside … stretching from the main gate with the [Gehry] chair museum to the other end of the factory site … Part of this landscape would be choreographic notations inscribing into the ground the ritualised fire exercises.'[57]

However, in the composition of *Aerial Painting* this influence expands to Weil am Rhein and the city of Basel, registered in the scatter of shapes beyond the representation of the scheme's roof forms – prompting consideration of the impact of the idea over the city. Hadid's programs for the Vitra Fire Station were not simply a recognition of contextual patterns of land use that reappear as decorative motifs within the site's environments. They inform the architectural programs that work to critique previous rigidity of the rational structures of the Vitra precinct grid and its urban context. Hadid continued this idea by reimagining the city. In a gesture toward Descartean rationality she hypothesised how within her approach the now 'anarchical developments' of the suburban context of Weil am Rhein could become differently 'meaningful', envisaged by her as perimeter housing blocks forming 'a solid podium 10 meters high'.[58] In this construct, influence from the landscape patterns would reappear not only as edges, but as

> cut outs and carefully placed voids, which would focus and frame the public life of the city much clearer than it would be possible in a loose suburban sprawl. This concept of podium, implying a reversal of the figure-ground relationship,

 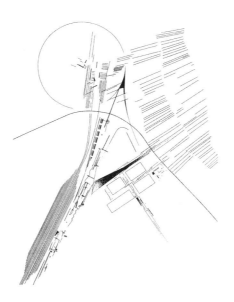 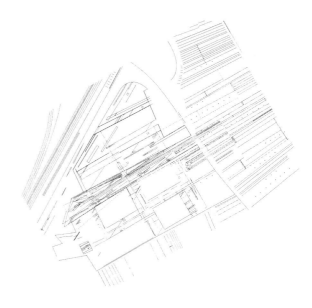

74 (a–c)
Zaha Hadid Architects
*Vitra Fire Station, Concept Drawings*, Weil am Rhein, Germany, 1990, from the catalogue *Vitra Fire Station*
Aedes Galerie, Berlin

(the individual building disappears into the framing mass of figural space), becomes the underlying hypothesis and common denominator for the approach.⁵⁹

This fictional or imagined city becomes fundamental within the project's conceptualisation as it 'frames' the context for developing an architectural program for Vitra. It is useful to remember that what Hadid understood as the suburban sprawl of Weil am Rhein included apartment towers, but like the single-family housing, these recent developments took the form of isolated buildings bounded by strips of open ground. Her idea was to reverse this model, in the same graphic manner of reversing the figure-ground to increase the dominance of the geometry of the agricultural fields – where the urban density of Weil am Rhein would acknowledge a counter spatiality in the unique relationship with its history.

Through layering these geometries Hadid could be seen to envisage a 'rational' spatial complexity for Weil am Rhein while recognising the impossibility of that resolution. The relationship she developed between landscape and built form would reflect the distinct opportunity embedded within the history of land patterns in the area. She explained: 'The relationship towards the landscape would take the character of an erosion of the podium and an inflow of nature into the city. This big open green space could contain a "free-floating" type of housing in between public recreational facilities. This idea becomes central to the new scheme.'⁶⁰

In *Aerial Painting*, the imagery, compositional layering and linearity work to project this idea toward the Vitra site, but it also implies a thrust toward Basel and Weil am Rhein, and in the processes defined by its composition, acts to subsume the existing dominance of the rail lines and their reinforcement of the international borders between nations. In the act of reinscribing these lines, patterns and their geometries into the Vitra precinct, Hadid was aware of the impossibility of gaining a unity. Like Benjamin, in recognising the 'madness' of the forms of the ancient city, the Vitra precinct too would transform by accretion over time. It was a visual gesture in this painting that implied deconstructive thought rather than the rationality demanded by Descartes. How this occurs requires broader consideration of the context of her thinking.

## The Spatial Role: Landscape and Architecture in the Figure-Ground of the City

There is an implied movement and thus temporality within both Vitra paintings: a trace of beginnings and propulsions forward, where the embodied energy of each visual element remains locatable, symbolically embedded within architecture's spaces and forms. In their gestural movements, it is as if architecture is projecting ideas beyond its physical forms and material realisation – influencing in equal measure the surrounding topographical formations, the urbanity of the distant city and town, and the industrial settings closely proximate. It is an idea reminiscent of the recognition of the distinct form of the metropolis of Hong Kong in The Peak scheme, but it also locates the context of Hadid's thinking during the late 1980s and 1990s, as it is in part reflecting ideas from deconstructivist theory.

To understand the context of Hadid's thinking of this time, a series of terms that she introduced into discussions of the Vitra scheme require explanation. They become layered within architecture's influence over the city. In interviews, texts and lectures, expressions like 'architectural program' continued to be refined, but others like 'the reversal of the figure-ground relationships', or the idea that 'individual buildings disappear into the framing mass of figural space', or the notion that 'landscape would take the character of an erosion', emerged during explanations of the Vitra Fire Station, and each has a unique meaning in that context.[61]

It was at this time that Hadid's engagement with the reconsideration of the city was at its height. Projects coinciding with Vitra, or indeed taking place just prior, included the urban 'map' studies for Berlin and London, and housing projects for Berlin.[62] It was also a time when her involvement in exhibitions and symposia increased, enabling the articulation of her ideas to international groups.[63] An example of this cross-pollination of thoughts was Hadid's involvement in the IBA projects for Berlin. The IBA was both the title of an exhibition in 1987 and the name of a development company motivating and showcasing the redevelopment of West Berlin.[64] By the 1987 exhibition many of the projects were already realised as buildings, so the form of the exhibition was a guide to walking through the schemes as well as an exhibit of the architectural drawings.[65] Hadid had been successfully awarded a scheme to complete in 1986 and so was not involved as an exhibitor.[66] However, the architectural basis of the IBA projects was debated at events like the Triennale of Milan held in early 1985, curated by Marco De Michelis, Pierluigi Nicolin, Werner Oechslin and Frank Werner. The Triennale's exhibition included Hadid's paintings of The Peak project.[67] It was in such contexts that Hadid developed particular themes that contributed to her ideas on the city. For her the city could be considered a 'metropolis', a 'field of fragments', of 'figure-ground relationships', or the notion of an urban 'figural mass'.[68] These are also terms she had used when describing the scheme for Vitra.

The trajectory from the Triennale of Milan through Hadid's own history traces these ideas and their meaning within her architectural vocabulary. The figure-ground studies of the urban perimeter block, predominant in the IBA and considered by Hadid for Weil am Rhein, for example, can even be traced in part to her student schemes completed for Léon Krier in her third year of the architecture course at the Architectural Association (AA), where considerations of figure-ground studies were instrumental as a principle in urban design. During the 1974/75 academic year in her project titled 'Urban Nucleus over Railway-Cutting in Swiss-Cottage South Hampstead', and the studies on 'Block Research, Greater London', Hadid had clearly referenced this approach.[69]

75
**Zaha Hadid Architects**
*Metropolis*, London, United Kingdom, 1988
Acrylic and coloured pencil on paper mounted on canvas, 246 × 95 cm (96⅞ × 37⅜ in)
San Francisco Museum of Modern Art, San Francisco

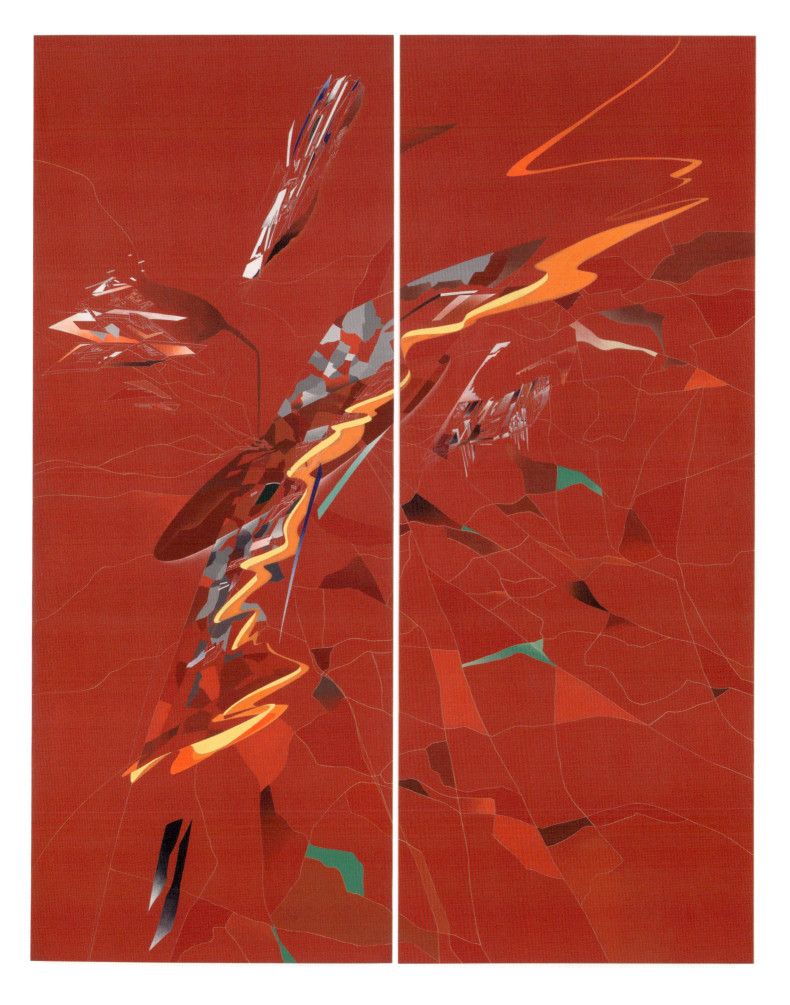

The idea of figure-ground analysis of the city is terminology that had also been central to Hadid's city mapping projects of the late 1980s, where the painting *Metropolis*, for example, depicting London as a series of differing figure-ground transformations (fig.75).⁷⁰ However, in this example the figure-ground 'principle' has been inverted and supports an idea of spatial experimentation. In the same year Hadid had been invited to take part in a consideration of Berlin in *Berlin 2000*, where she again experimented with reversals of figure-ground studies as a way to renegotiate spatial geometries and programs of the city.

These references not only recognise Hadid's own historical context, but introduce a connection to the IBA, and discussions on the city during the Triennale of Milan in 1985. It was in this context that the idea of figure-ground became important in a consideration of the city. Architects involved with the IBA were given individual sites within designated districts of Berlin with little requirement for continuity. Many IBA participants taking part in the Triennale of Milan argued the relevance of differing approaches to the city and its future development. Discussion questioned whether cities such as Berlin – due to war-time damage – could still be recognised as having a remnant of the figure-ground patterning evident within historical maps, or only as a series of vacant sites interspersed by remnant buildings. There were numerous studies of the underlying historic geometry of Berlin and its similarities with Roman planning, especially in the analytical studies of architect and urban planner Manuel de Solà-Morales.⁷¹ The characteristics of the figure-ground map enabled the outline of existing built development to be considered a 'figure' shown in solid black, hatched, or coloured, and the remaining open space to be considered as 'ground' and left untextured. Post-war Berlin complicated that understanding because of the decimation of the urban fabric after the Second World War bombing.

Each of the arguments proffered at the Triennale had long histories. Rowe and Koetter's *Collage City*, published in 1978, had informed reconsideration of figure-ground as a way for recognising the city as a 'bricolage' of patterns of development over time, and was brought into debates on Berlin at the Triennale by Marco De Michelis.⁷² Rowe and Koetter's book was popularised into architectural debates further by its core tenets being central to the 1978 *Roma Interrotta* symposium and exhibition, where Piero Sartogo, who had worked with Rowe and Eisenman,⁷³ invited architects to consider the loss of the subtlety of this type of urban texture in

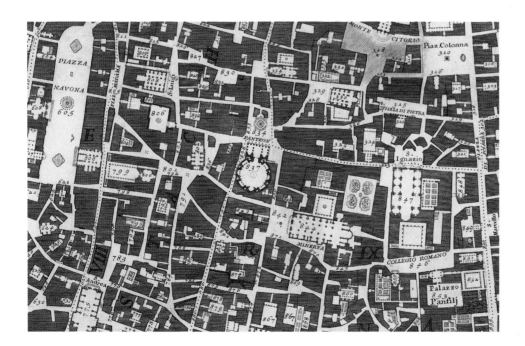

76
Giambattista Nolli
(detail) *Plan of Rome, La nuova topografia di Roma, Alla Santità Di Nostro Signore Papa Benedetto XIV La Nuova Topografia Di Roma Ossequiosamente Offerisce e Dedica l'Umilissimo Servo Giambattista Nolli Comasco / Nuova pianta di Roma*, 1748
Copper engraving, individual panels glued together overlapping and mounted, overall plan framed, 172 × 207 cm (67¾ × 81½ in)
Bibliotheca Hertziana Rome

Rome. Architects were invited to reconsider Rome from the basis of Giambattista Nolli's 1748 *La nuova topografia di Roma* or *Plan of Rome* (fig.76). It was Nolli's graphic formulation for describing Rome through figure-ground studies that had been lauded by Rowe and Koetter as a way for understanding the complex composition of a city.[74] Nolli's plan had been compiled over 12 sheets, defined by the size of printer's plates, and was printed within a border of Giambattista Piranesi's complex artworks. Each building was inscribed not as an individual form but amalgamated within a 'figure' that has distinctive visual characteristics. Each 'figure' is surrounded by the 'ground' of open streets, piazza, church interiors, and palazzi courtyards and their entry halls, making the 'figure' the remnant shape.[75] The contrast of dark to light in this map's construct is revealing. By including some interior spaces within his consideration of 'ground', Nolli introduced the volumetric quality of architecture into what was essentially a mapping exercise.[76]

The international profiling of *Roma Interrotta* continued with its publication in a double issue of the magazine *Architectural Design* becoming a vehicle for scholarly interest for Nolli's representation of Rome, and now entering mainstream English-speaking architectural debates.[77] While the exhibition reinforced the importance of figure-ground to the urban debates, Berlin's IBA redevelopment provided the vehicle for its testing. In consideration of Berlin at the Milan Triennale, figure-ground re-emerged as an idea when architects began to 'fictionalise' the historic city as a prompt for new developments. This act of 'fictionalising' from the past supported the retention of the fragments of the historic city still standing after the devastation of war – not simply as contextual 'monuments', but as meaningful traces to consider within a contemporary Berlin.

This potted history of just one of Hadid's adapted terms begins to explain her experimentation in the context of the Vitra Fire Station, in her ease of 'fictionalising' a construct for a future Weil am Rhein, and for reversing the figure-ground of the agricultural fields and the city alike. Its impact becomes implicit in the visual structures of the paintings and is most evident in the sketches that were shown at the Aedes Galerie, where figure-ground is reversed, and the agricultural fields are now considered as figures (seen prior in figure 74). However, as understood from Nolli's consideration of Rome, figure-ground, and its reversal, can have volumetric spatial consequences in a consideration of architecture. These ideas parallel Hadid's understanding of pictorial space that she had interpreted from the paintings of Malevich and the Suprematists. Her lectures at the time explained these not only for their pictorial consequences but also for their architectural programmatic complexity. It was a way of conceptually 'flipping' ideas, reversing hierarchies of thought to envisage new implications.

This emphasis directs an understanding of the composition of *Aerial Painting* where the distinction between figure and ground, complicated within architecture's topographic reach, now embeds the fields, buildings, rail lines and city beyond. It becomes a question of how new architectural 'figures' inform that space. This development transforms the idea of the architectural program at Vitra, implicating a context defined by a future city's fictional urbanity, as much as it was by inscribing the choreography of fire exercises within the lines now drawn onto the ground.[78] In the representational structure of *Aerial Painting*, architecture becomes an active protagonist, programmed not only to absorb linear forces from the land's dominating visual, historical and psychological lines, but also to redirect conceptual and ideological obstacles of the contemporary contexts of borders and industry, transforming them within a new spatiality of potential – one prompting a recognition of a distinctive future that is unobstructed by its past. Hadid recognises the importance of the 'chance' of this effect on the city, and its madness in terms of Andrew

Benjamin's discussions about deconstruction. Her use of the term 'program' here is introduced to be temporally continuous within the changing city, where time is implicated as an influence in architecture. The sense of movement and dynamic power of the painting circumscribes a way viewers might consider architecture's urban affect – its program – where lines of force redefine the ground's historical occupation and have been presented now as spatial and societal prompts.

To understand the implications of the narrative force of Hadid's gestures, it must be remembered that initially the Vitra director had commissioned Grimshaw to masterplan the new industrial complex. Its grid-like Modernist Euclidean rationality had been inscribed into the land as a sign of spatial efficiency, and it was only through the introduction of a sculpture by Oldenburg and discussions with Gehry that Fehlbaum had questioned the necessity of this alienating regularity.[79] His brief to Gehry for his Museum building, and to Hadid for her Fire Station, was that they reconsider the site as more urbanely complex, where the efficient flow of manufacturing was not the only visual prompt defining the company's values.

By redeploying the linearity and patterning of the surrounding landscape setting, used now to counter the rational power of the box-like Euclidean grid, Hadid's scheme radically reconceived the site's visual referencing. The Vitra complex was no longer defined by this grid formation, but now reflected a new spatial complexity. As evinced through the paintings, it is through inferred lines, as well as new geometries expressed within the materiality of its forms, that the Vitra Fire Station and its landscape critique the hierarchies expected within architecture's aesthetics and purpose by not only reversing their usual status but also reinserting and thus nullifying their spatial affect. Mirroring Derrida's claim for deconstruction in architecture, their imagery of architecture complicates 'the rational' as a point of origin.

# 6 From the Networked Object to the Fluidity of Histories: MAXXI, Rome

For the exhibition *Latent Utopias*, held in Graz in 2002, curators Zaha Hadid and Patrik Schumacher sought from their participants a level of experimentation more evident in artistic production than in architecture.[1] Linking participation to a sense of 'play' they aimed to explore new possibilities for architecture's material resolution anticipated by emerging computer technologies.[2] With a trace of deconstruction, Hadid and Schumacher explained the exhibits through this sense of the experimental:

> The radical architectural projects presented here are not offering themselves as utopian proposals in the sense of elaborated proposals for a better life. They do not claim to have a meaning in this sense. They pose questions and withdraw the familiar answers. They are open-ended mutations that at best might become catalysts in the coevolution of new life processes.[3]

Their own work within the exhibition included images of their scheme for what was then called the Contemporary Art Centre, Rome.[4] The final realisation of this project was not completed until 2008, with construction progressing more seriously after 2005. When the building opened under the name of Museo Nazionale delle arti del XXI Secolo (MAXXI) the forms of the design had changed quite significantly from those envisaged at the *Latent Utopias* exhibition. Consistent with their aims for the exhibition, their scheme at that time had explored the new possibilities of digital software and how these could transform architectural thinking and production.

It was during the period between 1993, when Vitra Fire Station was completed, and 2002, when the exhibition was held in Graz, that Hadid's office transformed their practice, increasingly relying on computer technologies to visualise architectural form.[5] Rather than focus on the Computer-Aided Design (CAD) software regularly used in commercial architecture, they adapted software from other design industries to explore the potential they could deliver for architectural experimentation. The complex line work and rendering style of their image published under the title *Computer Model from Above* (fig.77) shows techniques imported into architectural presentation from the film and advertising industries.

Of great importance within architectural discourses of this time were the visual effects achieved by the Wachowskis' film *The Matrix*, opening in the USA in March of 1999. Its formulation in prior years introduced many of the cinematic effects, including 'bullet time', to architectural discussions.[6] 'Bullet time' emphasised the smoothing of surfaces into a semi-abstracted continuity of movement inferring a duration of time that was in one sense extremely fast and in another, poised for effect as a static moment in that action. But tellingly, in architecture what was evident also were the limitations of adapting this type of software capability to interface with standard architectural software of that period. In architecture, the traditional conventions of architectural drawing, including the conventions underpinning the orthographic and perspective, were now encoded into CAD software systems that replicated agreed 'rules' based on a logic driven by Cartesian axiality; and also fundamental to the realisation of architecture, surfaces had to be resolved as material form relying in part on standardised building products rather than filmic

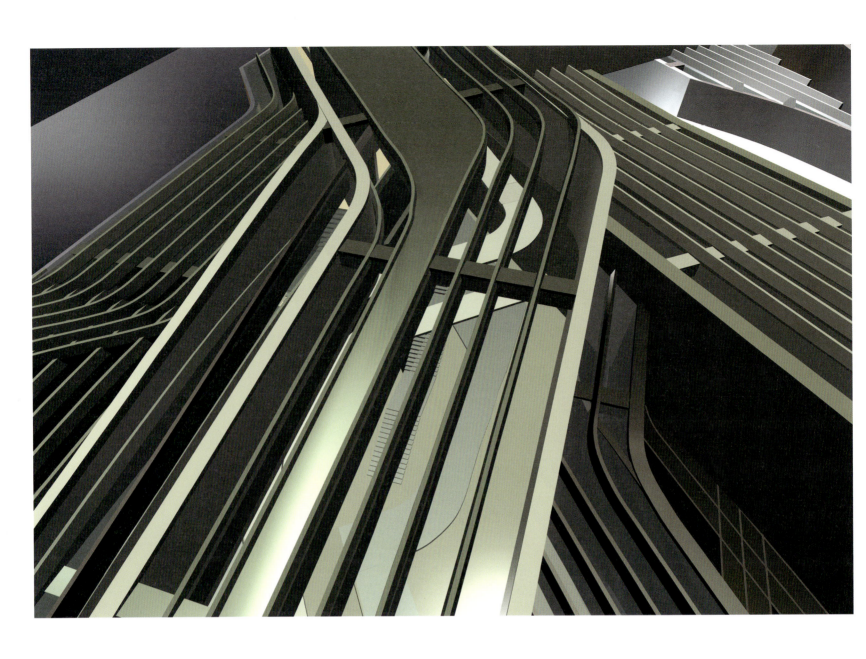

77
**Zaha Hadid Architects**
*MAXXI: Museum of XXI Century Arts, Computer Model from Above*, Rome, Italy, 1999
Digital rendering
Zaha Hadid Foundation

impressions. The problem for Hadid and Schumacher was the issues embedded within their desire for fluidly curving lines and volumes, for 'open-ended mutations', and the requirement to describe these for the scale and materiality of a realisable architecture.

Hadid and Schumacher's visualisation *Computer Model from Above* suggests a different process, one emerging from the abstract and linear effects of cinematic space as each set of curved ribs negotiates changing angles. Within this imagery, references like the staircase – located centrally in the view – suggest depth in an architectural interiority, its implied scale and volume, and yet these properties do not present as producing material resolutions. Their imagery remains semi-abstract.

Hadid spoke of the differing intellectual origins of these representational techniques later in her career, saying: 'I actually think things changed a lot with the arrival of computing. Something was lost, maybe related to scale, but something was also gained by letting architects see space as more complex.'[7]

She also claimed:

> I resisted digitisation for a very long time. The fascinating thing is that with a three-dimensional work, it wasn't very complicated because the computing almost imitated the way we worked. So, it was an interesting transition. Now it's less complex, less transparent, much more opaque and, let's say, real. I still think the work that was done in graphical presentation was originally more complex and less predictable.[8]

Informing the analysis within this chapter are the differences and the similarities between these computer-generated visualisations, the final documentation and realised building, and the paintings forming part of ZHA's submission for the architectural competition in 1998.

Many paintings now associated with Hadid's resolution of the MAXXI scheme were included within the Stage Two submission of the architectural competition (fig.78).[9] Within the submission panels, details from several paintings can be clearly seen collaged: placed alongside sketches, orthogonal drawings, photography of schematic physical models, and computer-generated three-dimensional visualisations. According to Steven Holl, an architect who also competed, the date of the presentations for Stage Two in Rome was 15 October 1998, suggesting that unlike most paintings for Hadid's other projects, those for the MAXXI were closely aligned with the process of design.[10]

The importance of the link between the exhibition *Latent Utopias* and Hadid and Schumacher's desire to explore non-Cartesian geometries through computer software defined a sense of experimentation in form and spatiality that was previously unseen in their architecture. Architectural interest in the implications of the computer's capacity to generate fluid curves as lines locatable in three-dimensional space emerged from the profession's historical fascination with the implied movement first experienced in 17th-century Baroque architecture. Contemporary interest in the Baroque and its sense of movement was also linked to developing philosophical interests in architectural theory, particularly the writings of contemporary philosophers Gilles Deleuze and Félix Guattari.

Bringing together an interest in these fluid geometries and the philosophical propositions of Deleuze and Guattari was architect Greg Lynn's guest editorship of *Architectural Design* (*AD*), in the 1993 special issue titled *Folding in Architecture*.[11] In this issue, an extract of Deleuze's text on the Baroque is included for its importance to other articles. For Deleuze the Baroque line 'twists and turns its folds, pushing them to infinity, fold over fold, one upon the other. The Baroque fold unfurls all the way to infinity.'¹² Comparing this to an organism he separated the notion of the organic fold from the Baroque curving form: 'It remains the case that the organic body thus confers an interior on matter . . . Folding-unfolding no longer simply means tension-release, contraction-dilation, but enveloping-developing, involution-evolution. The organism is defined by its ability to fold its own parts and unfold them, not to infinity, but to a degree of development assigned to each species.'¹³

The interest by architects in Deleuze was from their desire to replicate this idea of spatial and linear folding/unfolding into architecture. Their interest in the Baroque stemmed from two sources. The first was the movement implied in the use of curvilinear form in architecture. The second was Deleuze's recognition that within the curving lines of an organism there were both accidental and mechanical influences. Thus, there was an acceptance of what appeared to be accidental in architecture. His explanation became tied within the experimentation enabled by new software's capability to produce drawings having complex linearity from specific data as well as more idiosyncratic spatial prompts or accidents.

Within Lynn's edition of *Architectural Design*, essays are contextualised by an exploration of architectural projects that brought visual clarity to its difficult propositions. Frank Gehry's design drawings for the Lewis Residence of 1989–95 were included for their complex fluid geometries, where there is a claim that three-dimensional computer modelling could reintegrate the architect with the trades in the process of form-making.¹⁴ However, it must be remembered that his Dancing Building in Prague post-dated the edition. Designed in 1992 and completed in 1996, it was the first of Gehry's designs to adapt '3D CATIA' software, enabling complex curvilinearity to be 'seamlessly' integrated into construction documentation processes.¹⁵ Gehry observed this in the digital technologies used by a stonemason in his American Centre in Paris and was in the process of working through the implications of the software for architecture.¹⁶ His office was the first to integrate these sophisticated software packages and their data-referencing into architectural practices. By 1997 the completion of Gehry's Guggenheim Museum, Bilbao, using 'CATIA' and its development into the architectural software 'Design Project' made feasible a unification between the design's irregular curvilinear surface geometry and its materials and construction processes.¹⁷ However, the cost of 'CATIA' and its development remained beyond the scope of most architectural offices.

Also included within this *Folding in Architecture* edition of *AD*, and pivotal to this discussion of new geometric developments in architecture, was Peter Eisenman's Rebstockpark Masterplan for Frankfurt, which had been designed in collaboration with its editor, Greg Lynn.¹⁸ It is in the Rebstockpark Masterplan that Eisenman and Lynn approximated fluidly curving form through a series of complex straight-line geometries. Remembering that the desire was for more curvilinear forms that might imply movement, the same *AD* issue also included images of Lynn's 1992 exhibition project *Stranded Sears Tower*, a project using computer-generated fluid curvilinear forms, and introducing the software terminology of 'spline geometries'.¹⁹ A spline curve, unlike those developed using radial geometry, is based on composite forces where the resulting line takes a position of 'best fit' within a force field defined by weighted fulcrum points or vectors. Like Deleuze's description of the organic fold this curve had complex origins, some accidental and others more mechanically derived through 'weighting'.

Bringing this geometry into architectural discussions, Lynn had claimed that the 'spline curve' could more easily handle the multifarious requirements of large-scaled architecture in complex urban situations because each fulcrum force could be adjusted by changing influences over the design's programmes – each

78
Zaha Hadid Architects
*MAXXI: Museum of XXI Century Arts, Stage Two, Competition Panel 1*, Rome, Italy, 1999
Digital file
Zaha Hadid Foundation

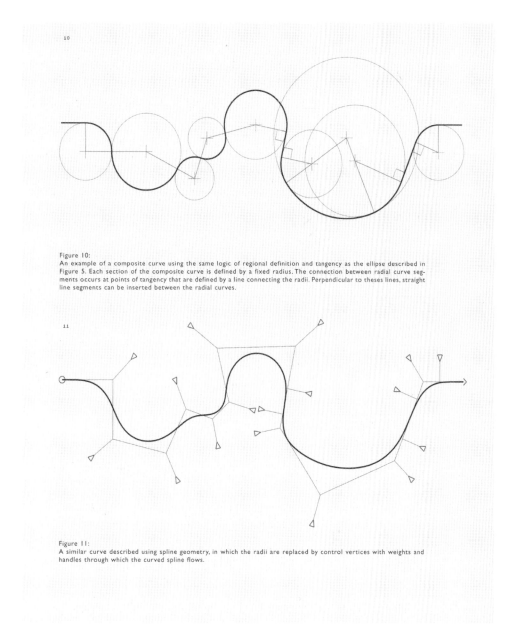

79
**Greg Lynn**
'Radial and Spline Geometry', from *Animate Form*, Princeton Architectural Press, New York, 1999, print, p.21

adjustment modifying the architectural outcome. However, it was not until 1999 that he published a graphic explanation of the 'complex spline curve', comparing it with similar curves generated through radial geometry (fig.79).[20] Returning to the Baroque architecture of the 17th century he explained that Baroque forms had not actually used 'spline' geometries for their sense of fluidity. He clarified further, that while the final imagery of complex radial geometries could appear similar to the 'spline', their actual conceptual basis stemmed from distinctively different intellectual origins. Explaining the spline to be closer to Deleuze's interests, Lynn used analogies found within natural organisms. He suggested the origins of spline geometries in patterns that could be construed from events like the murmuration of flocking birds or the movement of schools of fish or the responses seen after mixing differing fluids. The resulting spline line became a depiction of the fluidity of perceived space conceived as 'unfixed' and open ended.[21] This became compelling to 'test' architecturally.

During the years between the appearance of *Folding in Architecture* (*AD*) and Lynn's further explanation of spline geometries in his publication *Animate Form*, two-dimensional spline geometry and its extension through concepts of surface anatomy had become important to architectural debates at the Architectural Association (AA). This can be seen reflected in the founding of the AA's Design Research Lab (AADRL) in 1996, and in their continuing invitation for Greg Lynn's involvement.[22] The AADRL was founded by Hadid's colleagues Patrik Schumacher and Brett Steele. Its aim was to focus on research into digital technologies and their use in prompting experimentation in architecture.[23] Schumacher, Hadid and Lynn had met in 1993, when they were all part of the teaching program at Columbia University in New York.[24] Their architectural practices are linked within this context.[25] Hadid and Schumacher's hybrid geometric solutions for projects like the MAXXI took advantage of the speculative thought that digital technologies could offer.

By 1998, digital technologies still struggled with the complexity of documenting curvilinear architectural projects as three-dimensional models, especially fluid forms based on complex combinations of convex and concave surfaces. The operational capability of computers at the time remained an ambition rather than reality.[26] Schumacher's comments in 2017, when looking back on the project, confirm their more conservative approach taken when the office completed final documentation of the MAXXI. He recalled:

> In MAXXI we went back to much simpler geometries, even simpler than Vitra where we had used some spline-like space curves (albeit constructed without the aid of computers). In MAXXI everything was rationalized into straight lines, arcs, planes, cylinders and cones, while still achieving a considerable sense of dynamism and fluidity as we blended these simpler forms into a flowing composition. On this basis we could maintain and demonstrate buildability while increasing compositional complexity ... We made a bigger effort towards a comprehensive, rational, and realistic documentation and presentation.[27]

However, Schumacher's 'simpler geometries' for the documented MAXXI curves were not those portrayed in the imagery of *Computer Model from Above*, or later described in *Digital Hadid*, published in 2004. Here he revealed that the scheme was 'initially composed of 2D splines and then crucially lifted into 3D (in 3D

80
Zaha Hadid
*MAXXI: Museum of XXI Century Arts, Sketch*,
Rome, Italy, 1999
Ink on lined paper, dimensions unknown
Zaha Hadid Foundation

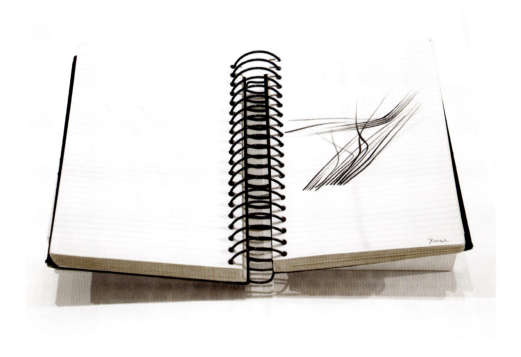

Studio Max)'.[28] It is this development that perhaps explains the term 'rationalised' in his quote above. Schumacher's comments hint at how difficult it was to transfer spline lines into architectural CAD drawings at that time, a process essential to enable building contractors and trades during the construction phase to reference the material implications of what was intended. Pinpointing these difficulties more precisely is one of the early conceptual sketches drawn by Hadid (fig.80). In this image she conceives a series of repeated and semi-parallel lines that become increasingly fluid, crossing each other as curved lines. Each line is independently thought and drawn while having a relation with others, conceived sequentially as her mind works through the spatial complexities of their repetition-differentiation. Of interest as well is that this sketch makes use of the horizontal lines embedded within the page. Their effect draws attention between the two geometries, the Cartesian geometry of the page and the fluidity of her sketched lines.[29]

A comparison between this sketch and the computer 'render' included in the *Latent Utopias* catalogue highlights the issues of transferability, between the desire to incorporate three-dimensional fluid volumes or linear spline curves into architecture at a time when CAD had become the preferred documentation tool in the architectural profession and for its consultants. The entry of the software 3D Studio Max into architectural practices developed some capacity for spline geometries to be easily drawn. But while these splines could further develop as meshed surfaces, they did not resolve the type of parallel line sequences envisaged in Hadid's sketch, nor did they resolve their architectural or material implications.[30] By the late 1990s the animation software Maya had supplanted others as the preferred design tool because of its capacity to handle the complex data and information that is inherent within any architectural line.[31] Maya was first released in 1997 for use in the animation industry. Its adaptation into architecture took time and was soon overtaken by simpler programs.

This context underpins any exploration of the paintings of the MAXXI but it is only part of the experimentation found. The Stage Two competition for the MAXXI project included Patrik Schumacher as design associate, alongside an expanded team.[32] In the drawings and renders completed using computer technologies, the change of hands and the importance of who 'sees' and who directs have become invisible, as drawers, renderers and architects are digitally transformed as one-and-the-same 'being'.[33] It becomes difficult to assign their roles. Not listed amongst Hadid's team referenced in publications was David Gomersall, who completed many of the larger paintings that were part of the Stage Two submission for the competition.[34] Gomersall had moved away from London in 1995, and during the course of intervening projects would complete works in his painting studio in Shropshire. Over several years of working together, he and Hadid had built a level of trust that supported this arrangement.

The two paintings selected for examination in this chapter show the breadth of the architectural experimentation in this project. Because there is little nomenclature with these paintings this chapter will use the titles *MAXXI: Museum of XXI Century Arts, Composite Aerial View* and *MAXXI: Museum of XXI Century Arts: Sketch Painting* for ease of discussion.[35] Their initial drawings are unattributed, emerging from manual adjustments of photographed computer renders. Gomersall was the lead painter of *Composite Aerial View* and undertook these adjustments, while he confirms that he and Hadid worked together as painters of *Sketch Painting*.[36]

## Fluidity of Architectural Networks:
### *MAXXI: Museum of XXI Century Arts, Composite Aerial View*

Like many previous paintings, *Composite Aerial View* combines at least two overlaid images to form the final composition (fig.81). Each layer uses pseudo-perspectival conventions that have been altered and distorted. While distortion was commonly used in Hadid's paintings, its origins here are in the screen-based imagery of the computer and its further manual manipulations into painting's spatial affect. Although not the creator of the MAXXI visualisations, Paul Brislin, when working as a young architect at the office, recalls that by 1994 computer technologies were increasingly embraced in their design and representational processes. He described one example of that process:

> We had one Macintosh computer in the office, and we had a program called ModelShop. We developed a way of using ModelShop which formed the basis for different ways of seeing. I experimented with ways to distort three-dimensional images by pushing the relationship between viewer and the scene's distances. The final view gained a type of Supremacist quality. It was quite abstract. Zaha responded really well to the images. However, each view needed to be printed... Computer memory could only contain one drawing at a time! So, once I printed the drawing it was deleted. The piece of paper that I printed became an original artwork. Many of these A4 prints were the basis of later paintings. Further manipulation took place in the painting process itself. What's interesting about ModelShop was that while it became a stepping stone to later computer use, its output as a single print was still deeply embedded within the hand-making process.[37]

Two examples of this technique of imaging can be seen in the Lycée Français Charles de Gaulle, Pancras Lane and Blueprint Pavilion projects of 1995.[38] Although a few years prior to the competition for the MAXXI, the type of experimentation that Brislin describes remained embedded within the visualisation processes of the office and loosened the tie between drawing by hand and the final paintings.

The total imagery for *Composite Aerial View* would have developed from screen-based visualisations that would have been manipulated on-screen and printed, continuing to develop through enlargement and further exaggeration by hand until suitable for incorporating into the final composition. The final drawing was then transferred onto black cartridge paper using carbon transfer methods, redrawn in white ink, and then painted with acrylics. Gomersall confirmed that colour was as much a result of the competition's requirement for black and white images as it was a negotiation of what might suit the project's representation, commenting that 'Zaha would always like to stretch the rules' when he explained the small coloured details of the painting.[39] The paintings are included in the first competition panel (fig.78). Although coloured in muted tones, the black and white print required for the competition panels worked tonally without disrupting its imagery.

The composition of this painting is structured pictorially into halves either side of an implied vertical axis, where the complexity of the right-hand side forms the major visual focus. This emphasis is reinforced through tonality where light/dark opposition mirrors the relationship between Rome's urban complexity and its natural landscape. Compositional balance is achieved through the continuous flow of fluid lines moving as a group right to left, from the dense urbanity of the right, toward the darkness of the landscape where they thicken and become more abstract. A depiction of the Tiber River arcs organically across the composition, its breadth

81
**Zaha Hadid Architects**
*MAXXI: Museum of XXI Century Arts,*
*Composite Aerial View*, Rome, Italy, 1999
Acrylic on paper, 93 × 172.5 cm (36 5/8 × 67 7/8 in)
Zaha Hadid Foundation

filled with a distinctive colour range of chrome yellow, and tints of green, mauve and blue, reinforcing important reminders of key visual symbols of Rome's forms.

Of the two main layers within the composition, the lower layer portrays the urban context as a semi-abstracted three-dimensional 'map' of Rome.[40] Its accuracy in locating various existing buildings, streets and the natural terrain, although abstracted, is fundamental to the painting's recognition of place. Important, for example, is the depiction of the nearby Palazzetto dello Sport by Pier Luigi Nervi in the upper sections of the image. The referencing of its form, although small, combined with radial street geometries, mountain and river, is used to reinforce Rome's symbolic registers. Within the logic of this map, in the lower half of the painting the scheme for the MAXXI defines the main emphasis due to its light, contrasting tonality. Its near white modulated forms appear as if an extrusion of elements crosses haphazardly over the site. When viewed more closely, both the scheme and the map appear as if the ground is slightly curved, where the heights of buildings are shown consistently as they respond to the earth's surface. It is an effect that introduces volume. The earth's curvature is emblematic and well understood in the oeuvre of Hadid, but uniquely in this painting the curvature determines the differing volumes of surrounding buildings as they fan out across the city's topography.

Onto this map an upper layer of parallel blade-like elements splay out toward the viewer, diminishing dramatically in perspective as they swerve toward a distant profile of Rome's buildings. These blades contract and expand in a dramatic manner, some highlighting the white 'whooshes' of their 'bullet' speed, while others are tonally reduced, shaded or left as transparent over the scenes below. Their imagery reinforces a cinematic sense of movement, a thrusting force whose invisible velocity originates from under and behind the viewer's gaze. Their painted 'whoosh' is dynamic, implying that the blades are the result of forms propelling past the viewer at great speed. It projects the idea in architecture of disappearing forms, and of the sense of the 'dissolution' of the fast speed of this action.[41]

Fundamental to this layer of the painting is a computer-generated 'model' that had been included within the competition panels. Its depiction is of the same curvilinear structure of blades, and as such, it draws attention to the continued back and forth between analogue practices – of the hand and the slow speed of painting – and those generated from the computer screen. The computer image has been tonally shaded using computer 'modelling' to make surfaces appear solid (fig.82). A second figure included still shows the geometric resolution of spline curves in each plane with the zig-zag dotted lines defining a bend in the plane still evident (fig.83).[42] As seen in the competition panels, both images seem to have been photographed from the computer's screen as there are light reflections from the office, seen in the backdrop of blank facades. In the context of comments like those of Brislin, these images were known for their fragility, often 'crashing' the computer model and the work being lost. Taking photographs from the screen provided some archive as ideas developed. Hadid was to comment on admiring the on-screen quality of the imagery: 'I think it is much nicer on the screen than when it is printed on to paper, because the screen gives you luminosity and the paper does not, unless you do it through painting.'[43]

When compared with this computer-derived view, the 'blades' in the final painting diverge and extend, transforming the computer model into the expressiveness of painting's affect. Hadid commented specifically of the ability of painting to direct attention to issues of importance:

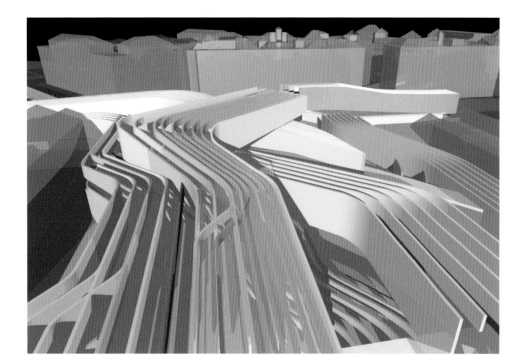

82
**Zaha Hadid Architects**
(detail) *MAXXI: Museum of XXI Century Arts, Stage Two, Competition Panel 1*, Rome, Italy, 1999
Digital file
Zaha Hadid Foundation

You can achieve certain things through technology, but you can't abstract in the same way. When drawing by hand you can decide what you want to show and edit out some things. It's not about wire-framing. Rather, you can decide to focus on the thing you want to study at the time while you are doing the drawing. It focuses you more on certain critical issues.[44]

In the reconsidering of this computer image for its transformation into painting, the extent of the linear blades and their tones are adjusted, reinforcing the cinematic impression of speed, as the 'whoosh' dissolves each form's solidity. The expression of the blades as painted reinforces Hadid's interest in sensation and the depiction of speed that dissipates form as it recedes from importance (fig.84). The origins of this effect for Hadid were with Malevich's paintings that she now extended technically through cinematic techniques derived from movies like *The Matrix*.

Further adjustments support this idea of speed where, between the solidity and transparency of each blade, the three-dimensional map of streets below becomes less comprehensible. The subtlety of spatial referencing in this juxtaposition of layers introduces visual effects, which partially reverse the relationship of foreground to background. Tones and pigments become indistinguishably assigned, as lines and shapes of the buildings on the 'map' intersect with the blades above. Viewers are prompted to question what they see.[45] While the image of the small model of the MAXXI scheme aids orientation, the area vertically above it is spatially indistinct. There is a potential for spatial illusion, where the differing architectural scales, originally implied by both the map and the blades, are unified within a pictorial space, registering simply as shapes or even a form of Cyrillic script that might have been seen in Russian avant-garde painting from the 1920s to the 1930s.

This effect develops importance for the narrative possibilities of the painting, complicating any deferment to represent the architecture as a complete or monumental object. Adapting Hadid's terminology, Schumacher defined this effect as the 'drift' of the architecture.[46] In this sense the painting becomes a response to the visual geometry and urbanity that is specific to Rome. However, the compositional emphasis is of fluidity and layering, introducing a specific instability. An example

83
**Zaha Hadid Architects**
(detail) *MAXXI: Museum of XXI Century Arts, Stage Two, Competition Panel 1*, Rome, Italy, 1999
Digital file
Zaha Hadid Foundation

84
Zaha Hadid Architects
(detail) *MAXXI: Museum of XXI Century Arts, Composite Aerial View*, Rome, Italy, 1999
Acrylic on paper
Zaha Hadid Foundation

can be seen in the fluidly drifting and bundled forms of the small rendering that are placed onto the radial triangular geometry of the Flaminio district of Rome, complicating its regularity. In this area of Rome, the close to equilateral geometry hinges from the nearby Piazza Gentile da Fabriano, with its central axis directed down Viale Pinturicchio, countering the resolution of angles defined by the tram lines along Via Masaccio curving onto Via Luigi Poletti. This complex radial geometry remains as a trace within the MAXXI, but there is a transformation suggested by the painting's structure. By introducing a complex three-dimensional solid volumetric geometry to the painting's imagery, one that combines fluidly linear elements with some lines mirroring the radial geometry of Rome, the MAXXI schema of the painting presents what Hadid and Schumacher describe as an 'open-ended mutation' or 'incomplete' form that 'speaks to' the city's historical typologies without replicating them.[47] It is the 'incompleteness' of the architectural geometry that asserts Hadid and Schumacher's experimentation in the context of Rome.

The idea of the historic centre of Rome as a 'model' for architects to discuss and explore was important to Hadid's intellectual milieu. Her MAXXI scheme was not simply considered in isolation as a building outside the ancient walls of the city, but as a response to Rome's role as a city where experiments with geometry have a long history. This understanding of Rome was commonly acknowledged within contemporary architectural debate. Venturi, Scott-Brown and Izenour's *Learning from Las Vegas* had used Rome, in comparison with Las Vegas, to discuss the complexity of geometry in urban forms.[48] Equally, Colin Rowe and Fred Koetter's *Collage City* had, through figure-ground studies of cities – including those from Rome – explored the spatial bricolage of a city, where the collision of geometries over time was accepted as essential to the composition of urban fabric.[49] These ideas had developed into the architectural discussions that generated the context for the *Roma Interrotta* project of 1978, when architects experimented with ways to rethink the implications of geometry observed in Rome's 'plan'.[50] It further prompted interest in the original 18th-century Nolli *Plan of Rome* and its 'bricolage' of geometries as the basis for contemporary experimentation.[51] Within contemporary debates, curator Mark Wigley's catalogue essay in *Deconstructivist Architecture* in 1988 had returned to examples from Rome, drawing attention to attributes of deconstruction's geometries in comparison. Opening his catalogue essay with Le Corbusier's illustration *The Lesson of Rome*, Wigley emphasised the importance of Le Corbusier's recognition that simple architectural forms derived from historic Rome were still recognised and used as a 'model' of thought to inform a consideration of contemporary architecture.[52] As a counter to Le Corbusier's line of argument, Wigley introduced deconstruction by critically exploring the use of complex geometries.[53]

The example of historic Rome was significant for this generation of architects. When Greg Lynn argued the uniqueness of attributes associated with spline geometry, he too referenced the geometries of 17th-century Baroque Rome's architecture to explain the uniqueness of the new geometry. For comparison Lynn used Francesco Borromini's geometric resolution for San Carlo alle Quattro Fontane, completed in 1646, to clarify the differences he saw in spline geometries.[54] For Lynn, the spline remained open ended. His explanation of San Carlo revealed its closed radial geometry. The implications of Lynn's explanation for San Carlo are revealed further through comparison with Donato Bramante's earlier Tempietto building at San Pietro in Montorio of 1502 (fig.85). This comparison provides an understanding of the radicality of Borromini's design and consequently the radicality of the initial use of spline geometry of Hadid's project for the MAXXI.

The radial geometry of Bramante's Tempietto is based on a series of concentric circles developed from the same central point where spatial divisions for columniation in the arcade are symmetrical, and, where the geometry is perceptually verifiable in its cylindrical form, capped by a half-spherical dome. For this reason, in architectural history it is considered compositionally pure, having a closed geometric system. It was judged at the time to be equivalent geometrically to the idealism of rediscovered antiquity.[55] Architecture emanating from a single point was privileged during the Renaissance because of its spatial integrity, where the circle's referencing of a 'monad', a singular entity without further division, assured an architecture symbolic of sacred, as well as classical, origins.[56] Unifying the spatiality between architecture and viewer, each viewer took part in this unity, easily perceiving the geometry of the whole from their first partial view only to be confirmed by walking around its circular form.[57] The symbolism is idealised in representations like Raphael's painting *The Marriage of the Virgin* of 1504 (fig.86). By turning Bramante's perspectively based geometry into representational power, Raphael's Tempietto radiates lines into the foreground setting of the piazza, visually reinforcing the authority of the geometric resolution of the architecture in a precise way, embracing the viewer and the group depicted within its geometry.[58]

Borromini's San Carlo stepped away from this desire for purity by introducing radial geometries, where more than one centre point is used as their origin (figs 87, 88 and 89). This resulted in a complex set of geometric relationships based on composite curves derived from the multiple centre points and their radii. These geometries could not be conceived without the transformation of a world view accepting a more nuanced relationship between geometry, its representation and society. While from antiquity, the plan of the Colosseum derived from two circles placed side by side forming an oval, Borromini could still claim the classical origins of his geometry while resolving a more nuanced result. Unlike Bramante's desire for purity Borromini's geometric complexity reinforces the way lines are implied within surfaces and textures and reinforced by lighting effects.[59] Each linear 'force' within the interior's surfaces implied directionality and movement as spatial attributes rather than the static idealism of the object evident in the Tempietto. Unlike the unity implied in the Tempietto, for San Carlo, the complexity of geometric layering

85
Donato Bramante
Tempietto, San Pietro in Montorio, Rome, 1502

86
Raphael
*The Marriage of the Virgin*, 1504
Oil on panel,
170 × 118 cm (66⅞ × 46½ in)
Pinacoteca di Brera, Milan

87
Francesco Borromini
San Carlo alle Quattro Fontane, dome interior, Rome, 1646

88
Francesco Borromini
San Carlo alle Quattro Fontane, site plan showing radial geometries, Rome, 1646
Graphite on paper,
87.9 × 53.1 cm (34⅝ × 21 in)
Albertina, Vienna

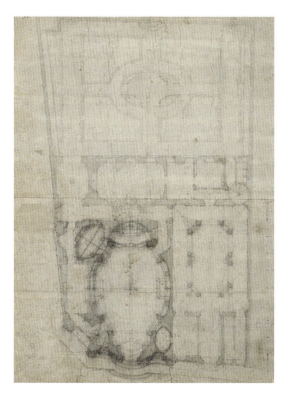

defined the relationship of a building's interior and exterior as separately conceived. Using complex and multiple structures of radial geometry, the architecture of the exterior sits independently, addressing the discrete and heterogeneous forces of the urban context. In the example of San Carlo, exterior forms may 'speak' from the same language as the interior; however, the facade's role in the city dominates the resolution of surface geometries and modulation.[60]

The significance of this change is made explicit within an argument that Lynn raised in his consideration of contemporary spline geometries, and specifically implicated in his example of Stranded Sears Tower.[61] He alluded to the far richer logic of curvilinearity that spline geometries permitted, bringing a 'cunning pliability' through 'smoothing difference' in architectural form where in Stranded Sears Tower, for example, its integration with the urban interface along Lake Shore Drive in Chicago could mesh within its multitudinous interfaces with the city. Lynn's interest in spline geometries and 'folding' (an idea developed from Deleuze) moves architectural form from a focus on 'the architecturally discrete' to emphasise what he terms the 'urbanistically' continuous.[62]

Hadid's painting *Composite Aerial View* considers the changing geometry within Rome's urbanity as a series of precise juxtapositions and implies the importance of this historical setting. For her, questions for architecture in this location were not only related to negotiating issues of representation in its forms and spaces, but more fundamentally related to the complex layering of Cartesian and non-Cartesian geometries of Rome's past. Through spline geometry, a third distinctive geometry is introduced into Rome's urban formation. It was not only immediately symbolic of change in Rome's urban complexity but also an idea centrally engaging within its society's palimpsest of historic formations. Hadid's painting references how architecture could move conceptually beyond Rowe's notion of bricolage, Le Corbusier's recognition of formal purity, or Lynn's contemporary interpretation of the Baroque. The MAXXI presents as an architecture of linear force that 'drifts' across its geometrically organised urban environment. The painting's reference to geometry does not imply a closed system that would define architecture as a completed object but remains open ended. Hadid explained the MAXXI as a form of 'incomplete composition, the idea that the configuration is not final'.[63]

In many ways this notion of incompleteness extends the ideas of pictorial space into architecture, ones that Hadid first found evident in Malevich and which she explored in her early designs. Malevich recognised that relationships enabled within an abstract sense of pictorial space supported a concept of interdependency between forms in a composition, without controlling relationships by a sense of perspectival stability. In his proposition of pictorial space, relationships between forms remained continuously modifiable as viewers engage with a painting. When Hadid introduced these ideas into an experimentation with space and form in architecture, the fluidity of relationships equally implicated time and viewer engagement. For the MAXXI, spline geometry enabled experimentation with figure-ground elements reminiscent of Malevich's ideas, where space as volume and form as material could be conceptually and architecturally reversed or were interchangeable.

This referencing of open-ended spatial, formal and geometric relationships in *Composite Aerial View* represents the importance of the project's origins in spline geometries and their referencing of Malevich's notions of pictorial space to introduce a 'drifting' incomplete type of geometry into architecture. Hadid's resolution extended the focus in architectural debate away from issues of representation and the confines of Cartesian/Euclidean geometry to emphasise the possibility of an open relationality in architecture's space–form configurations. In *Composite Aerial*

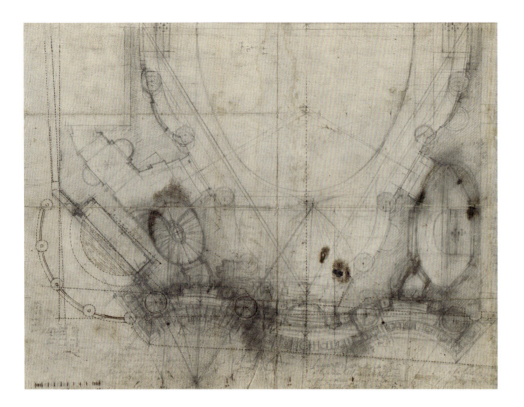

89
**Francesco Borromini**
San Carlo alle Quattro Fontane, facade plan showing radial geometries, Rome, 1646
Graphite on paper, 52 × 40.7 cm (20½ × 16 in)
Albertina, Vienna

*View* there is a visual 'playing out' of this logic. The painting highlights the decisive role that geometry has for Rome while defining the possibility to extend the idea of experimentation so essential to its historical urban forms.

What remains to be considered is whether the MAXXI campus, as finally realised, fulfilled these ideas given its ultimate change from spline to radial geometry. As Schumacher explained, the fluid curvilinear forms of the competition entry were later 'rationalised' into a radial geometry during the documentation process and in the instructions to building contractors.[64] The question arises, did this act return the MAXXI as realised to the geometry of Bramante or Borromini? In a sense, a response falls between yes and no. The subtlety of the MAXXI's architecture relies in part on Lynn's explanation of the visual similarity of complex radial geometries and those of the spline. But extending this is the notion of the interdependence of forms within a pictorial space. In Hadid's MAXXI, the spline had become a shorthand tool for navigating a relationship with the geometric structuring of Rome's urbanity, without adopting its Cartesian regularity. Her design proposed an architecture seen as contiguous yet open ended within this context. It drifts. This idea flowed consistently throughout the interior–exterior relations of the architecture, for how the gallery was entered as a porous set of 'events', and for how galleries were spatially interwoven and navigated. For these reasons, the analogy of the spline remains fundamental within the space–form relationships of the final realised form of the museum campus.

### Architecture's Spatial Weave:
### MAXXI: Museum of XXI Century Arts, Sketch Painting

In isolation, the composition of *Sketch Painting* presents as pure abstraction: a collection of intersecting clusters of loosely parallel planes, portrayed as they fluidly swerve, and spatially fold, from different angles across a pictorial surface (fig.90).

It is in this imagery that the issues of representation and spatiality in architecture are considered as a question. Reinforcing the painting's abstraction is the black background, a notion of void space within which the rib-like forms float, folding on their own time and space. Similarity can be drawn immediately with the imagery of the *Confetti – Suprematist Snowstorm* painting completed for The Peak scheme more than 20 years earlier. There is an evocative tension that keeps these lines poised in place. Unlike *Confetti*, and refining the abstraction of this painting, is the absence of any visual referent that would assign it as a 'representation' of architecture: of site boundaries, material form's relation to ground surface, tectonics, plans, spatial cohesion of interiority and exteriority, or references to Rome's topologies, monuments or geometries.

Through this painting's imagery, as intersections occur between the elongated ribbed planes, there is interpenetration: a woven sense of spatiality rather than hierarchies of one cluster over the other. However, in the array of its fluid and interpenetrating planes there is one contrasting element. In the top right of the composition there is an equilateral triangle. It is isolated, located beside the painting's main linear force and remaining distinct from other elements. Upon closer inspection, and with the architecture in mind, its imagery gives the appearance of an 'end profile' where the shape infers the triangular 'cross section' of a fluid form.[65] Its inclusion introduces a visual complexity to the image as all other linear planes, while chamfered at the same angle, give the appearance of being 'vertically' aligned within the 'axonometric' logic of the painting's abstract space.

The geometry of this contrasting shape has implications for the whole image. In architecture, its equilateral shape references the most stable of geometries, for its resolution of both statics and structural forces. Its theoretical meaning was derived from the earliest writer on architecture, first century BCE Roman 'architect' Vitruvius in his *Ten Books on Architecture*. It is even in the form of these ten 'books' when piled as ten rolls of papyrus that a tetractys is implied, and their simple physical positioning symbolised a deep principle of stability in architectural geometry.[66] In Hadid's painting, however, the triangle is separated and tilted away from the perpendicular, poised geometrically as a counterpoint to the fluid linear effect dominating the composition. Its reference may be closer to the street geometries of contemporary Rome and the district of Flaminio. While the triangle would return the imagery of the painting to Cartesian references, its separation and tilt in this painting suggests its difference and visual critique of both references.

In *Sketch Painting*, visual diagramming distils the simplicity of the 'origin' or 'conceptual force' of the MAXXI schema as one that, while registering the Cartesian geometry of Rome, proffers the idea that architecture can be configured conceptually as geometrically and formally 'incomplete'. As a result, the painting's messaging develops three visual 'events', each referencing distinct geometries: the multi-directional weaving together of interpenetrating planar geometry; the void space of the background; and the tilted triangle. It is the relationship of these pictorial 'events' that becomes fundamental to its consideration.

In the catalogue for the *Latent Utopias* exhibition, in the section *Space VS Object*, Hadid's aspirations for a complex spatial geometry are stated: 'Our project offers a quasi-urban field, a "world" to dive into rather that a building as signature object. The Campus is organised and navigated on the basis of directional drifts and the distribution of densities rather than key points.'[67]

The terms 'directional drifts' and 'distribution of densities' reinforce the idea of the irregular juxtaposition between the elements of this painting. Their complexity is further explored:

This is indicative of the character of the Centre as a whole: porous, immersive, a field space. An inferred mass is subverted by vectors of circulation. The external as well as the internal circulation, follows the overall drift of the geometry. Vertical and oblique circulation elements are located at areas of confluence, interference and turbulence.

The move from object to field is critical in understanding the relationship the architecture will have with the content of the artwork it will house ... it is important here to state that the premise of the architectural design promotes a disinheriting of the 'object' oriented gallery space. Instead, the notion of a 'drift' takes on an embodied form. The drifting emerges, therefore, as both architectural motif and also as a way to navigate experientially through the museum.[68]

Her expressions 'overall drift to geometry', and 'move from object to field' provide a way for understanding the linear agency of the ribbon-like planes centrally located within *Sketch Painting*, where in the geometric make-up of the architecture, ideas of spatial 'confluence, interference and turbulence' can coexist. Hadid explained that for this project it had been important to keep 'the relation of part to whole ambiguous'.[69] It is an approach to architecture that is not immediately 'monumental' but negotiates the geometries of Rome's historic fabric. She continued, 'Rome is a kind of woven space ... when you weave in this way, you constantly intersect with others.'[70] There is a consistency with other terms like 'field' and 'drift', where each term touches on philosophies explored in relation to 'the digital' in architecture; they also build on terms like 'matrix' and 'conflicting layers' as planning strategies that appeared in her teaching at Columbia University during 1993.[71] The complexity of how Hadid described her work was seen in her encoding of each term with a number of meanings. An example is how she described a 'matrix' as a graphic on a page, but her text also implies that a reader will understand the linking context of this term, without directing attention to the writings of Jean-François Lyotard and the use of this term in his 1985 exhibition catalogue to explain her work.[72] When Hadid uses the terms 'drift' and 'woven space' in the context of the MAXXI, there is equally an image of woven lines as well as an implied derivation from the contemporary debates in architecture that reference Deleuze and Guattari. But what is portrayed in the inclusion of the triangle is recognition that the 'drift' is the result of an occurrence from 'somewhere'.

In architecture, spline geometry was not simply a new formal geometry that could now be deployed through CAD. It also relied in part on interest in the philosophical writings of Deleuze and Guattari whose explorations of the implications of spatial structuring changed the way 1990s' architects considered and conceptualised spatial complexity. Their notion of 'smooth space' as a 'meandering linear subjectivity' showed how navigation of new spatial programs in the city's urbanity could be considered beyond the idea of 'bricolage' or 'collage', and, critically, outside the conceptual framework of city planning professions.[73]

For Deleuze and Guattari, 'smooth space' had been countered with the idea of 'striated space', one aligned with closure, hierarchy and determined structures of order, where the allocation of meaning reflected architecture's monumentality and its reinforcement of ideas of an ordered society. It was this attribute of 'striated space' that had been accepted as part of the urban bricolage of historic cities – or as Rowe explains: 'a tension between quasi-integrated whole and quasi-segregated parts' – where patterns of ordering and monumentality were evident in the recognisability of cities.[74] Deleuze and Guattari's 'smooth space' described the open, fluid and responsive attribute of nomadic spatial experience, increasing the interest in an

90
Zaha Hadid Architects
*MAXXI: Museum of XXI Century Arts, Sketch Painting*, Rome, Italy, 1999
Teppachi watercolour with acrylic on paper,
65 × 90 cm (25⅝ × 35½ in)
Zaha Hadid Foundation

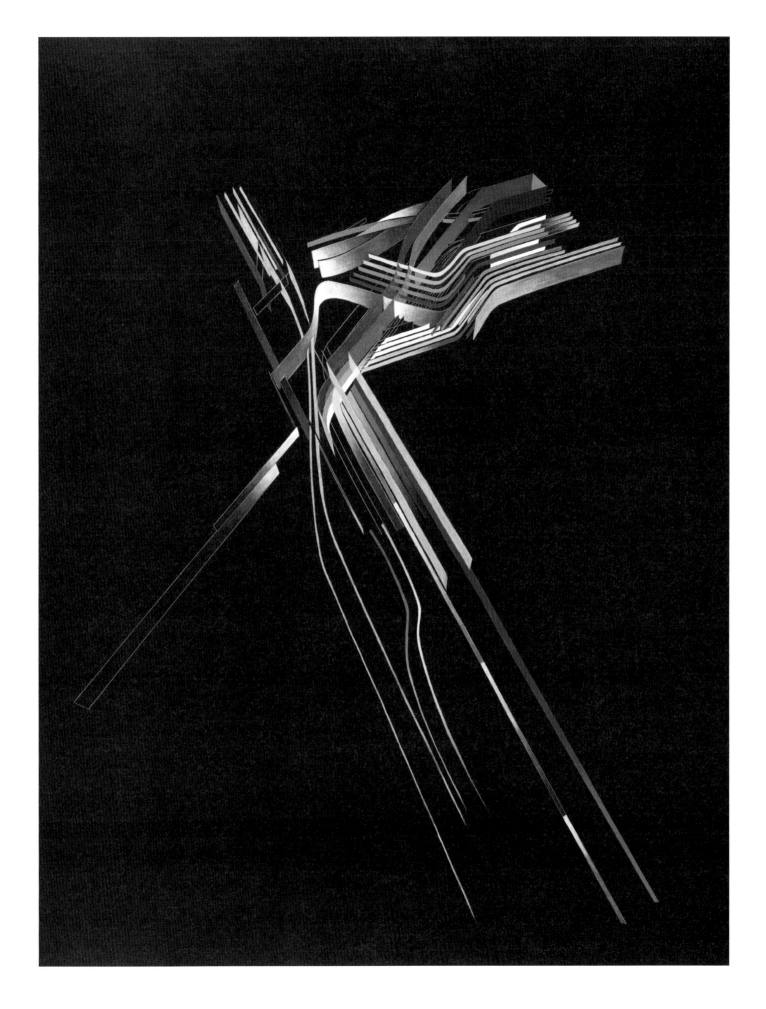

architecture of fluid and drifting geometries that could fold back on themselves. This proposition shifted attention in architecture from the spatial order implied by monuments, where axial coordinates and static geometries defined spatial usage. There was a growing interest for accepting a more nebulous set of relationships where time and motion could be expressed as a response to multiplicitous and small but influential forces.[75]

For the architectural audience of the *AD* special issue of 1993, the implications of Deleuze's writing on the fold were explored by architectural theorist John Rajchman.[76] For him, to weave, as an architectural and spatial idea, reinforced the possibility of architecture having a logical and directional force over time, where a line is no longer prescribed as the joining of two points but instead emerged as a dynamic negotiation of forces. In many ways it has similarities with how Hadid had conceived the term 'program' in architecture, where architecture became defined through a negotiation and enfolding of forces both internally and externally. This concept of negotiated resolution became integral to discussions of how spline geometry could work in architecture as notions of time and direction became implicated by its linearity. So when in 2004 Hadid explained her MAXXI scheme as 'a kind of woven space', she inferred this concept of 'woven lines', with the fluid linearity of the spatial fold found in her painting contrasting with Rome's stable triangular and radial geometries.[77]

In the imagery of the painting *Composite Aerial View* an intensity is proposed for architecture's role in the city. However, there is no reduction of architecture to an image of unity that would reinforce single oppositions of origins and ends, or a new monumentalism to merge contextually within the environments of Rome's suburbia.[78] The layering of images in this painting provides a virtual space proposing geometric relationships for the future of Rome, where, by implication, the palimpsest of past traditions can be retained as a trace. Curvilinear effects derived from the scheme transform those regular geometries evident from an aerial view, into the experiential geometry of the filmic effect of movement and a nomadic sense of time and space.

In *Sketch Painting* this idea extends further, introducing the power of abstraction to negotiate Hadid's Suprematist understandings of pictorial space networked within the possibility of an open-ended architecture. In this painting the fluid linearity of the spline, and its relationship to straight radially informed geometries of Rome's urban landscape, suggests a tension. Their juxtaposition implies that the architecture of the MAXXI takes part in Rome's spatial weave in a precise manner. The questions of architecture, of where to build and how to consider program, negotiates angles and forces from the landscape, bringing influence from some geometries and extending influences back to the city through others. What emerges in *Sketch Painting* is an absence, where the actual site boundaries, street patterns and historical buildings are recorded only in the stark juxtaposition of the interface between the void ground, the allusion to the equilateral triangle, and the end conditions of the splines/lines re-emerging within a pictorial tension. Forms remain implicit, returned to the void space of the pictorial ground to become real but immaterial at the same time.

When Malevich spoke of 'pictorial space' having an infinite number of relationships that could be structured through colour or each shape's spatial proximity, relative size and directionality, he recognised a sense of visual 'weight' and tension within a painting's composition.[79] Each shape implied an energy held in tension. Within Hadid's MAXXI paintings this idea is now merged with Deleuze's concept of weaving and folding of a line on itself. The result affords an architecture that accepts the density of forces interpenetrating in a drifting spatiality, never centred, always relational.

In many ways *Sketch Painting* forms a 'bookend' to Hadid's early painting *Confetti – Suprematist Snowstorm*. Their bracketing conceptually encloses the sequence of paintings in this period as one framed by Suprematism, while appearing in differing theoretical contexts. *Confetti*'s composition relied on an absence of architectural and/or urban references. Where plans were incorporated, they too took the characteristics of confetti falling freely in space but kept in precise juxtaposition through their relational tension. There was no 'gravity' to force resolution into a binary opposition between space and form, but instead there remained a conceptual structure where each shape's 'energy' was supported only through the void implied within the pictorial surface. Elements became a collective, self-referential as a system, reinforcing a link to the spatiality described by Malevich for Suprematism.[80] The imagery of *Confetti* signified proximity to what Hadid would suggest was the 'cosmos' necessary for an apprehension of this new juxtaposition of elements and ideas.[81] She used the term cosmos widely, an example being her description of the placement of Suprematist paintings within a group, overlapping and layered so that there was an indeterminacy of association rather than defined as single objects: 'The Suprematist paintings, for example, were never intended to be isolated in the white cube: they were part of a field or cosmos.'[82]

Within *Sketch Painting*, the lines portray a constant negotiation that is implicitly architectural, a delivery of representational and non-representational spatial effects. Internal to its imagery there is the linear referencing of the tonally ribbed blades. Their lines are fluid and structured in clusters that intersect, weave, interpenetrate and then are released. They take on a porosity and change angle to introduce ideas of drifting between space/void relationships. Through their collective juxtaposition with the equilateral triangle, there remains a frisson of fluid and Cartesian geometries – the triangle isolated in its depiction of 'the other'. In the void-space of the background these juxtapositions become a powerful visualisation of compositional forces where, as a painting, each plane's linear complexity strikes across the pictorial surface and, by implication, across an implied Rome. Externally, the forms of the painting – its linear events – become traces within the MAXXI as a realised environment, and in taking this representational force, the lines and linear effects of painting inform a way for understanding its programmatic complexity.

It is as if in a return to origins, Hadid's *Sketch Painting* ensured that the stability of the conceptual process had endured. The internal and external inferences symbolised by this painting draw to a close the consideration of painting as fundamental to Hadid's development of her architectural propositions. In 2010, Hadid was to reflect that with the MAXXI: 'drawing technique, became design technique, became building'.[83] The complex imagery she initiates raises questions of diagramming, the purpose of lines, and their relation to abstract spatial constructs in response to the context of discourses in the discipline of architecture – all acting as a prompt as much as a reply.

# Conclusion: Of Painting and Architecture

Zaha Hadid was asked over many years to respond to questions concerning the *purpose* of her architectural paintings. It is an enduring question, one which Brett Steele, then director of the Architectural Association, returned to in his homage to Hadid in 2016.[1] His quoting of many of her responses to this question is telling – as none are conclusive or direct. Rather than closing the prescience of the issue, each response invites further inquiry of how her paintings defined an approach to architecture. Such interests prompt the more general question of *what is the purpose of painting to architectural thought*?

In this book, each chapter has proposed that there is a complicated and changing association between these very different activities: from the level of the image and its diagrammatic intent to theoretical propositions exposed by its subject; and further, beyond the realisation of buildings to the different ways of conceiving the 'project' of architecture. One statement Hadid made focuses the concluding comments of this book. It was made in a lecture to students in 1997 and was directed to explaining an early painting titled *The World, 1983*:[2]

> I made these paintings to have a record of what I was thinking at the time. That's why I decided to call it *The World*, because that's what it was for me – a world of projects I had designed by 1983. I originally thought that the subject of the painting was the buildings it showed. The strange thing is, looking back now much later, I realise that its actually the surface of the ground, everything between them, the shaping and building and manipulation of the ground, the arranging of a continuous surface, [*how you inject a kind of new life into these segments*] that became for me such a big project for many years since.[3]

In the lecture, Hadid continues that the paintings were to explore the idea of spatial manipulation and how this attribute of her works 'represented a certain kind of non-hierarchy … to create a degree of freedom, of liberty, and also imply the buildings are so light that they are non-gravitational, no longer adhering to the idea of the kind of grid, or the idea of an orthogonal kind of life'.[4] What is immediately recognisable is the way she looked back at her earlier paintings, and that in explaining them she morphed ideas from the past within her architectural inquiry of the present. This is made precise in *The World, 1983*. While in her lecture she displayed the copy that was included in her *GA Architect* publication of 1986,[5] shown here is a 1984 version of the image that became titled *The World, The Eighty-nine Degrees* (fig.91).[6] It remains unclear which came first. It becomes an example of this continual return and reconsideration, where each painting modifies, in part adapting for new relevance in its author's consideration of architecture, a relevance once so clearly defended in a different manner.

It is a unique attribute of painting, that each image has a diagrammatic force remaining open to differing types of engagement from each viewer, whether the focus is on the explanation of a building that is portrayed, an inquiry of ideas that inform the architecture, or an explanation of the spatiality of the composition and painting's sense of representation. When the effect of imagery within one painting

91
Zaha Hadid
*The World, The Eighty-nine Degrees*, 1984
Print with hand-applied acrylic and wash,
69.9 × 57.5 cm (27.5 × 22.7 in)
Alvin Boyarsky Archive, inscribed:
'*To Alvino, with affection Zaha 26/3/84*'

is seen in the context of others, each portraying aspects of the same architectural project, this is further complicated. Their differences can present a dialogue of ideas further enriching viewer apprehension of potential architectural propositions. Each painting tells a partial story, therefore, 'speaking' to other paintings, models and drawings, and to ideas that are equally 'painting' and 'architecture' – inferring a complex and layered juxtaposition of thoughts and approaches that lie between those referents.

Hadid's paintings evidence an architectural inquiry that adapted with new interests, new terminology and for each new project. Her aims for architecture were not easy to articulate and there remains a risk of returning her paintings – the expectations for their imagery and questioning of conventions – to a level of inquiry that only questions their equivalency to traditional architectural drawing techniques. Through this process there will always be a tendency for interpretation to 'naturalise' their experimentation. Yet these paintings avoid the ease of such neutralising acts. They remain tangential to architectural traditions of drawing, guiding the fluidity of the interpretive eye – of who is looking, and how they see those figures and effects that embed their strangeness. Unlike other more easily quantifiable acts, her architectural paintings do not reinforce closure comforted by knowledge of realised architecture. They remain discomforting fragments that attract engagement while avoiding architecture's requirement for material resolve and completion.

These paintings presume a role that remains distinctive if compared with presentation drawings, architectural renders, or technical drawings. In their step away from the practices usually inscribed as 'architectural', Hadid's paintings frame both a critique and a reflection that while personal, also reach a broader audience. The act of painting became an act of meditation and thought, a slow process of applying layers of hue with a brush, but the act of painting was also an architectural self-communication: attempting new levels of inquiry relying on the prompts of others in her atelier setting. She made the comment that, in the act of layering the paint, or drawing the details to be painted, there was time to focus on certain critical issues of architecture.[7] In this sense painting could be considered an act of architecture. Time was spent in focused development with others sharing the table. Colour matching, tonality and precision were mixed with storytelling, jokes, moments of fury, and more profound discussions and arguments, often taking place well into the night while sharing a meal. The questions raised by this way of working within an atelier prompted new thought, of painting while thinking about the architecture and its ideas, thought freely mixed within painting's spatiality, materials, tectonics and their differing scales of operative intent.

Hadid's thinking into architecture through painting favoured abstraction, spatial movement, interpenetration, space–form relationships and their juxtaposition – all those notions fundamental within a response to the pictorial surface and its implied geometries. Like the Suprematists, she would question how a new social construct could be imagined now through painting and inscribed into architecture. When Malevich spoke of the 'intuitive reason' of experience as an attribute of painting, he inferred a new understanding of the two-dimensional surface of the canvas and its capacity for a different logic.[8] Painting for the Suprematists was beyond Cartesian logic.[9] For Hadid, Malevich's concepts for pictorial space enabled her to escape the authority of architectural drawing conventions and the problem of recognising the new.

Over 20 years, the changing context of contemporary thought in architecture modified the way that Hadid's practice approached Suprematism. Her responses, whether more directly influenced by the politics of city planning in London, the spatiality of urban experiences and sensations, the question of the role of architecture in the city, or the nature of the architectural program, can be seen morphing throughout the developments of her paintings. While many of these ideas have been explained in this book using the proper names of philosophers and their texts, Hadid's immersion within these ideas came as much through meeting, engaging and speaking with individuals – whether students, her many assistants or those named figures who were so important to architectural debates of the period.

To return to the ideas expressed by Walter Benjamin about 'representing buildings using painterly means', where through architectural drawing the architecture is apprehended and 'imagined as an objective entity', Hadid's paintings present an 'apprehension' of architecture that remained incomplete or just beyond reach.[10] These paintings represent more than an objective appearance of an imagined 'realisable' building and its spaces. When examining the paintings of Rem Koolhaas and Zaha Hadid, Jean-François Lyotard claimed the representational act was 'the real place of architecture', and Robin Evans was to argue that a complex relationship was proffered between the architectural drawing and its realised building – where drawings remained 'repositories of effects and the focus of attention'.[11]

For Hadid, painting was an act of distilling complex architectural and urban thought into a series of co-relational visual statements. Painting's understandings of colour, linear effects, spatial diagramming, and the relationships between objectivity and non-objectivity are woven into architecture's sense of space – form interdependencies. She, like Lyotard, considered these paintings as the project of architecture. Her paintings entered spatially into the locus of her architectural thought. They presented a way to shock each viewer into a consideration of architecture; a prompt to question their own 'place' within a new construct of space–form relationships. Viewers of her paintings were invited to question their own instinctive privileging or naïve attachments to an 'orthogonal life'.[12] For Hadid – the world was *always* at eighty-nine degrees.[13]

# Notes

Introduction
Experimentation Through Painting

1. Hadid, Zaha, and Futagawa, Yoshio, in Futagawa, Yukio, ed., *Zaha M. Hadid, GA Document Extra 03*, A.D.A Edita, Tokyo, 1995, p.17.
2. Sebastiano Serlio was the first to explain the conventions of architectural documentation through drawing. Serlio, Sebastiano, *Regole generali di architetura sopra le cinque maniere de gliedifice cioè, Thoscano, Dorico, Ionico, Corinthio, et Composito, con gliessempi dell'antiquita, che, per la magior parte concordano con la dottrina di Vitruvio*, Francesco Marcolini, Venezia, 1537, Libro Terzo, p.v. The implications of this connection are expressed most clearly in the century to follow in Viollet-le-Duc, Eugène-Emmanuel, *Histoire d'un dessinateur: comment on apprend à dessiner* (*Learning to Draw: or The Story of a Young Designer*), J. Hetzel, Paris, *ca*.1880. See it translated in Hearn, Millard Fillmore, *The Architectural Theory of Viollet-le-Duc: Readings and Commentary*, The MIT Press, Cambridge, Mass., 1992, pp 127–39.
3. Evans, Robin, 'Translations from Drawing to Building', *AA Files*, no.12, Summer 1986, pp 3–18. It is reprinted in his *Translations from Drawing to Building and Other Essays*, Architectural Association, London, 1997, pp 185–6.
4. Woods, Lebbeus, 'Drawn into Space: Zaha Hadid', *Architectural Design (AD) Special Issue: Protoarchitecture: Analogue and Digital Hybrids*, vol.78, no.4, July/August 2008, p.31.
5. Hadid's former student and close friend Simon Koumjian III recalled her reminiscence of visiting exhibitions with her father including Picasso's paintings in London and an architectural exhibition in Baghdad. Confirmed in conversations, 8 October 2023.
6. In conversations with Simon Koumjian III, 7 October 2023; Justyna Karakiewicz, 22 June 2020; and Mya Manakides and Camilla Ween, 23 November 2019.
7. For usage of this term, see Benjamin, Walter, 'The Rigorous Study of Art', in Jennings, M., et al., eds, *Walter Benjamin: Selected Writings*, trans. Livingstone, R., vol.2, Belknap Press of Harvard University, Cambridge, Mass., 1999, pp 669–70.
8. This is also discussed in an interview with Hadid. See Levene, Richard, and Cecilia, Fernando, 'Interview with Zaha Hadid', *El Croquis 52: Zaha Hadid 1983/1991*, El Croquis Editorial, Madrid, 1991, p.11.
9. In conversation with Michael Wolfson, Piers Smerin and Nicola Cousins, 18 December 2019. While many were architectural students who had been taught by Hadid at the Architectural Association, Smerin did his undergraduate degree at the Polytechnic of Central London (now Westminster University).

1
From Lines to the Tactile Surface: *Malevich's Tektonik* to 59 Eaton Place

1. This is a claim considered by Walter Benjamin as he responded to the idea of architectural drawing. See Benjamin, Walter, 'The Rigorous Study of Art', in Jennings, M., et al., eds, *Walter Benjamin: Selected Writings*, trans. Livingstone, R., vol.2, Belknap Press of Harvard University, Cambridge, Mass., 1999, pp 669–70. To gain some sense of the different expectations of architectural drawing, see Benjamin, Andrew, *Architectural Philosophy*, Athlone Press, London, 2000, especially Chapters 5 and 6. In artistic practices, see Petherbridge, Deanna, *The Primacy of Drawing: Histories and Theories of Practice*, Yale University Press, New Haven, Conn., 2010.
2. Comment by Unit Leaders, Zenghelis, Elia, and Koolhaas, Rem, 'Student File, Zaha Hadid', Architectural Association School of Architecture, London. See Architectural Association Archive.
3. Koolhaas, Rem, and Zenghelis, Elia, 'Diploma Unit 9', *Architectural Association School of Architecture, Projects Review 1975–76*, Architectural Association, London, July 1976, pp unnumbered. See also Zenghelis's reminiscences of the period in Zenghelis, Elia, 'Text and Architecture: Architecture as Text', in van Schaik, Martin, and Máčel, Otaker, eds, *Exit Utopia: Architectural Provocations 1956–76*, Prestel Verlag, Munich, 2005, pp 255–62.
4. See Koolhaas, Rem, *Delirious New York*, Oxford University Press, New York, 1978, p.214. Much of the writing for this publication was done during 1973 and 1974 while Koolhaas was on a Harkness Scholarship to North America working at Cornell University with Oswald Mathias Ungers and at Columbia University.
5. See student projects in Koolhaas and Zenghelis, 'Diploma Unit 9', 1975–76, op.cit. Steven Holl, a member of the examining panel, remembers the impact of Hadid's scheme. See Holl, Steven, 'New Journey into Space', in Gad, Amira, and Gryczkowska, Agnes, eds, *Reflections on Zaha Hadid*, Serpentine Sackler Gallery, London, 2016, p.54.
6. It is unclear whether this date reflects the completion of the painting or the portfolio. For the earlier scheme of 'Tektonik in Thames', see the axonometric printed in Koolhaas and Zenghelis, 'Diploma Unit 9', 1975–76, op.cit., that was published in July 1976. For Zenghelis's comment see, 'Report' dated 7 January 1977, Architectural Association Archives, where he states that the Malevich bridge project needs to be completed to the same precision as the museum. The portfolio for 'Hotel Malevitch London' [*sic*] incorporates small projects from the 1976/77 academic year. See Koolhaas, Rem, and Zenghelis, Elia, 'Diploma Unit 9', *Architectural Association School of Architecture, Projects Review 1976–77*, Architectural Association, London, July 1977, pp unnumbered.
7. While much larger and with colouration slightly different to the earlier signed copy, the SFMOMA example displays a similar tonal value with photographic negatives, held in the Image Archives of the Architectural Association, and was thus most likely the copy included in Hadid's exhibition *Planetary Architecture Two* in 1983. There is no guarantee that the dating of this painting is correct other than to say the project was concluded at the AA by mid-1977. SFMOMA purchased their painting in 1998 when Aaron Betsky – as their first Architecture and Design Curator – curated the exhibition *Retrospective, Zaha Hadid, The Complete Buildings and Projects*. See the catalogue Zaha Hadid Architects with Betsky, Aaron, *Zaha Hadid: The Complete Buildings and Projects*, Thames and Hudson and Rizzoli, London and New York, 1998.
8. Koolhaas and Zenghelis, 'Diploma Unit 9', 1975–76, op.cit.
9. Koolhaas and Zenghelis, 'Diploma Unit 9', 1975–76, op.cit.
10. Koolhaas, *Delirious New York*, op.cit.
11. Koolhaas, *Delirious New York*, op.cit.
12. Obrist, Hans Ulrich, 'Zaha Hadid in Conversation', in Hadid, Zaha, and Schumacher, Patrik, *Zaha Hadid and Suprematism*, Hatje Cantz, Zurich, 2012, p.43.
13. Obrist, 'Zaha Hadid in Conversation', ibid.
14. Nakov, Andrei, *Tatlin's Dream: Russian Suprematist and Constructivist Art 1910–1923*, Fischer Fine Art Limited, London, 1973.
15. See review Kosloff, Max, 'Malevich as a Counterrevolutionary (East and West)', *Artforum International*, January 1974, pp 30–38, https://www.artforum.com/print/197401/malevich-as-a-counterrevolutionary-east-and-west-37388 (accessed 23 August 2023). Hadid had the use of her brother's apartment in New York and could easily have seen the exhibition.
16. Hadid, Zaha, *Rendering Speculations*, Part II, 7/5/2010, AA Lecture Archive, https://www.youtube.com/watch?v=63GbLuWNt_Q (accessed 15 November 2019).
17. By 1977 this image had been used with Kenneth Frampton's critique of OMA's work on New York and would have been well known. See Frampton, Kenneth, 'Two or Three Things I Know About Them: A Note on Manhattanism', *OMA Architectural Design (AD)*, vol.47, no.5, 1977, pp 315–25.
18. The folio submission's title page calls the scheme *Hotel Malevitch, London*. The folio is kept in the Zaha Hadid Foundation, Image Archive.
19. An explanation of these drawing types can be found in Fraser, Iain, and Henmi, Rod, *Envisioning Architecture: An Analysis of Drawing*, Van Nostrand Reinhold, New York, 1994, especially their 'Explanatory Notes' throughout.
20. See interview, 'Zaha Hadid interviewed by GA', with Futagawa, Yoshio, in Futagawa, Yukio, ed., *Zaha M. Hadid: GA Document Extra 03*, Global Architecture, A.D.A. Edita, Tokyo, 1995, pp 12ff.
21. Hadid and Futagawa, 'Zaha Hadid interviewed by GA', ibid.
22. Hadid and Futagawa, 'Zaha Hadid interviewed by GA', ibid., p.17.
23. *Planetary Architecture* was held at Galerie van

Rooy Amsterdam from November 1981 until January 1982. The catalogue contains black and white drawings only. See Hadid, Zaha, *Zaha M. Hadid: Planetary Architecture, Projects 77–81*, Galerie van Rooy, Amsterdam, first published in 1981. It is reprinted in Jacobson, Clare, ed., *Pamphlet Architecture 1–10*, Princeton Architecture Press, New York, 1998, pp 59–77. See also Drawing Matter, https://www.drawingmatter.org/sets/drawing-week/luce-van-rooy-drawing-architecture/; and Kauffman, Jordan, *Drawing on Architecture: The Object of Lines, 1970–1990*, The MIT Press, Cambridge, Mass., 2018, pp 256–63. Hadid's scheme was awarded the 'Gold Medal for the AD British Architecture Award', in 1982. See Papadakis, Andreas, 'Architectural Design Project Awards', *British Architecture 1982, Architectural Design (AD)*, Academy Editions, London, 1982, pp 26–7.

24 These titles were used first when the project was included for publication in Futagawa, Yukio, ed., *GA Architect*, Global Architecture, Tokyo, 1986, pp 50–57. Sizes are taken from the 'Image Credits' found in Gad, Amira, and Gryczkowska, Agnes, eds, *Zaha Hadid: Early Paintings and Drawings*, Serpentine Galleries and Koenig Books, London, 2016, p.160.

25 This exhibition opened from 8 to 26 June 1982. See Cook, Peter, 'Reviews of AA Exhibitions: Larger than Life Cedric Price: The Home / Zaha Hadid: 59 Eaton Place', *AA Files*, no.3, January 1983, pp 78–83.

26 The inclusion of Hadid's paintings in this exhibition coincided with her scheme being considered for the 'Gold Medal for the AD British Architecture Award'. See this recognition in Papadakis, *British Architecture 1982*, op.cit.

27 In conversations with Nan Lee, 22 July 2019.

28 Those involved with the design were Jonathan Dunn, Bijan Ganjei and Kasha Knapkiewicz, while those completing the painting and exhibition settings included Nan Lee, Wendy Galway and Nabil Ayoubi. See catalogue for the exhibition reprinted in Jacobson, ed., *Pamphlet Architecture 8*, op.cit. See also Kauffman, *Drawing on Architecture*, op.cit., p.78.

29 In conversation with Jonathan Dunn, 14 February 2020.

30 The necessity to question the traditions of architecture and its representation as a general concern of experimentation in architecture of the period is explicitly addressed by Peter Eisenman, interviewed in the film *Beyond Utopia: Changing Attitudes in American Architecture*, Blackwood Productions, 1983.

31 The work of M.C. Escher is well known. In architecture, it should be remembered that Peter Eisenman's 'House' series explored this effect using the axonometric. His experimentation is seen especially in House X, 'Axonometric Model, Scheme H'. See Eisenman, Peter, *House X*, Rizzoli, New York, 1982, pp 163–7. His interest responded in part to a more general exploration of the axonometric technique by De Stijl architects during the 1920s, including the drawings of Theo van Doesburg and Gerrit Rietveld.

32 It is a strategy for colour that Gerrit Rietveld had used in his Schröder-Schräder house of 1924. See Luscombe, Desley, 'Illustrating Architecture: The Spatiotemporal Dimension of Gerrit Rietveld's Representations of the Schröder House', *The Journal of Architecture*, vol.18, no.1, 2013, pp 25–58.

33 See the more contemporary experimentation in Eisenman, Peter, 'Notes on Conceptual Architecture', *Casabella*, no.359–60, November/December 1971, pp 48–58. Eisenman's House I and II were published in 1975 within Drexler, Arthur, *Five Architects: Peter Eisenman, Michael Graves, Charles Gwathmey, John Hejduk, Richard Meier*, Oxford University Press, New York, 1975. Beyond Hadid's understanding of Eisenman's work through publications she would have met him and attended his lectures on numerous occasions when he visited the Architectural Association. See, for example, Peter Cook's *Conceptual Architecture Symposium* at the Art Net Gallery 1975, where AA students attended. Alvin Boyarsky also interviewed Eisenman in January of 1975, see https://www.youtube.com/watch?v=rhQLaMoQ11g (accessed 11 February 2020).

34 Eisenman's axonometric drawings had first been published in 1973, associated with Eisenman, Peter, 'Notes on Conceptual Architecture II A', *On Site*, no.4, 1973, pp 41–4. Eisenman's House I and House II were also published in Drexler, *Five Architects*, ibid. These drawings were later brought together in Eisenman, Peter, *House of Cards*, Oxford University Press, New York, 1987, pp 82–7.

35 See Evans, Robin, 'Architectural Projection', in Blau, Eve, and Kaufman, Edward, eds, *Architecture and its Image: Four Centuries of Architectural Representation, Works from the Canadian Centre for Architecture*, CCA, and The MIT Press, Montreal, 1989, p.34. See also Bois, Yve-Alain, 'Lissitzky, Malevich, and the Question of Space', *Suprematisme*, Gallery Jean Chauvin, Paris, 1977, pp 29–43.

36 Bois, 'Lissitzky, Malevich, and the Question of Space', ibid., p.34.

37 Carroll, Lewis, *Alice in Wonderland*, Macmillan & Co., London, 1865.

38 See this described in Jay, Martin, 'Scopic Regimes of Modernity', in Foster, Hal, ed., *Vision and Visuality*, Bay Press, Seattle, Wash., 1988, pp 3–27.

39 See discussion in Kemp, Martin, *The Science of Art: Optical Themes in Western Art from Brunelleschi to Seurat*, Yale University Press, New Haven, Conn., 1990, pp 167ff.

40 See discussion of Renaissance architectural theorist Daniele Barbaro's critique of placing 'strained, dizzily steep, deformed, or awkward' elements within a perspective in Elkins, James, *The Poetics of Perspective*, Cornell, Ithaca, N.Y., 1994, pp 173ff.

41 See interest in this idea in Wittkower, Rudolph, *Architectural Principles in the Age of Humanism*, Academy Editions, London, 1973.

42 See discussion in Elkins, *The Poetics of Perspective*, op.cit., pp 8ff.

43 See Evans, 'Architectural Projection', op.cit., pp 18–35.

44 See Alberti, Leon Battista, *On the Art of Building in Ten Books*, trans., Rykwert, Joseph, Leach, Neil, Tavernor, Robert, The MIT Press, Cambridge, Mass., 1988, Book II, Chapter I, 34. Further discussions on his methods are found in the explanatory translators notes of Leon Battista Alberti, *On Painting*, trans., Spencer, John R., Yale University Press, New Haven, Conn., 1966, pp 100–117 esp.

45 See Elkins's discussion of this effect in Tintoretto's *Removal of the Body of Saint Mark*, in Elkins, *The Poetics of Perspective*, op.cit., pp 174ff.

46 See the geometric techniques of his methods explained in, Pozzo, Andrea, *The Rules and Examples of Perspective Proper for Painters and Architects*, John James, Greenwich, 1707.

47 Hadid, Zaha, 'Conversion of 59 Eaton Place, AD Project Award, Gold', in Papadakis, *British Architecture 1982*, op.cit., p.28.

48 See Malevich's discussion in Malevich, Kazimir, 'From Cubism and Futurism to Suprematism: The New Painterly Realism, 1915', in Bowlt, John, ed., and trans., *Russian Art of the Avant-Garde: Theory and Criticism 1902–1934*, Viking Press, New York, 1976, pp 116–35.

49 See Hadid, Zaha 'The Calligraphy of the Plan', in Middleton, Robin, ed., *Architectural Associations: The Idea of the City*, The MIT Press and AA, Cambridge, Mass., 1996, p.65.

50 See Zaha Hadid on Kazimir Malevich – *Secret Knowledge*, 2/2/2014, https://www.youtube.com/watch?v=Lg1b_n9IKU0, (accessed 5 September 2019). Hadid assigned great influence to the lectures given by Gerrit Oorthuys at the AA on the work of Russian avant-garde architect Ivan Leonidov. In 1974 Koolhaas was to publish his first study on Leonidov, see Koolhaas, Rem, 'Ivan Leonidov's Dom Narkomtjazjprom, Moscow', *Oppositions*, no.2, 1974, pp 96–102. Leonidov's drawings for the city were finally published in Frampton, Kenneth, and Kolbowski, Silvia, eds, *Ivan Leonidov*, IAUS and Rizzoli, New York, 1981, pp 68–79. Frampton acknowledges Koolhaas and Oorthuys as the initiators of this project. He states that, 'Koolhaas publicly declared his affinity for neo-Suprematism in his entry for the Centre Pompidou competition of 1973', p.1.

51 Hadid, Zaha, 'The Calligraphy of the Plan', op.cit., p.66.

52 As an architectural element, this curved form can be verified in the catalogue drawings for Hadid, *Planetary Architecture*, in Jacobson, ed., *Pamphlet Architecture 8*, op.cit., where there are three small drawn perspectives: 'Perspective of Dining Room', 'Perspective of Dining Room and Lobby', and 'Perspective of Dining Room Screened'.

53 See Zaha Hadid, *Planetary Architecture*, in Jacobson, ed., *Pamphlet Architecture 8*, op.cit., p.59.

2
Pictorial Space and the Transformation of Architecture: The Peak

1 In March 1983, Bernard Tschumi had been announced as winner of the Parc de la Villette competition with OMA as second. Later that month Zaha Hadid was announced as winner of The Peak, Hong Kong. See review in Wilson, Peter, 'The Park and the Peak – Two International Competitions', *AA Files*, no.4, July 1983, pp 76–87.

2 Examples can be seen in Unit descriptions. See *The Architectural Association's Projects Reviews* from 1976 to 1986, AA Archive, London. The term Modernism is explored by Evans, Robin, '1975–1980 Projects: From Axes to Violins', *AA Files*, no.1, Winter 1981–82, pp 115–20.

3 See Kauffman, Jordan, *Drawing on Architecture: The Object of Lines, 1970–1990*, The MIT Press, Cambridge, Mass., 2018.

4 *Sparkling Metropolis* had included three paintings by Hadid for her Museum of the Nineteenth Century student project. See the Solomon R.

Guggenheim Museum's 'Works in Exhibition List, OMA: The Sparkling Metropolis, Nov (16) 17 – Dec 17, 1978', Archive No. A0023B709909_OMA_Checklist.
5. *Planetary Architecture* was open from November 1981 to January 1982. Its catalogue was later republished as Hadid, Zaha, *Zaha Hadid, Planetary Architecture, Projects 77–81, Pamphlet Architecture 8*, William Stout, San Francisco, 1981.
6. *Planetary Architecture Two* was open from 18 November to 16 December 1983.
7. For a full list of these folio editions see, Marjanović, Igor, and Howard, Jan, *Drawing Ambience: Alvin Boyarsky and the Architectural Association*, Mildred Lane Kemper Art Museum, St. Louis, Museum of Art, Rhode Island, and University of Chicago Press, Chicago, 2014, p.151.
8. Hadid, Zaha, and Boyarsky, Alvin, *Zaha Hadid: Planetary Architecture Two*, Architectural Association, London, 1983. See also Marjanović and Howard, *Drawing Ambience*, ibid., for others.
9. See Boyarsky, Nicholas, 'We Fight the Battle with the Drawings on the Wall', in Marjanović and Howard, *Drawing Ambience*, ibid., pp 139–41.
10. Until recently these remained in the ownership of Alfred Siu in Hong Kong. Confirmed in correspondence with Siu, 11 July 2020.
11. The Hong Kong architectural magazine *Vision, Architecture + Design* published a special issue on the competition. See Sharma, Suresh, et al., eds, *Vision, Architecture + Design*, vol.1, no.4, April 1983.
12. The judging of the competition was held from 14 to 20 March 1983. The jury had finalised its selection by 19 March, see, *South China Morning Post*, 20 March 1983, p.8. An exhibition of selected submissions was held in the Far East Exchange Building until 16 April. See the review by Cameron, Nigel, 'Club Designs Raise Ribaldry', *South China Morning Post*, 22 March 1983, p.22. Hadid's visit to Hong Kong was confirmed in correspondence with Alfred Siu, 25 July 2020, and with her friend Justyna Karakiewicz, 22 June 2020. Siu's meeting with Hadid and centrality to the project followed his success establishing *The I Club* in the Admiralty district of Hong Kong. See interview with Zheng Shengtian, 8 April 2013, http://yishu-online.com/wp-content/uploads/mm-products/uploads/2013_v12_04_zheng_s_p043.pdf (accessed 25 June 2020). See Warhol's account http://warholpolaroids.blogspot.com/1982/10/ (accessed 28 June 2020). Hadid's commission for The Peak Leisure Club was still active in 1984, see McLean, John, 'Futuristic Project Still Pending', *South China Morning Post*, 27 March 1984, p.12. Hadid was later to consider the rift in Sino-British politics as the major cause of its financial difficulties. See her interview with Charlie Rose, 21/06/1999, https://charlierose.com/videos/14851 (accessed 13 December 2021).
13. Prior to the competition, Hadid's experience of Hong Kong had been on a tour of the People's Republic of China in 1981. See, Hadid, Zaha, *Zaha Hadid: To a New Modernism*, a film by Pidgeon Digital Audio Visual, London, 1988, Producers Monica Pidgeon in association with Leonie Cohn. Transcript https://www-pidgeondigital-com.ezproxy.lib.uts.edu.au/talks/to-a-new-modernism/chapters/ (accessed 6 March 2020).
14. In conversation with Camilla Ween, 23 November 2019.
15. ibid.
16. Michael Wolfson had studied with Hadid in 1980/81 and after graduating in 1982 joined her studio; Jonathan Dunn studied with Hadid in 1977/78, 1978/79 and 1979/80, and worked in her studio from 1979 to 1984; Nabil Ayoubi had been her student in 1979/80 and 1980/81, and joined her studio in 1981; and Marian van der Waals studied with Hadid in 1980/81 and 1981/82. Alastair Standing studied with Hadid 1981–1983 and continued to work in her office after graduating. See *The Architectural Association's Projects Reviews* for those years.
17. In conversation with Jonathan Dunn, 14 February 2020.
18. In conversation with Michael Wolfson, 19 December 2016. This is further explained in a recent filmed interview with Nicholas Boyarsky. See https://youtu.be/wYVTD_H9K9w (accessed 20 October 2021).
19. In conversation with Wolfson, ibid.
20. ibid.
21. ibid.
22. ibid. The story goes that Hadid had secured a number of these long rulers on one trip to Paris.
23. In conversation with Michael Wolfson, Piers Smerin and Nicola Cousins, 18 December 2019.
24. ibid.
25. The imagery correlated in most attributes when measured by Wolfson and the author at the Serpentine Gallery in 2016.
26. ibid.
27. Apart from those listed here, are a group of students listed in the advertising of the catalogue for the exhibition in *Architectural Association Projects Review 1983–84*, Architectural Association, London, 1984, p. unnumbered.
28. Lee and Galway were graduate students at Central Saint Martins in textile design. In conversations with Nan Lee and Wendy Galway, 22 July 2019.
29. Some initial experiments are held in Wolfson's private collection.
30. In conversation with Wolfson, Smerin and Cousins, op.cit.
31. ibid.
32. In conversation with David Gomersall, 22 November 2019.
33. In conversation with Dunn, op.cit.
34. In conversation with Wolfson, Smerin and Cousins, op.cit.
35. In conversation with Gomersall, op.cit.
36. Hadid, Zaha, 'Colour Programme', *Architectural Association Projects Review 1983–84*, Architectural Association, London, July 1984, pp unnumbered.
37. In correspondence with Nan Lee, 6 May 2020.
38. See further discussion in Chapter 4, p.80ff.
39. Hadid returned to explain these terms in her lecture at the Architectural Association in *Rendering Speculations Symposium*, 2010, https://www.youtube.com/watch?v=63GbLuWNt_Q (accessed 24 May 2020).
40. The title for *Confetti* and *Slabs* follows contemporary usage. Where possible, painting titles are directed to their first appearance in published form. For The Peak project they follow, Futagawa, Yukio, ed., *GA Architect 5, Zaha M Hadid*, Global Architecture, Tokyo, 1986.
41. See the settings in the competition's promotion material. See *The 'Peak' Architectural Competition Hong Kong, 1982*, HKIA, Hong Kong, 1982.
42. Hadid and Boyarsky, *Zaha Hadid: Planetary Architecture Two*, op.cit., p. unnumbered.
43. Kai Tak Airport closed in 1998 as it was no longer able to service the international needs of Hong Kong.
44. In correspondence with Lee, op.cit.
45. See Hadid speaking at SCl-Arc, Los Angeles, 21 February 1985, https://channel.sciarc.edu/browse/zaha-hadid-february-21-1985 (accessed 28 August 2023).
46. The term 'graft' appeared in Koolhaas's Unit description from the 1975/76 academic year at the AA, when Hadid was his student. It is referred to in Chapter 1, p.17.
47. Hadid and Boyarsky, *Zaha Hadid: Planetary Architecture Two*, op.cit., p. unnumbered. In her diploma studies Hadid had proposed a thesis titled 'Malevich and Suprematism'. Although the work failed in assessment it had included essays on Malevich and Leonidov. See AA Archive, Zaha Hadid Report.
48. Comprehensive lists can be seen in the Events Calendar for each year but more critical engagement of debates during Hadid's student years is seen in the student publication, Pawley, Martin, ed., *Ghost Dance Times*, Architectural Association, London, 1974–75.
49. This is explained in Boyarsky, Nicholas, 'We Fight the Battle with the Drawings on the Wall', op.cit., pp 139–41.
50. The translation available in English at the time would have been *Vitruvius: The Ten Books on Architecture*, Morgan, Morris Hicky, trans., Dover, London, 1960. A significant example in the context of the AA's discussion of meaning had been Jencks, Charles, and Baird, George, *Meaning in Architecture*, Braziller, New York, 1970.
51. Rykwert's books reinforced Vitruvian themes. See Rykwert, Joseph, *On Adam's House in Paradise: The Idea of the Primitive Hut in Architectural History*, The MIT Press, Cambridge, Mass., 1981, originally published in 1972; and, *The Idea of a Town: The Anthology of Urban Form in Rome, Italy and the Ancient World*, Princeton University Press, Princeton, N.J., 1976.
52. Rykwert, *On Adam's House in Paradise*, ibid., cover and pp 45 and 104.
53. See Cesare Cesariano's translation of Vitruvius, *Di Lucio, Vitruvio Pollione de architectura libri dece: traducti de latino in vulgare affigurati: comentati: & con mirando ordine insigniti*, trans., Cesare Cesariano, Gottardo da Ponte, Como, 1521, Book II, XXXI.
54. This is Rykwert's term, *On Adam's House in Paradise*, op.cit., p.105.
55. Frontispiece of Laugier, Marc-Antoine, *Essai sur l'architecture*, second edition, Chez Duchesne, Paris, 1755. Drawing by Charles Eisen (1720–78).
56. Rykwert, *On Adam's House in Paradise*, op.cit., p.44.
57. The complete image can be found at https://photolib.noaa.gov/Collections/Coast-Geodetic-Survey/Geodesy/Topography-Mapping-the-Shoreline/Photogrammetry/emodule/957/eitem/45622 (accessed 16 August 2023) where its original has been lost. This image was the one that both Libeskind and Koolhaas accessed and reproduced details from the original. It was first published in *Life* magazine, 1 September 1947, pp 14–16.
58. See Jung, Carl, *Man and His Symbols*, Doubleday, Garden City, N.Y., 1964, p.39. See https://static1.squarespace.com/static/5e265eb50aee2d7e8a81ae69/t/634606d40132590366e0e838/1665533663009/man-and-

his-symbols%2BA.pdf (accessed 1 November 2023). It is subsequently seen in Libeskind, Daniel, 'Intermediate Unit 9', *Architectural Association School of Architecture, Projects Review 1975–76 and 1976/77*, London, AA, 1976/77, n.n. Jung's essay arose after his death and in response to a BBC television program he had done called *Face to Face*, airing in 1959.

59  Jung's use of the image was to frame a comparison with an image of Hiroshima after the atomic bomb. His reference was to present an idea that humankind had not yet learned to control their own nature. See the caption of the images as presented, ibid.

60  Koolhaas, Rem, 'Life in the Metropolis or The Culture of Congestion', *Architectural Design, OMA*, vol.47, no.5, 1977, p.319.

61  Hadid continued to show this image for Hong Kong at a lecture given at SCI-Arc in Los Angeles in 1985. See https://channel.sciarc.edu/browse/zaha-hadid-february-21-1985 (accessed 25 August 2023).

62  Zaha Hadid, 'Competition Report, The Peak Hong Kong', 1982. Zaha Hadid Foundation Archive.

63  The drawing by Barry Marshall for the competition entry of PDCM is an example of a more traditional form, see *Vision, Architecture + Design*, vol.1, no.4, April 1983, pp 48–9. This image appeared in Anon., 'The Peak Architectural Competition', *Architectural Record*, vol.171, no.11, September 1983, p.56.

64  Hadid, Zaha, 'The Calligraphy of the Plan', in Middleton, Robin, ed., *Architectural Associations: The Idea of the City*, The MIT Press and AA, Cambridge, Mass., 1996, p.65.

65  Hadid assigned great influence to the lectures given by Gerrit Oorthuys at the AA on the work of Russian avant-garde architect Ivan Leonidov. In 1974 Koolhaas was to publish his first study on Leonidov, see Koolhaas, Rem, 'Ivan Leonidov's Dom Narkomtjazjprom, Moscow', *Oppositions*, no.2, 1974, pp 96–102. Leonidov's drawings for the city were finally published in Frampton, Kenneth, and Kolbowski, Silvia, eds, *Ivan Leonidov*, IAUS and Rizzoli, New York, 1981, pp 68–79. Frampton acknowledges Koolhaas and Oorthuys as the initiators of this project. He states that, 'Koolhaas publicly declared his affinity for neo-Suprematism in his entry for the Centre Pompidou competition of 1973', p.1.

66  Hadid, Zaha, 'The Calligraphy of the Plan', op.cit., p.66.

67  Malevich, Kazimir, '1/42 Non-Objectivity', in Andersen, Troels, ed., *K.S. Malevich, The World as Non-Objectivity: Unpublished Writings 1922–25*, trans., Glowacki-Prus, Xenia, and Little, Edmund T., Borgen, Copenhagen, 1976, p.49. See discussion in Benjamin, Andrew, 'Malevich and the Avant-Garde', *Malevich: Art and Design Profile 15 (AD)*, vol.5, no.5/6, 1989, pp 55–7.

68  Argued in Malevich, Kazimir, 'From Cubism and Futurism to Suprematism: The New Painterly Realism, 1915', in Andersen, Troels, ed., *K.S. Malevich, Essays on Art, 1915–1933*, trans., Glowacki-Prus, Xenia, and McMillin, Arnold, Rapp & Whiting, London, 1968, p. 35 and 'The Question of Imitative Art, 1920', ibid., p.173.

69  See Malevich, 'From Cubism and Futurism to Suprematism', ibid., p.36.

70  Malevich saw this as a return to representational 'death'. See Malevich, 'From Cubism and Futurism to Suprematism', ibid., p.34.

71  Malevich's *Landscape with a Yellow House (Winter Landscape)* can be seen more clearly at https://rusmuseumvrm.ru/data/collections/painting/19_20/malevich_k.s._peyzazh_s_zheltim_domom_zimniy_peyzazh._okolo_1906._zh-9411/index.php?lang=en. However, because geopolitics in current years has limited activities with Russia I have relied on secondary sources.

72  In Malevich's description of *Suprematism: 34 Drawings*, he makes the claim that 'friends' had published the book. It is unclear quite what this meant for the selection and orientation of images. See 'Suprematism, 34 Drawings', in Andersen, ed., *K.S. Malevich, Essays on Art*, op.cit., p.123.

73  'Suprematism, 34 Drawings', ibid.

74  This is the focus of Malevich, 'Non-objective Creation and Suprematism', in Andersen, Troels, ed., *K.S. Malevich, Essays on Art*, ibid., pp 120–22.

75  Shatskikh, Aleksandra, 'Malevich, Curator of Malevich', in Petrova, Yevgenia, ed., *The Russian Avant-Garde: Representation and Interpretation*, Palace Editions, St Petersburg, 2001.

76  See Hadid's reminiscences of this effect in Malevich in her presentation 'Zaha Hadid and Suprematism: Tate Talks', a discussion between multiple award-winning architect Zaha Hadid and Achim Borchardt-Hume, Head of Exhibitions at Tate Modern and curator of Malevich Exhibition, 30 October 2014, https://www.youtube.com/watch?v=GF_qPKnrrH0 (accessed 13 December 2021).

77  See Hadid, Zaha, 'Recent Work', lecture delivered at the Architectural Association, November 1997, https://www.youtube.com/watch?v=ZcoY4i4P6no (accessed 26 May 2020).

78  Unpublished transcript of a conversation between Alvin Boyarsky and Zaha Hadid, held in the Boyarsky family archive. It is dated 1987.

79  Unpublished transcript, Boyarsky, ibid.

80  This will be shortened to *Confetti* in the remainder of the text.

81  In conversation with Gomersall, op.cit. He attributed the drawing to Alistair Standing.

82  As early as 1930, Rodchenko had lectured on the distinction between 'photo stills' and 'photo pictures'. His interest in photo stills was used to register the instantaneity of spatial experience, rather than the Social Realism in paintings of the period. See Tupitsyn, Margarita, 'Fragmentation versus Totality: The Politics of (De)framing', in Solomon R. Guggenheim Museum, et al., *The Great Utopia: The Russian and Soviet Avant-Garde, 1915–1932*, Guggenheim Museum, et al., New York, 1992, pp 482–96.

83  See Obrist, Hans, 'Zaha Hadid in Conversation', in Hadid, Zaha, and Schumacher, Patrik, *Zaha Hadid and Suprematism*, Hatje Cantz, Zurich, 2012, p.45.

84  Zaha Hadid quoted in Wilson, 'The Park and the Peak', op.cit., pp 76–87.

85  In an interview with Nicholas Boyarsky, Michael Wolfson, who completed many final drawings, claims it was partly in response to Madelon Vriesendorp's drawing of naked boxers eating oysters published in *Delirious New York*. See Dialogues 5 May 2020 FILM 003 – YouTube, https://www.youtube.com/watch?v=wYVTD_H9K9w (accessed 10 July 2020). However, the spatial construct is very different.

86  See Burns, Karen, and Morgan, Paul, 'Interview with Zaha Hadid', *Transition*, vol.20, May 1987, pp 17–21.

87  Hadid and Boyarsky, *Zaha Hadid: Planetary Architecture Two*, op.cit., p. unnumbered.

88  See her comments in Hadid and Boyarsky, *Zaha Hadid: Planetary Architecture Two*, op.cit., p. unnumbered.

89  See *Vision, Architecture + Design*, op.cit.

90  While extended to architecture in the projects of Leonidov and El Lissitzky this is a pictorial understanding in Hadid's work. See the explanation of their approaches in Burgos, Francesco, and Garrido, Ginés, *El Lissitzky: Wolkenbügel, 1924–25*, Edición, Ministero de Vivienda, Madrid, 2004.

91  See Tschumi, 'An Urban Park for the 21st Century', in Wilson, 'The Park and the Peak', op.cit., p.80.

92  See Koolhaas, 'The Layers', in Wilson, 'The Park and the Peak', op.cit., p.78.

93  Unpublished transcript, Boyarsky, op.cit.

94  Burns and Morgan, 'Interview with Zaha Hadid', op.cit., pp 17–21.

95  Cedric Price's architecture was mentioned as important to her development of ideas in Hadid's interview with Boyarsky. See Hadid and Boyarsky, *Zaha Hadid: Planetary Architecture Two*, op.cit., p. unnumbered.

96  Cook, Peter, 'Reviews of AA Exhibitions: Larger than Life Cedric Price: The Home / Zaha Hadid: 59 Eaton Place', *AA Files*, no.3, January 1983, p.78.

97  See Burns and Morgan, 'Interview with Zaha Hadid', op.cit. The term programmatic is discussed further in Chapter 3, p.59 ff.

98  See Hadid, 'Competition Report', op.cit.

99  Seen in later documents and publications produced by ZHA.

100  Hadid and Boyarsky, *Zaha Hadid: Planetary Architecture Two*, op.cit., p. unnumbered.

3
Politicising the Urban Character of London: Grand Buildings

1  Anticipation for the competition was covered in the architectural press, Anon., 'Grand Competition', *Building*, vol.246, no.7340 (17), 27 April 1984, p.9; and 'Tight Brief for Grand Buildings', *Building*, vol.246, no.7336 (13), 30 March 1984, p.11. However, the actual architectural competition seems to have been finally opened in 1985.

2  See the debates as remembered by Koolhaas, Rem, and Jencks, Charles, 'Radical Post-Modernism and Content: Charles Jencks and Rem Koolhaas Debate the Issue', *Architectural Design (AD)*, vol.81, no.5, September 2011, pp 32–45.

3  This project became the focus of their segment of the film *Deconstructivist Architects*, Michael Blackwood, 1989, https://www.michaelblackwoodproductions.com/project/deconstructivist-architects/ (accessed 10 October 2019).

4  See Krier, Léon, *Rational Architecture Rationelle: The Reconstruction of the European City*, Archives d'Architecture Moderne, Brussels, 1978.

5  This occurred after his being appointed the first director of the new SOM Foundation in the USA. See https://somfoundation.som.com/about/history/ (accessed 1 November 2023). For discussion on his involvement with the aftermath of the competition for the extension to The National Gallery, see his explanation in Krier, Léon, 'Open Letter to Joseph Rykwert', *Architectural Review*, 4 July 2013, https://www.architectural-review.com/essays/points-of-

order (accessed 2 May 2023). See also HRH The Prince of Wales, *A Vision of Britain: A Personal View of Architecture*, Doubleday, London, 1989.
6   See Tschumi, Bernard, *The Manhattan Transcripts: Theoretical Projects*, Academy Editions, London, 1981. Parc de la Villette increased its critical acclaim with its exhibition in the Centre Pompidou, Paris, in 1983 and publication of Derrida, Jacques, 'Point de Folie – Maintenant l'Architecture. Bernard Tschumi: La Case Vide – La Villette, 1985', *AA Files*, no.12, 1986, pp 65–75. See Special Issue, *Urbanité/Urbanity: Projects Exhibited at the Paris Biennale's First International Exhibition of Architecture* (*AD*), no.11/12, 1980, pp 4 and 22 regarding Tschumi.
7   In terms of the Architectural Association the celebration of Tschumi's win of the competition for Parc de la Villette coincided with the announcement of Hadid's win of the competition for The Peak; see, Wilson, Peter, 'The Park and the Peak – Two International Competitions', *AA Files*, no.4, July 1983, pp 76–87.
8   Texts of interest at the time include: De Certeau, Michel, *The Practice of Everyday Life*, trans., Rendell, Steven, University of California Press, Berkeley, Calif., 1984; Lefebvre, Henri, *The Production of Space*, trans., Smith, Donald, Blackwell, Oxford, 1991 (1974, 1984); Debord, Guy, *The Society of the Spectacle*, trans., Nicholson-Smith, Donald, Black & Red, London, 1970; Barthes, Roland, especially his comments directly on architecture, 'Sémiologie et Urbanisme', *Architecture d'Aujourd'hui*, no.153, December 1970/January 1971, pp 11–13; and the many publications of Jacques Derrida and Michel Foucault. See discussed in Martin, Louis, 'Architectural Theory after 1968, Analysis of the Works of Rem Koolhaas and Bernard Tschumi', submitted in partial fulfilment for the Degree of Master of Science in Architectural Studies, The MIT Press, 1988, and his 'The Search for a Theory in Architecture: Anglo-American Debates, 1957–1976', PhD thesis, Princeton University, 2002, UMI 3067009. See also, Martin, Louis, 'Transpositions: On the Intellectual Origins of Tschumi's Architectural Theory', *Assemblage*, no.11, April 1990, pp 22–35. More generally, in 2014 Patrik Schumacher was to recall, 'All of them were closely related in their search for radically new concepts which were to imply more intensity, dynamics and complexity than the concepts of classical Modernism.' See, 'Thomas Redl speaks with Patrik Schumacher, Vienna, 30.01.2014', *C-Live Magazine*, Architektur/Raum/Kunst, Graz-Wein-Hamburg, June 2014. See, https://www.patrikschumacher.com/Texts/C%20Live%20MAGAZINE_english%20text.html (accessed 20 August 2023).
9   See Derrida, 'Point de Folie', op.cit.
10  See the working documents of the AA including their weekly published *Events List*, and their annual *Prospectus* and *Projects Reviews*.
11  Rowe, Colin, and Koetter, Fred, *Collage City*, The MIT Press, Cambridge, Mass., 1978; and Rossi, Aldo, *The Architecture of the City*, trans., Girardo, Diane, and Ockman, Joan, The Graham Foundation for Advanced Studies in the Fine Arts, The Institute for Architecture and Urban Studies, and The MIT Press, Chicago, New York and Cambridge, Mass., 1982.
12  For transcripts of Rowe's early presentations associated with the AA, see *1975 NET*, Art Net, London, 1975. See also Krier, *Rational Architecture Rationelle*, op.cit.
13  See Sunwoo, Irene, 'Between the "Well Laid Table" and the "Marketplace": Alvin Boyarsky's Experiments in Architectural Pedagogy', PhD dissertation, Princeton University, 2013, UMI 3604509.
14  Hadid's Unit descriptions prior to this time had used terminology like 'housing for the masses', 'no elitism', 'the metropolis', each term clearly retained from her tutoring under the leadership of Koolhaas and Zenghelis. There is an important change in Hadid's approach seen after the 1981/82 academic year. See 'Diploma Unit 9', *Architectural Association, School of Architecture Prospectus, 1978 to 1981–82*, Architectural Association, London.
15  Hadid, Zaha, 'Diploma Unit 9', *Architectural Association, School of Architecture Prospectus, 1983–84*, Architectural Association, London, 1983, p. unnumbered.
16  Hadid, 'Diploma Unit 9', ibid.
17  Hadid, 'Diploma Unit 9', ibid.
18  See Williams, Stephanie, 'A New Round in the Battle of Trafalgar', *Blueprint*, March 1985, p.5. This summarises the conditions of the architectural competition. It also lists the jury members as Sir Hugh Wilson, Nicholas Grimshaw, John Miller, William Whitfield, Sir John Boynton and Ian Henderson of Land Securities.
19  Williams, 'A New Round', ibid.
20  HRH The Prince of Wales, 'A Speech by HRH The Prince of Wales at the 150th Anniversary of the Royal Institute of British Architects (RIBA)', Royal Gala Evening at Hampton Court Palace, 30 May 1984, https://web.archive.org/web/20070927213205/http://www.princeofwales.gov.uk/speechesandarticles/a_speech_by_hrh_the_prince_of_wales_at_the_150th_anniversary_1876801621.html (accessed 5 February 2021).
21  The scheme can be seen at: https://www.architecture.com/explore-architecture/inside-the-riba-collections/abk-national-gallery-models (accessed 26 October 2023).
22  See commentary and explanation of the failure of this scheme in Krier's open letter to Joseph Rykwert, ibid. The scheme has been published in Krier, Léon, *Léon Krier: Architecture & Urban Design 1967–1992*, Academy Editions, London, 1992, pp 200–201.
23  HRH The Prince of Wales, 'A Speech by HRH', op.cit.
24  It was not until April 1985 that the competition for the extension to The National Gallery was recommenced. See https://www.nationalgallery.org.uk/about-us/history/about-the-building/the-sainsbury-wing-20th-anniversary (accessed 21 July 2021).
25  Anon., 'Grand Buildings Trafalgar Square', *Architectural Design*, vol.56, no.4, 1986, pp 24–9.
26  This date was announced in Anon., *Building*, 8 March 1985, p.7. The scheme submitted by Hadid and Zenghelis first appeared in the editorial, Anon., 'Grand Exits, a Selection of the 278 Failed Schemes Submitted to the Grand Buildings Competition', *Architects' Journal*, vol.182, no.34/35, 21–28 August 1985, pp 20–25. See explanation of their earlier partnership in http://concretestew.blogspot.com/2016/04/zaha-hadid-and-taoiseachs-house.html (accessed 6 February 2020). Discussion on her British citizenship was still active in the unpublished transcript of a conversation between Alvin Boyarsky and Zaha Hadid, held in the Boyarsky family archive, dated 1987, pp 7ff.
27  Hadid, Zaha, and Boyarsky, Alvin, 'Post Peak Conversations with Zaha Hadid, 1983 & 1986', in Futagawa, Yukio, ed., *GA Architect 5, Zaha M. Hadid*, A.D.A. Edita, Tokyo, 1986, p.18. This outcome eventuated in the final selection explored in Anon., 'Grand Buildings Trafalgar Square', op.cit.
28  Hadid and Boyarsky, 'Post Peak Conversations', op.cit. For Krier's influence see Krier, Léon, 'Houses, Palaces, Cities', *Architectural Design*, vol.54, no.7/8, 1984, complete issue. For his continued connection see, HRH The Prince of Wales, *A Vision of Britain*, op.cit.
29  Hadid and Boyarsky, 'Post Peak Conversations', op.cit., p.19.
30  For the analysis of The Peak, see Chapter 2 of this volume.
31  See Anon., 'Grand Exits', op.cit., p.25.
32  It had opened on 28 September 1985. See Futagawa, *GA Architect 5*, op.cit., p.7.
33  See Futagawa, *GA Architect 5*, op.cit.
34  See Hadid and Boyarsky, 'Post Peak Conversations', op.cit., p.19.
35  Brian Ma Siy recounts this as his sketch. A later rendition, included in *GA Documents*, was larger and interpreted from his original. See Futagawa, *GA Architect 5*, op.cit., p.104. In conversation with Ma Siy, 27 November 2019.
36  Latham, Ian, 'Grand Tour (2)', *Building Design*, no.756, 20 September 1985, pp 26–7.
37  C. Lim and S. Tandon are added. Hadid, Zaha, 'Dynamiser L'Urbain, Concours pour Trafalgar Square, London', *Architecture d'Aujourd'hui*, no.242, December 1985, pp 4–11.
38  Hadid, 'Dynamiser L'Urbain', ibid.
39  Lyotard, Jean-François, *Les Immatériaux*, 28 March to 15 July 1985, Centre de Création Industrielle, Grande Gallerie du Centre national d'art et la culture George Pompidou, Paris. There were a series of catalogues and publications that can be seen at https://www.centrepompidou.fr/fr/programme/agenda/evenement/cRyd8q (accessed 24 November 2021).
40  In conversation with Ma Siy, op.cit.
41  Titles use those in Futagawa, *GA Architect 5*, op.cit.
42  See *City of London, Local Development Framework, Core Strategy*, Policy CS 13, pp 70–71; https://democracy.cityoflondon.gov.uk/Data/Court%20of%20Common%20Council/20100715/Agenda/$A%20-%20Annex1%20Core%20Strategy%20Final.DOC.pdf#:~:text=WHAT%20IS%20THE%20CORE%20STRATEGY,develop%20to%202026%20and%20beyond (accessed 6 May 2023).
43  See the importance to concepts of modernity discussed in Jay, Martin, 'Scopic Regimes of Modernity', in Foster, Hal, ed., *Vision and Visuality*, Bay Press, Seattle, Wash., 1988, pp 3–27.
44  Alberti, Leon Battista, *On the Art of Building in Ten Books*, trans., Rykwert, Joseph, Leach, Neil, and Tavernor, Robert, The MIT Press, Cambridge, Mass., 1988, Book II, Chapter I, 34.
45  See discussion of the technical development of perspectival geometry in Pérez-Gómez, Alberto, *Architecture and the Crisis of Modern Science*, The MIT Press, Cambridge, Mass., 1984.
46  See discussion of perspectival techniques in Chapter 1, p.26ff.
47  Panofsky, Erwin, *Perspective as Symbolic Form*,

48 Panofsky, *Perspective as Symbolic Form*, ibid., pp 30–31.
49 See discussion in Elkins, James, *The Poetics of Perspective*, Ithaca, Cornell, N.Y., 1994, pp 8ff.
50 See Evans, Robin, 'Architectural Projection', in Blau, Eve, and Kaufman, Edward, eds, *Architecture and its Image: Four Centuries of Architectural Representation, Works from the Canadian Centre for Architecture*, CCA and The MIT Press, Montreal and Cambridge, Mass., 1989, pp 18–35.
51 See Hadid and Boyarsky, 'Post Peak Conversations', op.cit.
52 For drawings and models of the competition schemes, see https://www.ribapix.com (accessed 11 May 2023). While the author of this drawing was not named, Krier was soon after appointed to director of the SOM Foundation in Chicago, only to leave shortly after to become advisor to HRH The Prince of Wales; https://somfoundation.com/about/history/ (accessed 16 May 2023).
53 This date determined by his description of events in Krier, 'Points of Order', *Architectural Review*, 4 July 2013, see AR online, https://www.architectural-review.com/essays/points-of-order. See the representation of the Masterplan in Krier, Léon, 'National Gallery Extension, A Trafalgar Square Masterplan', in *Léon Krier*, op.cit., pp 200–201. Coincidentally, it was only after the comment in 1984 by HRH The Prince of Wales, who had been on the Board of Trustees to the gallery and was aware of debates, that Krier was invited to become his personal advisor, and to complete a 'Masterplan for The National Gallery and Trafalgar Square Precinct'.
54 See, Hadid, 'Diploma Unit 9', *Prospectus, 1983–84*, op.cit.
55 De Certeau, Michel, 'Walking in the City', in *The Practice of Everyday Life*, op.cit., pp 92–3.
56 De Certeau, 'Walking in the City', ibid., p.92.
57 Obrist, Hans Ulrich, 'Zaha Hadid in Conversation', in Hadid, Zaha, and Schumacher, Patrik, *Zaha Hadid and Suprematism*, Hatje Cantz, Zurich, 2012, p.45. Although this interview is conducted many years after the scheme for Grand Buildings, its discussion of projects ranges freely to her earlier schemes. Broader issues of temporality in Rodchenko's photographs were discussed in Chapter 2 in relation to The Peak.
58 Obrist, 'Zaha Hadid in Conversation', ibid.
59 See Hadid speaking at SCI-Arc, Los Angeles, 21 February 1985, https://channel.sciarc.edu/browse/zaha-hadid-february-21-1985 (accessed 28 August 2023).
60 See, for instance, the front and back cover of *Novyi LEF*, no.9, 1928, where two differently oriented views from the ground looking skyward up a building's facade are placed horizontally on the page.
61 Rodchenko, Alexander, 'Foto-vopros', Пионер (*Pioneer*), no.13, July 1933, p.4.
62 Rodchenko, Alexander, 'Doklad Rodchenko o sotial'nom znachenii forografii', 1930, A. Rodchenko and V. Stepanova Archive Moscow, see discussed in Tupitsyn, Margarita, 'Fragmentation versus Totality: The Politics of (De)framing', in Solomon R. Guggenheim Museum, et al., *The Great Utopia: The Russian and Soviet Avant-Garde, 1915–1932*, Guggenheim Museum, et al., New York, 1992, p.496.
63 Rodchenko, Alexander, 'Predosterezhenie', *Novyi LEF*, no.11, 1928, p.37. See Tupitsyn, 'Fragmentation versus Totality', op.cit., p.486.
64 Tupitsyn, 'Fragmentation versus Totality', ibid.
65 Tupitsyn, 'Fragmentation versus Totality', ibid., p.485.
66 Lyotard, Jean-François, and Roberts, Mark, 'Plastic Space and Political Space', *Boundary 2*, vol.1/2, no.14, Autumn 1985 / Winter 1986, p.220. It was originally published as Lyotard, Jean-François, 'Espace plastique et espace politique' (1970), reprinted in *Dérive à partir de Marz et de Freud*, U.G.E., Paris, 1973, p.300.
67 See discussion of The Peak, for example, in Chapter 2, p.45ff.
68 Rossi, *The Architecture of the City*, op.cit.; Rowe and Koetter, *Collage City*, op.cit.
69 Krier, *Rational Architecture Rationelle*, op.cit.
70 Rowe and Koetter, *Collage City*, op.cit., p.142.
71 Rowe and Koetter, *Collage City*, op.cit., pp 143–4.
72 Rossi, *The Architecture of the City*, op.cit., p.128.
73 Rossi, *The Architecture of the City*, op.cit., p.130.
74 Krier, *Rational Architecture Rationelle*, op.cit., p.58. The capitalisation is Krier's.
75 Lyotard, Jean-François, *Les Immatériaux*, op.cit.. There were a series of catalogues and publications that can be seen at https://www.centrepompidou.fr/fr/programme/agenda/evenement/cRyd8q (accessed 24 November 2021).
76 See Szacka, Léa-Catherine, 'The Materiality of the Immaterial: S,M,L,XL, as Postmodern Manifesto?', *Journal of Architectural Education*, vol.69, no.2, 2015, pp 163–5.
77 Discussed in review Anon., 'Glorious Failure', *Building Design*, no.742, 7 June 1985, n.p.
78 Anon., 'Glorious Failure', ibid. See also Hofer, Nina, and Kipnis, Jeffrey, eds, *Peter Eisenman: Fin D'Ou T Hou S*, Folio 5, Architectural Association, London, 1985.
79 The Grand Buildings first stage results were known by August 1985, and the development of the paintings for the scheme was completed for hanging at the GA Gallery Tokyo in late September that year.
80 See Lyotard, *Les Immatériaux*, op.cit. Discussed in review by Pelissier, Alain, 'Les Immatériaux', *Techniques et Architecture*, vol.359, April/May 1985, pp 134 and 141.
81 See Lyotard, *Les Immatériaux*, op.cit. Discussed in review Pelissier, 'Les Immatériaux', op.cit.
82 Lyotard, Jean-François, *The Postmodern Condition: A Report on Knowledge* (1979 in French), trans., Bennington, Geoffrey, and Massumi, Brian, University of Minnesota Press, Minneapolis, Minn., 1984.
83 See explanations in Rajchman, John, 'Jean-François Lyotard's Underground Aesthetics', *October*, no.86, Autumn 1998, pp 3–18.
84 There were different paths through the exhibition. Viewers were given headsets where recorded sound/music was delivered in differing manners in relation to the path chosen. Viewers were also given a magnetic strip that recorded their passage and physical response to what happened on their passage through the exhibition. See Hudek, Anthony, 'From Over- to Sub-Exposure: The Anamnesis of Les Immatériaux', *Tate Papers*, Tate's Online Research Journal, no.12, 2009, https://www.tate.org.uk/research/tate-papers/12/from-over-to-sub-exposure-the-anamnesis-of-les-immateriaux (accessed 23 November 2021).

4
Body, Sensation and the Immaterial in Architecture: Office Building on Kurfürstendamm 70, Berlin

1 Lyotard, Jean-François, *Les Immatériaux*, 28 March to 15 July 1985, Centre de Création Industrielle, Grande Gallerie du Centre national d'art et la culture George Pompidou, Paris. There were a series of catalogues and publications that can be seen at https://www.centrepompidou.fr/fr/programme/agenda/evenement/cRyd8q (accessed 24 November 2021).
2 See Obrist, Hans Ulrich, 'Philippe Parreno in interview with Hans Ulrich Obrist', in *Gasthof 2002 Städelschule Frankfurt/M*, Staatliche Hochschule, Städelschule, Frankfurt am Main, 2003, pp 98–106.
3 See the summation in McDowell, Tara, 'Les Immatériaux: A Conversation with Jean-François Lyotard and Bernard Blistène', *e-flux Criticism*, https://www.e-flux.com/criticism/235949/les-immatriaux-a-conversation-with-jean-franois-lyotard-and-bernard-blistne. The extended interview was published as Blistène, Bernard, 'A Conversation with Jean-François Lyotard', *Flash Art*, vol.121, 1985, pp 32–5.
4 See discussion in Chapter 3, p.73.
5 See Koolhaas, Rem, *Delirious New York*, Oxford University Press, New York, 1978. See also Hadid, Zaha, 'Diploma Unit 9', *Architectural Association, School of Architecture Prospectus, 1981–82 and 1983–84*, Architectural Association, London, 1981 and 1983, p. unnumbered.
6 See Lyotard, Jean-François, 'After Six Months of Work... (1984)', in Hui, Yuk, and Broeckmann, Andreas, eds, *30 Years After Les Immatériaux: Art, Science, and Theory*, Meson Press, Hybrid Publishing, Lüneburg, 2015, pp 46ff. There is a note after this translation that becomes important to Hadid's possible attendance; the text is based on the transcript, in French, of a talk that Jean-François Lyotard gave in Spring 1984, ibid., p.66.
7 Virilio, Paul, 'Une ville surexposée', *Change International*, vol.1, December 1983, pp 19–22; and Daghini, Giairo, 'Babel-Métropole', *Change International*, vol.1, December 1983, pp 23–6.
8 See Lyotard, 'After Six Months of Work', op.cit.
9 The date for submission of the final designs was 22 July 1986 and judging was concluded on 28 July 1986. See Zaha Hadid Architects and Betsky, Aaron, 'Project Information', *Zaha Hadid: The Complete Buildings and Projects*, Thames and Hudson and Rizzoli, London and New York, 1998, p.172. Good graphic coverage of this scheme can be found in Levene, Richard, and Cecilia, Fernando, eds, *El Croquis 52: Zaha Hadid 1983/1991*, El Croquis Editorial, Madrid, 1991, pp 58–65.
10 While most participating architects were from Germany, Zaha Hadid (UK) and Helmut Jahn (USA) were the two international architects to be invited.
11 The full list of members was supplied in briefing documents and included: Jürgen Laschinski, Bernd Faskel, Professor Heinrich Klotz, Rem Koolhaas, Peter Schiansky, Stefan Schroth, Hartmut Behrendt, Friedrich Finkmann, Alfons Geisler, Horst-Georg Lüders and Herbert Fink. ZHF Archive RUB 16, Folio 5, KB 864.
12 Zaha Hadid Architects, 'Zaha Hadid, Office Building in Berlin', *AA Files*, no.12, Summer 1986, pp 29–34.

13 The poster for the exhibition, 'Entwurf Zaha M. Hadid at the Aedes, Gutachten Kurfürstendamm 70/ Adenauerplatz' gives the dates as 23 September to 10 October 1986. Copies of the poster are held by Piers Smerin, Michael Wolfson and Brian Ma Siy.

14 The exhibition was titled *Zaha Hadid, the Tension Builds*, Max Protetch Gallery, New York, 9 June to 10 July 1987. Brian Ma Siy has a print of the exhibition poster and catalogue from Zaha 20/3/87 signed with a note. The exhibition included Grand Buildings, IBA Block 2, West Berlin, Kurfürstendamm Office Building, West Berlin. A review of the exhibition noted that there were 87 drawings in the exhibition. See Phillips, Patricia C., 'Zaha Hadid', *Artforum International*, vol.26, no.2, October 1987, https://www.artforum.com/print/reviews/198708/zaha-hadid-61905 (accessed 25 February 2022).

15 The critique of the working capabilities of, and general misogyny toward, Hadid as a female architect became more explicit in Hadid's project for the Cardiff Bay Opera House some years later, see Crickhowell, Nicholas, *Opera House Lottery: Zaha Hadid and the Cardiff Bay Project*, University of Wales, Cardiff, 1997.

16 See review, Dietsch, Deborah, 'Beyond the Peak', *Architectural Record*, June 1987, p.120.

17 Lebbeus Woods's review of this exhibition responded directly to this quotation in Dietsch's review, suggesting that such claims from the profession were based on Hadid's growing influence in architecture schools and amongst young practitioners. See Woods, Lebbeus, 'Zaha Hadid: The Tension Builds at Max Protetch Gallery', *A+U Architecture and Urbanism*, vol.9, no.204, 1987, pp 4–8.

18 Hadid discussed this more extensively with Alvin Boyarsky in 1986. See Hadid, Zaha, and Boyarsky, Alvin, 'Post Peak Conversations with Zaha Hadid, 1983 & 1986', in Futagawa, Yukio, ed., *GA Architect 5, Zaha M. Hadid*, A.D.A. Edita, Tokyo, 1986, p.19.

19 Brian Ma Siy remembers searching for the new office, in correspondence with Ma Siy, 9 June 2020.

20 Noted in ZHA, 'Zaha Hadid, Office Building in Berlin', op.cit.; ZHA and Betsky, *Zaha Hadid: The Complete Buildings and Projects*, op.cit., p.172.

21 In correspondence with Michael Wolfson, 21 September 2023.

22 ZHA, 'Zaha Hadid, Office Building in Berlin', op.cit., pp 30–31 especially.

23 In correspondence with Piers Smerin, 25 September 2023.

24 In correspondence with Michael Wolfson, 21 September 2023.

25 Each of the group retains a copy of this poster.

26 In correspondence with David Gomersall, 20 September 2023.

27 In conversation with David Gomersall, 22 November 2019.

28 In correspondence with Piers Smerin, 11 July 2022.

29 It was Kurfürstendamm 70 that was included in the publications by Academy Press for this symposium. See Papadakis, Andreas, ed., *Deconstruction in Architecture*, *Architectural Design* (*AD*), vol.58, no.3/4, 1988, pp 40–45; and cover; Papadakis, Andreas, Cooke, Catherine, and Benjamin, Andrew, eds, *Deconstruction Omnibus Volume*, Academy Editions, London, 1989, pp 208–13; and Norris, Christopher, and Benjamin, Andrew, *What is Deconstruction?* Academy Editions/St. Martin's Press, London, 1988, p.7.

30 See Johnson, Philip, and Wigley, Mark, *Deconstructivist Architecture*, Museum of Modern Art, New York, 1988.

31 See Zaha Hadid in conversation with Nicolai Ouroussoff, in *Artforum*, February 1995, https://www.artforum.com/print/199502/urban-flight-zaha-hadid-s-modern-cities-33255 (accessed 29 October 2021).

32 Virilio, Paul, 'The Overexposed City', in Crary, Jonathan, et al., eds, *Zone 1:2*, Urzone, New York, 1986, pp 15–31.

33 Both Eisenman and Koolhaas are included in the 'Questionnaire' section of *Zone 1:2*, ibid., pp 440 and 448 respectively.

34 See Virilio, 'The Overexposed City', op.cit., pp 29–30. See also Venturi, Robert, Scott-Brown, Denise, and Izenour, Steven, *Learning from Las Vegas*, The MIT Press, Cambridge, Mass., 1977.

35 By 1985 Hadid had travelled with students and colleagues from the AA to Russia several times. In conversation with Michael Wolfson, Brian Ma Siy, Madelon Vriesendorp and Zoe Zenghelis from 2016 to 2019. She had also frequented many Suprematist exhibitions in North America, Europe and England.

36 See comments on Alexander Rodchenko in previous chapter, p.68ff.

37 See 'Zaha Hadid and Suprematism: Tate Talks', a discussion between multiple award-winning architect Zaha Hadid and Achim Borchardt-Hume, Head of Exhibitions at Tate Modern and curator of Malevich Exhibition, 30 October 2014, https://www.youtube.com/watch?v=GF_qPKnrrHo (accessed 13 December 2021).

38 'Zaha Hadid and Suprematism: Tate Talks', ibid.

39 The one used in this chapter was presented to Alvin Boyarsky and is dated September 1986. See Marjanović, Igor, and Howard, Jan, ed., *Drawing Ambience: Alvin Boyarsky and the Architectural Association*, Mildred Lane Kemper Art Museum, St. Louis, Museum of Art, Rhode Island, and University of Chicago Press, Chicago, 2014, p.77.

40 ZHA, 'Zaha Hadid, Office Building in Berlin', op.cit. See titles in ZHA and Betsky, *Zaha Hadid: The Complete Buildings and Projects*, op.cit., p.37.

41 See review, Dietsch, 'Beyond the Peak', op.cit.

42 See discussions of the 'whoosh' in earlier chapters, p.40ff.

43 Woods, 'Zaha Hadid: The Tension Builds', op.cit., p.8.

44 'Zaha Hadid and Suprematism: Tate Talks', op.cit.

45 See comments by Gomersall, op.cit.

46 Hadid, Zaha, 'Plane Sailing', *The Royal Academy of the Arts Magazine*, 22 July 2014, see https://www.royalacademy.org.uk/article/zaha-hadid-ra-on-the-influence-of (accessed 3 March 2022).

47 Hadid, Zaha, and Schumacher, Patrik, *Zaha Hadid and Suprematism*, Hatje Cantz, Zurich, 2012. This Malevich painting is owned by the gallery so may have been preferred in their exhibition. *The Great Utopia* catalogue is an important difference in their consideration of Russian art. Although Hadid had been commissioned to design the exhibition and its hanging for the Guggenheim, she had less curatorial influence. For comparison of inclusions, see Calnek, Anthony, in Solomon R. Guggenheim Museum, et al., *The Great Utopia: The Russian and Soviet Avant-Garde, 1915–1932*, Guggenheim Museum, et al., New York, 1992.

48 Malevich's *Yellow Plane in Dissolution* is more typically the example from this period used. It had been published in Golding, John, 'The Black Square', *Studio International Journal of Modern Art*, March/April 1975, p.103, a copy of which is in the AA Library suggesting Hadid would be aware of it as an example from her student days.

49 For Alexander Rodchenko's *Non-Objective Composition*, see Nakov, Andrei, *Avant-Garde Russe*, Universe Books, New York, 1986, Plate 60. Nakov was to later write an essay for Hadid's exhibition at Galerie Gmurzynska in 2012. See Hadid and Schumacher, *Zaha Hadid and Suprematism*, op.cit.

50 Schmidt, Katharina, and Salzmann, Siegfried, eds, *Alexander Rodtschenko und Warwara Stepanowa*, Ministerium für Kultur der UdSSR, Moskau, Wilhelm Lehmbruck Museum der Stadt Duisburg und Staatliche Kunsthalle Baden-Baden, Duisburg, 1983.

51 In discussion with Nicholas Boyarsky, 26 November 2019. In the catalogue the image is photographed on the cover as well as included on p. 139. See Schmidt and Salzmann, eds, *Alexander Rodtschenko und Warwara Stepanowa*, op.cit.

52 Douglas, Charlotte, 'Supremus – The Dissolution of Sensation', in Hadid and Schumacher, *Zaha Hadid and Suprematism*, op.cit., pp 84–9.

53 See Lyotard, 'After Six Months of Work', op.cit.

54 Virilio, 'The Overexposed City', op.cit., p.29.

55 Venturi, Scott-Brown, and Izenour, *Learning from Las Vegas*, op.cit, p.13.

56 Virilio, 'The Overexposed City', op.cit., p.25.

57 While the *AA Files* article reproduced this in black and white, it was printed in colour in Dietsch, 'Beyond the Peak', op.cit., p.129. By the 1988 publication of *Deconstruction in Architecture*, there is further development of its elements into a more abstracted version titled *Main Facade and Balcony Study*. See Hadid, 'Two Recent Projects for Berlin and Hong Kong', in Papadakis, ed., *Deconstruction in Architecture*, *Architectural Design*, op.cit., pp 44–5. The unrendered drawing for this painting was reproduced in Levene and Cecilia, eds, *El Croquis 52*, op.cit., p.64. It is in the collection of the Deutsches Architekturmuseum, Frankfurt.

58 An alternative example where this is emphasised can be seen in techno-fantasies of Archigram from the 1970s or by Richard Rogers and Renzo Piano for the drawings of the Centre Pompidou completed in 1977.

59 Like Malevich's *Dissolution of a Plane*, his *Red Square* was prominently displayed in Hadid and Schumacher's exhibition at Galerie Gmurzynska in 2010. See Hadid and Schumacher, *Zaha Hadid and Suprematism*, op.cit.

60 See Nakov, Andrei, 'Kazimir Malevich, Carré Rouge', in Hadid and Schumacher, *Zaha Hadid and Suprematism*, op.cit., pp 94–5.

61 It is this story that Hadid wanted to include in the context of her exhibition in 2010. See Nakov, 'Kazimir Malevich, Carré Rouge', ibid.

62 The art of casting shadows in architecture is known through sciagraphy. It was commonly learned through texts like Ronald A. Center, *Sciagraphy: Architectural Shadow Projection*, Cassell, Melbourne, 1967, or similar.

63 Methods explained in architectural drawing books at the time, such as Reekie, Fraser, *Draughtsmanship: Drawing Techniques for Graphic Communications in Architecture and Building*, Edward Arnold, London, 1969, pp 153ff.

64 See Levene and Cecilia, *El Croquis 52*, op.cit., p.64.

65 Rykwert lectured at the AA, but also by that time had a following of his ex-students who would have used similar analogies. See his discussions

66 Vesalius, Andreas, *De humani corporis fabrica libri septem* (*On the Fabric of the Human Body in Seven Books*), Johannes Oporinus, Basel, 1543, p.181.
67 Rykwert in *The First Moderns*, op.cit., uses an engraving from James Winslow's 'The Anatomised Human Body on a Locational Grid', p.44.
68 See Lyotard's catalogue entries for the room where Hadid and Koolhaas's paintings were exhibited in Part 3, 'Introduction: Architecture's Mediated Presence', *Les Immatériaux, Inventaire*, Centre de Création Industrielle, Grande Gallerie du Centre national d'art et la culture George Pompidou, Paris, 1985, pp 4–5.
69 This title was used by Lyotard, see Lyotard, 'Architecture Plane', *Les Immatériaux, Inventaire*, ibid., pp nn.
70 See Lyotard, 'Architecture Plane', ibid., pp nn.
71 See Lyotard, 'Architecture Plane', ibid., pp nn.
72 Evans, Robin, 'Translations from Drawing to Building', *AA Files*, no.12, Summer 1986, pp 3–18. Reprinted as Evans, Robin, 'Translations from Drawing to Building', in *Translation from Drawing to Building and Other Essays*, Architectural Association, London, 1997, pp 160ff.
73 Buchanan, Peter, and Davis, Colin, 'Ambience and Alchemy, Alvin Boyarsky Interviewed', *Architectural Review*, vol.174, October 1983, p.28. This approach is discussed by Boyarsky, Nicholas, 'We Fight the Battle with the Drawings on the Wall', in Marjanović and Howard, *Drawing Ambience*, op.cit., pp 139–41.
74 There is no direct allusion to Lyotard in Evans's text, but he would have been aware of the exhibition as it had involved both Hadid and Koolhaas from the AA, and Peter Eisenman who visited the AA to lecture coincident with the exhibition opening in Paris.
75 Evans, 'Translations from Drawing to Building', op.cit., p.180.
76 Evans, 'Translations from Drawing to Building', op.cit., p.186.
77 Quoted in a review of the *Deconstruction in Art and Architecture* symposium at the Tate. See Hatton, Brian, 'Fractal Geometry', *Building Design*, vol.879, 1 April 1988, p.2.
78 Hadid, Zaha, 'Plane Sailing', op.cit.
79 While saying this there is one early 20th-century film that experimented with this spatiality. It is Hans Richter's *Vormittagsspuk* (*Ghosts Before Breakfast*) of 1928, where there is a similar sense of staccato reception of movement. See https://www.youtube.com/watch?v=bc2eDeYRglM (accessed 30 March 2022).
80 Virilio, 'The Overexposed City', op.cit., p.21. There are reflections of Malevich in these statements. See Chapter 2 for Malevich's statements on speed, p.46.
81 Virilio, 'The Overexposed City', ibid., p.29.
82 This is discussed in Chapter 2, p.46. See Malevich, Kazimir, *From Cubism and Futurism to Suprematism: The New Painterly Realism*, 1915; although dated on the cover as 1916, it was released in November of 1915. See its inclusion in translation in Andersen, Troels, ed., *K.S. Malevich, Essays on Art, 1915–1933*, trans., Glowacki-Prus, Xenia, and McMillin, Arnold, Rapp & Whiting, London, 1968, pp 19–41.
83 See Boyarsky's approach crystalised in his interview in Buchanan and Davis, 'Ambience and Alchemy', op.cit., pp 27–31. See also the exploration of this in Marjanović, Igor, 'Drawing Ambience', in Marjanović and Howard, *Drawing Ambience*, op.cit., pp 23–57.

5
Spatial Force – Architecture as Urban Impact: Vitra Fire Station

1 Johnson, Philip, and Wigley, Mark, *Deconstructivist Architecture*, Museum of Modern Art, New York, 1988, pp 68–79.
2 Drawings in the ZHF Archive are dated from December 1988. However, the scheme is already quite developed by this stage suggesting a commissioning date earlier in that year.
3 See the interest developed at conferences during 1988 with symposia and exhibitions held in London and North America. There was also a symposium at the Tate earlier in 1988. Its inclusions were the focus of Papadakis, Andreas, ed., *Deconstruction in Architecture*, *Architectural Design* (*AD*), vol.58, no.3/4, 1988. It was later to be combined as *Deconstruction in Architecture II and III* in Papadakis, Andreas, Cooke, Catherine, and Benjamin, Andrew, eds, *Deconstruction Omnibus Volume*, Academy Editions, London, 1989. In response to the need for further explanation after *Deconstruction in Architecture*, Papadakis also commissioned the booklet Norris, Christopher, and Benjamin, Andrew, *What is Deconstruction?* Academy Editions/St. Martin's Press, London, 1988.
4 Apart from the writings by Jacques Derrida, some of which had been translated into English, for English-speaking audiences of the 1980s, deconstruction was primarily introduced through the writings of Christopher Norris. See Norris, Christopher, *Deconstruction: Theory & Practice*, Methuen, London and New York, 1982; *The Deconstructive Turn: Essays in the Rhetoric of Philosophy*, Methuen, London and New York, 1983.
5 See https://www.moma.org/calendar/exhibitions/2044 (accessed 1 February 2022). This was later to be developed into the book Hitchcock, Henry-Russell, and Johnson, Philip, *The International Style: Architecture Since 1922*, W.W. Norton, New York, 1932, and then to Hitchcock, Henry-Russell, and Johnson, Philip, *The International Style*, W.W. Norton, London and New York, 1966.
6 See poster in Papadakis, *Deconstruction in Architecture*, *Architectural Design*, op.cit, p.6.
7 Johnson and Wigley, *Deconstructivist Architecture*, op.cit. Wigley had previously published an article exploring the changing status of architecture in recent philosophical discussion. See Wigley, Mark, 'Postmortem Architecture, the Taste of Derrida', *Perspecta*, vol.23, 1987, pp 156–72.
8 There were a number of published reviews for the Tate symposium: see Lodge, David, 'Deconstruction: Will Deconstruction be the Architectural "ism" of the 1990s?', *The Guardian* (London), 8 April 1988, p.25 (this was later printed in full within Papadakis, Cooke and Benjamin, eds, *Deconstruction Omnibus Volume*, op.cit., pp 88–90); Hatton, Brian, 'Fractal Geometry', *Building Design*, vol.879, 1 April 1988, p.2; and Bolle, Eric, 'Deconstructivisme, Probleem of Plezier?', *De Architect*, vol.19, no.5, 1988, pp 32–5; amongst others. The speakers at the symposium held in New York at MoMA can be found at https://www.moma.org/momaorg/shared/pdfs/docs/press_archives/6561/releases/MOMA_1988_0064_65.pdf (accessed 23 September 2023).
9 The publication of the interview in full was not included in the initial publication associated with the symposium but became prominent in the 1989 edition, Papadakis, Cooke and Benjamin, *Deconstruction Omnibus Volume*, op.cit., pp 71–5.
10 See Papadakis, Cooke and Benjamin, ibid., pp 76–8.
11 Jacques Derrida, quoted within the review of the symposium by Hatton, 'Fractal Geometry', op.cit. It differs slightly from the complete interview as printed in Papadakis, Cooke and Benjamin, op.cit.
12 Derrida in discussion with Norris, in Papadakis, Cooke and Benjamin, op.cit., p.73.
13 See 'Interview, Alvin Boyarsky Talks with Zaha Hadid (October and December 1987)', in Celant, Germano, and Ramirez-Montagut, Mónica, eds, *Zaha Hadid*, Guggenheim Museum Publications, New York, 2006, p.49.
14 See *Deconstructivist Architects*, Michael Blackwood Productions, 1989; https://michaelblackwoodproductions.com/project/deconstructivist-architects/ (accessed 6 September 2023).
15 *Deconstructivist Architects*, ibid.
16 See Derrida in discussion with Norris, in Papadakis, Cooke and Benjamin, op.cit., p.73. The statement 'form follows function' derived from Sullivan, Louis, 'The Tall Office Building Artistically Considered, 1896', see Benton, Tim, and Benton, Charlotte, with Sharp, Dennis, *Form and Function: A Source Book for the History of Architecture and Design 1890–1939*, Crosby Lockwood Staples, London, 1975, pp 11–14.
17 Hadid's interview is published as Hadid, Zaha M., 'Heut gibt es keinen Plaz mehr für Visionen, für visionäres Denken', in Noever, Peter, *Weiner Architektur-gespräche*, Ernst & Sohn, Berlin, 1991, pp 23–30.
18 In presenting her projects in a lecture at SCI-Arc, Los Angeles, USA, Hadid avoids this link. See https://channel.sciarc.edu/browse/zaha-hadid-march-16-1993 (accessed 6 September 2023).
19 It was a critique of attitudes narrated most clearly by Rykwert, Joseph, *The Idea of a Town: The Anthology of Urban Form in Rome, Italy and the Ancient World*, Princeton University Press, Princeton, N.J., 1976 and The MIT Press, Cambridge, Mass., 1988, as well as those of Krier.
20 From Descartes, René, *Discourse on Method*, as quoted by Benjamin, Andrew, 'Derrida, Architecture and Philosophy', in Papadakis, *Deconstruction in Architecture*, *Architectural Design*, op.cit., p.8.
21 Benjamin, 'Derrida, Architecture and Philosophy', ibid., p.9. This section of Descartes had also been used by Lyotard in his rationalisation of the exhibition *Les Immatériaux* in 1984; see Lyotard, Jean-François, 'After Six Months of Work… (1984)', in Hui, Yuk, and Broeckmann, Andreas, eds, *30 Years after Les Immatériaux: Art, Science, and Theory*, Meson Press, Hybrid Publishing, Lüneburg, 2015, pp 34–5.
22 Molteni, Enrico, 'Architettura per tutti gli usi: la collezione Vitra a Weil am Rhein' ('Architecture for a Multitude of Uses: The Vitra Campus in Weil am Rhein'), *Casabella*, vol.74, no.788, April 2010, pp 16–37 and 107–9.

23. Molteni, 'Architettura per tutti gli usi', ibid.
24. Molteni, 'Architettura per tutti gli usi', ibid.
25. See Noever, Peter, ed., *Architecture in Transition: Between Deconstruction and New Modernism*, Prestel Verlag, Munich, 1991, pp 60–61.
26. This point is confirmed in his interview, but also in the interview 'Zaha Hadid interviewed by GA', with Futagawa, Yoshio, in Futagawa, Yukio, ed., *Zaha M. Hadid, GA Document Extra 03*, Global Architecture, A.D.A. Edita, Tokyo, 1995, p.66. It is confirmed by Rolf Fehlbaum in later interviews, see Adam, Hubertus, 'The Client as Curator', in Mateo Kries, ed., *The Vitra Campus: Architecture Design Industry*, Vitra Design Museum, Weil am Rhein, 2013, p.188. See also Bingham, Neil, 'Collected by the Chairman', *Apollo: The International Magazine for Collectors*, September 2007, pp 26–30.
27. Molteni, 'Architettura per tutti gli usi', op.cit.
28. The modification of the Fire Station by Hadid to turn it into an exhibition/visitors' centre was announced in the architectural press in a note titled 'Chairs Take over Zaha's Fire Station', *Building Design*, 12 May 1995. A Vitra spokesperson confirmed that the city of Weil am Rhein had enlarged their fire brigade and that the factory no longer had need for an internal service.
29. Hadid in Noever, *Architecture in Transition*, op.cit., p.61.
30. See Nägeli, Walter, ed., *Zaha Hadid: Vitra Fire Station*, Aedes, Berlin, 1992, p.48.
31. It is included in Levene, Richard, and Cecilia, Fernando, eds, *El Croquis 52: Zaha Hadid 1983/1991*, El Croquis Editorial, Madrid, 1991, p.111.
32. Nägeli, *Zaha Hadid: Vitra Fire Station*, op.cit., p.30.
33. See Jodidio, Philip, *Hadid: Complete Works 1979–2009*, Taschen, Hong Kong, 2009, p.137.
34. In correspondence with Brian Ma Siy, 17 April 2022. The MAK had reopened in stages. The exhibition of architectural drawings of contemporary architects was most likely included at the same time as the opening of Vito Acconci's *The City Inside Us*, from 29 August 1993. See Noever, Peter, *Vito Acconci: The City Inside Us*, Österreichisches Museum für Angewandte Kunst, Vienna, 1993. In an article in *The New York Times* the sequencing of openings is mentioned. See Hofmann, Paul, 'Vienna's Decorative Spirit in Tables and Teapots', *The New York Times*, Section 5, p.23.
35. Hadid and Futagawa, *GA Document Extra 03*, op.cit., p.72.
36. In correspondence with Ma Siy, op.cit.
37. In correspondence with Nicola Cousins, 27 April 2022.
38. Within the Zaha Hadid Foundation Archive there are a series of coloured swatches that test the colours and tones. The largest is the final chartreuse green carefully completed using several vertically and horizontally layered washes to achieve a solid colour. See RUB 8/ Portfolio 4/ VI 901.
39. Zaha Hadid Architects and Betsky, Aaron, *Zaha Hadid: The Complete Buildings and Projects*, Thames and Hudson and Rizzoli, London and New York, 1998, p.24. See discussion of the terminology of this aerial view in the Conclusion to this book.
40. Zaha Hadid speaking at SCI-Arc, Los Angeles, 21 February 1985, op.cit.
41. Hadid speaking at SCI-Arc, ibid.
42. Hadid and Noever, *Weiner Architektur-gespräche*, op.cit., p.25.
43. These comments are discussed at the beginning of Chapter 1.
44. Hadid and Futagawa, *GA Document Extra 03*, op.cit., pp 67 and 70.
45. Hadid and Noever, *Weiner Architektur-gespräche*, op.cit., p.25.
46. Hadid and Futagawa, *GA Document Extra 03*, op.cit., p.67.
47. Hadid and Futagawa, *GA Document Extra 03*, op.cit., p.70.
48. Hadid and Noever, *Weiner Architektur-gespräche*, op.cit., pp 24–5.
49. See discussion on Michel de Certeau's claim in Chapter 3, p.68. By this time Hadid's personal knowledge of Virilio is confirmed by their both being involved at the symposium *Architecture Today* chaired by Peter Noever in Vienna in 1990, see Noever, Peter, *Architecture in Transition*, op.cit.
50. Virilio, Paul, 'The Overexposed City', in Crary, Jonathan, et al., eds, *Zone 1:2*, Urzone, New York, 1986, p.30.
51. This title is first used in Jodidio, *Hadid: Complete Works 1979–2009*, op.cit., p.137.
52. In correspondence with Ma Siy, op.cit.
53. Hadid, 'Interview 2004', in Obrist, Hans Ulrich, *Zaha Hadid: The Conversation Series*, Verlag der Buchhandlung Walther König, Cologne, 2007, p.80.
54. See explanation of the history of these agricultural patterns in Braudel, Fernand, *La Méditerranée et le monde méditerranéen à l'époque de Philippe II*, second edition, 2 vols, Armand Colin, Paris, 1966; and *Civilisation matérielle, économie et capitalisme*, Armand Colin, Paris, 1979; and, *L'identité de la France*, 3 vols, Arthaud-Flammarion, Paris, 1986.
55. Nägeli, *Zaha Hadid: Vitra Fire Station*, op.cit.
56. Unpublished papers in the Zaha Hadid Foundation Archive, RUB 21, Portfolio 8, 'Vitra and Landscape'.
57. Unpublished papers, ibid.
58. Unpublished papers, ibid.
59. Unpublished papers, ibid.
60. Unpublished papers, ibid.
61. Unpublished papers, op.cit., 'General Urbanistic Strategy'.
62. These are listed in ZHA and Betsky, *Zaha Hadid: The Complete Buildings and Projects*, op.cit., 'Project Information', pp 172–4.
63. These are listed in 'The Pritzker Architecture Prize 2004', presented to Zaha Hadid, https://usmodernist.org/Hadid-pritzker.pdf (accessed 9 September 2023).
64. Nakamura, Toshio, ed., 'Introduction', *International Building Exhibition Berlin 1987*, A+U, Tokyo, 1987, p.7.
65. Two guides were produced: Nakamura, ibid., focusing on the built schemes, and Kleihues, Josef P., and Klotz, Heinrich, eds, *International Building Exhibition Berlin 1987: Examples of a New Architecture*, Academy Editions, London, 1986, focusing on the architectural drawings.
66. This date is included in ZHA and Betsky, *Zaha Hadid: The Complete Buildings and Projects*, op.cit., pp 38–41 and 172.
67. Its propositions are recounted in De Michelis, Marco, et al., eds, *La Ricostruzione della Città: Berlino – IBA 1987*, XVII Trienalle di Milano and Electa, Milan, 1987, © 1985.
68. Unpublished papers ZHF, op.cit., 'General Urbanistic Strategy'.
69. Krier, Léon, 'Intermediate School Unit 10, Projects on the City', *Architectural Association School of Architecture, Projects Review 1974–75*, Architectural Association, London, 1975, unnumbered.
70. Blazwick, Iwona, 'Acknowledgements', in Brown, Linda, and Sudjic, Deyan, eds, *Metropolis: New British Architecture and the City*, Belmont Press, London, 1988.
71. See De Michelis, Marco, et al., *La Ricostruzione della Città*, op.cit., pp 42–3.
72. Rowe, Colin, and Koetter, Fred, *Collage City*, The MIT Press, Cambridge, Mass., 1978.
73. See the recounting of their association in Szacha, Léa-Catherine, 'Roma Interrotta: Postmodern Rome as the Source of Fragmented Narratives', in Holdaway, Dom, and Trentin, Felippo, eds, *Rome, Postmodern Narratives of a Cityscape*, Routledge, London, 2015, p.161.
74. See Beck, Haig, ed., and Graves, Michael, guest ed., *Roma Interrotta*, Architectural Design Profile 20 (*AD*), vol.49, no.3–4, 1979.
75. For an investigation of the original survey drawings and different states of the final plan, see Bevilacqua, Mario, *Roma Nel Secolo Dei Lumi: Architecture erudizione scienza nella Pianta di G.B. Nolli 'celebre geometra'*, Electa Napoli, Naples, 1998.
76. See submissions in Sartogo, Piero, ed., *Roma Interrotta*, Incontri Internazionali D'Arte, Rome, 1978; https://monoskop.org/images/a/a5/Roma_interrotta_1978.pdf (accessed 9 September 2023).
77. See Beck and Graves, *Roma Interrotta*, op.cit. The exhibition was bought to the AA in 1979.
78. Unpublished papers, op.cit., 'Vitra and Landscape'.
79. See Molteni, 'Architettura per tutti gli usi', op.cit.

6
From the Networked Object to the Fluidity of Histories: MAXXI, Rome

1. Hadid, Zaha, and Schumacher, Patrik, 'Latent Utopias', in *Latent Utopias: Experiments with Contemporary Architecture*, Steirischer Herbst, Springer Verlag, Vienna, 2002, p.7.
2. Hadid and Schumacher, *Latent Utopias*, ibid., p.7.
3. Hadid and Schumacher, *Latent Utopias*, ibid., p.8
4. Hadid and Schumacher, *Latent Utopias*, ibid., pp 154–6.
5. During the symposium associated with *Latent Utopias*, software discussed included C++, HTML, 3D Studio Max, Max-script and Maya. By this time ZHA had used 3D Studio Max, Form Z and ModelShop as modelling tools. For the symposium discussion, see Brett Steele and others in Riewe, Roger, ed., *Space Condition: International Architecture Symposium*, Springer, Vienna, 2005, p.151.
6. See The Flash Pack, 'A Brief History of Bullet Time: Aka The Matrix Effect', https://itstheflashpack.com/the-lens/a-brief-history-of-bullet-time-aka-the-matrix-effect/ for a description (accessed 6 October 2023).
7. Hadid responding to questions at a lecture in 2012. Seen in Steele, Brett, 'Anecdote as Evidence: Zaha's World', in Gad, Amira, and Gryczkowska, Agnes, eds, *Reflections on Zaha Hadid*, Serpentine Sackler Gallery, London, 2016, p.140.
8. Hadid, Zaha, 'Interview 2006', in Obrist, Hans

Ulrich, *Zaha Hadid: The Conversation Series*, Verlag der Buchhandlung Walther König, Cologne, 2007, p.89.

9. The competition for MAXXI was a two-staged event with 15 architectural teams shortlisted for Stage Two. Patrik Schumacher dates the announcement of the competition's outcomes as early in 1999. See Schumacher, Patrik, 'The Place of MAXXI in the Œuvre of Zaha Hadid', in Ciorra, Pippo, and Guccione, Margherita, eds, *Zaha Hadid in Italy*, Quodlibet, Rome, 2017, p.32.
10. Architect Steven Holl, an entrant, included a photograph in his reflection of Hadid's career dating the close of Stage Two as 15 October 1998, when he, Jean Nouvel and Hadid had a dinner together to celebrate the close of their presentations. See Holl, Steven, 'New Journey into Space, to Zaha Hadid 31 October 1950 – 31 March 2016', in Gad and Gryczkowska, *Reflections on Zaha Hadid*, op.cit., p.63.
11. See Lynn, Greg, guest ed., *Folding in Architecture*, *Architectural Design Profile* (*AD*), no.102, 1993, which also advertises a translation of Deleuze, Gilles, *The Fold: Leibniz and the Baroque*, trans., Conley, Tom, Athlone Press, London, 1993.
12. Deleuze, Gilles, 'The Fold, Leibniz and the Baroque, The Pleats of Matter', in Lynn, *Folding in Architecture*, ibid., p.17.
13. Deleuze, 'The Fold, Leibniz and the Baroque', ibid., p.19.
14. See Gehry, Frank, and Johnson, Philip, 'Lewis Residence, Cleveland Ohio', in Lynn, *Folding in Architecture*, op.cit., pp 68–73. Explored also in Lynn, Greg, ed., *Archaeology of the Digital: Peter Eisenman, Frank Gehry, Chuck Hoverman, Shoei Yoh*, CCA, Montreal, 2013, pp 147–211, and, https://cca-bookstore.com/collections/e-pub/products/gehry-lewis-residence-gehry-lewis-residence (accessed 18 September 2023).
15. See the wire-framed imagery in Fialová, Irena, ed., *Frank Gehry and Vlado Milunić: Dancing Building*, Zlaty rez, Prague, 2003, pp 127ff.
16. Fialová, *Dancing Building*, ibid., p.127.
17. See these explorations discussed in Jencks, Charles, 'Nonlinear Architecture: New Sciences = New Architecture', in Jencks, Charles, ed., *New Science = New Architecture, AD Profile 129* (*AD*) vol.67, September/October 1997, pp 6–9. See also Carpo, Mario, *The Digital Turn in Architecture 1992–2012*, John Wiley & Sons, West Sussex, 2013, pp 80–107. The focus on new geometries is explored in Davidson, Peter, and Bates, Don, guest eds, *Architecture After Geometry*, *Architectural Design Profile 127* (*AD*), vol.67, no.5/6, May/June 1997.
18. Eisenman, Peter, 'Folding in Time: The Singularity of Rebstock', in Lynn, *Folding in Architecture*, op.cit., pp 22–8. See also Eisenman, Peter, *Unfolding Frankfurt*, Aedes and Ernst & Sohn, Berlin, 1991.
19. The project was first published in Lynn, Greg, 'Multiplicitous and Inorganic Bodies', *Assemblage*, no.19, December 1992, pp 32–49. See also Lynn, *Folding in Architecture*, op.cit., pp 82–5.
20. See Lynn, Greg, *Animate Form*, Princeton Architectural Press, New York, 1999. His earlier lectures at the Architectural Association and his publications discussed the ideas behind curvilinearity but this is the first published graphic explanation.
21. Discussed in Lynn, 'Multiplicitous and Inorganic Bodies', op.cit.
22. Amongst others, see Lynn, Greg, 'Animated Form', Part 1 and 2, 21 January 1997, https://www.aaschool.ac.uk/publicprogramme/whatson/animated-form (accessed 16 February 2022).
23. Many of these experiments and commentary by leading theorists of the period are summated in Steele, Brett, ed., *Corporate Fields: New Office Environments by the AA DRL, AA DRL Documents 1*, Architectural Association, London, 2005.
24. Confirmed in conversation with Patrik Schumacher, 12 February 2020.
25. See Hadid's chronology of lectures and teaching posts listed in 'The Pritzker Architecture Prize 2004', https://usmodernist.org/hadid-pritzker.pdf (accessed 15 August 2023). Many exhibitions coincided with symposia where a broadening group interested in new geometries could openly speculate on its future implementation in architecture.
26. For a summation of pertinent texts of the period, see Carpo, Mario, *The Digital Turn in Architecture*, op.cit. Lynn's presentation at the Architectural Association was combined with philosopher Andrew Benjamin. See Benjamin, Andrew, and Lynn, Greg, 'The Fold 1/2', 14 June 1993, https://www.aaschool.ac.uk/publicprogramme/whatson/the-fold-1-2 (accessed 16 February 2022). This was followed by discussion with Jeff Kipnis and Mark Cousins. See also Lynn, Greg, 'Architectural Curvilinearity: The Folded, the Pliant and the Supple', in Lynn, *Folding in Architecture*, op.cit., pp 8–14.
27. Schumacher, 'The Place of MAXXI in the Œuvre of Zaha Hadid', op.cit., p.33.
28. Schumacher, Patrik, *Digital Hadid: Landscapes in Motion*, Birkhäuser, Basel, 2004, pp 33–4.
29. For discussion of this sketch, see Luscombe, Desley, 'Zaha Hadid's Notebooks: The Role of the Sketch in Architecture's Representation', *The Journal of Architecture*, vol.25, no.3, 2020, pp 252–75.
30. See Elliott, Steven, et al., *Inside 3D Studio Max 2*, vol.1, New Riders Publishing, Indianapolis, Ind., 1998, Chapters 13 and 23 for this capability.
31. Schumacher is quoted in Seabrook, John, 'The Abstractionist', *The New Yorker*, 13 December 2009, http://www.newyorker.com/magazine/2009/12/21/the-abstractionist.
32. Hadid and Schumacher, *Latent Utopias*, op.cit., p.295. The team included: Gianluca Racana, Barbara Pfenningstorff, Ana M. Cajao, Lars Teichmann, Raza Zahid, Adriano De Gioannis, Ken Bostock, Gernot Finselbach, Dillon Lin and Caroline Voet.
33. This was discussed in relation to developments in the office with Paulo Flores, 18 July 2019.
34. In discussion and correspondence with David Gomersall, 26 July 2022 and 22 November 2019.
35. A detail of *Composite Aerial View* is depicted in the Stage Two competition panels, confirming its completion prior to November 1998. There is no nomenclature for these paintings. The term 'Competition Painting' was given for all paintings in Racana, Gianluca, and Janssens, Manon, eds, *MAXXI: Zaha Hadid Architects*, Skira, New York, 2010, pp 24, 25 and 28.
36. Confirmed in correspondence with Gomersall, 26 July 2022. Two panels are missing from the photographed set submitted. This second painting, although not used within the competition panels that are extant, is collated within the ZHA Archive with those completed at that time and may have been featured on the final panels.
37. In conversation with Paul Brislin, 30 November 2019.
38. Zaha Hadid Architects and Betsky, Aaron, *Zaha Hadid: The Complete Buildings and Projects*, Thames and Hudson and Rizzoli, London and New York, 1998, pp 104, 105 and 115.
39. In conversation with Gomersall, 22 November 2022.
40. While assumptions may be made about the apparent visual similarity to images now regulated by software such as Google Earth, it must be remembered that this searchable map engine was launched publicly only in 2005.
41. Especially after the important discussions on sensation, immateriality and speed proffered by Virilio during the late 1980s, see discussion in Chapter 4, pp 93–4.
42. Most likely the result of 3D Studio Max.
43. Mostafavi, Mohsen, in conversation with Hadid, Zaha, 'Landscape as Plan' (2001), in Cecilia, Fernando, and Levene, Richard, eds, *El Croquis: Zaha Hadid 1983–2001*, El Croquis Editorial, Madrid, 2004, p.51.
44. Mostafavi with Hadid, 'Landscape as Plan', ibid.
45. For an exploration of this notion of diagram in painting, see Deleuze, Gilles, *Francis Bacon: The Logic of Sensation*, trans., Smith, Daniel W., University of Minnesota Press, Minneapolis, Minn., 2005, see especially pp 99–110 for the notion of the diagram in painting.
46. See the term used in Hadid and Schumacher, *Latent Utopias*, op.cit., pp 154–5, and also in Schumacher, *Digital Hadid*, op.cit., pp 33–4.
47. It was the 'incomplete' in architectural form that had been discussed by Peter Eisenman, Charles Jencks and Stan Allen in their writings. See a collection of these in Carpo, Mario, *The Digital Turn in Architecture*, op.cit.
48. Venturi, Robert, Scott-Brown, Denise, and Izenour, Steven, *Learning from Las Vegas*, The MIT Press, Cambridge, Mass., 1977, p. 18.
49. Rowe, Colin, and Koetter, Fred, *Collage City*, The MIT Press, Cambridge, Mass., 1978, esp. pp 106ff.
50. See Beck, Haig, ed., and Graves, Michael, guest ed., *Roma Interrotta*, *Architectural Design Profile 20* (*AD*), vol.49, no.3–4, 1979.
51. See Chapter 5 in this book for discussion. See Szacka, Léa-Catherine, 'Roma Interrotta, Postmodern Rome as the Source of Fragmented Narratives', in Holdaway, Dom, and Trentin, Filippo, eds, *Rome, Postmodern Narratives of a Cityscape*, Routledge, London, 2015, pp 155–69.
52. Wigley, Mark, 'Deconstructivist Architecture', in Johnson, Philip, and Wigley, Mark, eds, *Deconstructivist Architecture*, Museum of Modern Art, New York, 1988, p.10.
53. Johnson and Wigley, *Deconstructivist Architecture*, ibid., p.11.
54. Lynn, *Animate Form*, op.cit., pp 16–17.
55. See its inclusion and explanation for why he includes the building amongst the antiquities of Rome in Serlio, Sebastiano, *Book III, On Antiquities*, fol., 67r, 67v, 68r and 68v. See Hart, Vaughan, and Hicks, Peter, trans., *Sebastiano Serlio on Architecture*, vol.1, Yale University Press, New Haven, Conn., 1996, pp 131–4.
56. Its ideality was mentioned by architect Andrea Palladio during the late Renaissance, see Palladio, Andrea, *The Four Books on Architecture* (1570), trans., Tavernor, Robert, and Schofield, Richard, The MIT Press, Cambridge, Mass., 1997, book 3,

Chapter xvii, p.276. For the argument of classical buildings, see the influence of Pythagorean symbolism in buildings like the Pantheon in Rome, argued in Joost-Gaugier, Christiane L., *Measuring Heaven: Pythagoras and His Influence on Thought and Art in Antiquity and the Middle Ages*, Cornell, Ithaca, New York, 2006, pp 166–81.

57 See the argument presented by Wittkower, Rudolf, 'Brunelleschi and "Proportion in Perspective"', *Journal of the Warburg and Courtauld Institutes*, vol.16, no.3/4, 1953, pp 275–91.

58 Analysis of this type of geometry in painting and architecture would have been known to contemporary audiences through Panofsky, Erwin, *Perspective as Symbolic Form*, trans., Wood, Christopher S., Zone, New York, 1997.

59 See Rajchman's discussion of Deleuze's use of Libniz in Rajchman, John, *Constructions*, The MIT Press, Cambridge, Mass., 1998, pp 14–15.

60 Although when constructed this notion was not complete, the building's association with the Four Fountains, defining the intersection of roads, signified urban concerns. See Guerra, Giovanni, and Nebbia, Cesare, *Perspective View of Rome*, Fresco, Salone Sistino, Vatican Library, Vatican, 1588–89; see Frutaz, Pietro Amato, *Le Piante di Roma*, Instituto di Studi Romano, Rome, 1962.

61 It is an idea explored earlier in Lynn, 'Architectural Curvilinearity: The Folded, the Pliant and the Supple', and also in the explanation of 'Stranded Sears Tower', in *Folding in Architecture*, op.cit., pp 8–15 and 83.

62 See Lynn, Greg, 'An Advanced Form of Movement', in Davidson, Peter, and Bates, Donald, guest eds, *Architecture After Geometry*, *Architectural Design* (*AD*), vol.67, no.5/6, May/June 1997, pp 54–7.

63 See Mostafavi with Hadid, 'Landscape as Plan', op.cit., p.48.

64 See the transformation and data sheets in Racana and Janssens, eds, *MAXXI: Zaha Hadid Architects*, op.cit.

65 The triangle when drawn in axonometric would infer either. It is only with other visual cues that resolution would be known.

66 See this presented by McEwan, Indra, *Vitruvius: Writing the Body of Architecture*, The MIT Press, Cambridge, Mass., 2003.

67 Hadid and Schumacher, *Latent Utopias*, op.cit., p.154.

68 Hadid and Schumacher, *Latent Utopias*, op.cit., pp 154–5.

69 Mostafavi with Hadid, 'Landscape as Plan', op.cit., p.42.

70 Hadid, 'Interview 2004', in Obrist, *Zaha Hadid: The Conversation Series*, op.cit., p.19.

71 See Wong, Tony, et al., eds, *Ubiquitous Urbanism, Total Architecture: The Tokyo Experiment: A Studio in Global Master Planning with Zaha M. Hadid at Columbia University Graduate School of Architecture, Planning and Preservation*, Columbia Books of Architecture, New York, 1994.

72 Lyotard, Jean-François, *Les Immatériaux*, 28 March to 15 July 1985, Centre de Création Industrielle, Grande Gallerie du Centre national d'art et la culture George Pompidou, Paris. There were a series of catalogues and publications that can be seen at https://www.centrepompidou.fr/fr/programme/agenda/evenement/cRyd8q (accessed 24 November 2021). See Chapters 3, 4 and 5 for discussion.

73 See Deleuze, Gilles, and Guattari, Félix, *A Thousand Plateaus: Capitalism and Schizophrenia*, trans., Massumi, Brian, University of Minnesota Press, Minneapolis, Minn., 1987.

74 See Rowe and Koetter, *Collage City*, op.cit., p.116.

75 See Lynn, *Animate Form*, op.cit., pp 8–43. Lynn was at pains to include what he called the two-degree spline that resulted in a poly-line of 'straights'. These introduced concepts of weaving that could be achieved in forms with obtuse and acute angles. See, for example, Eisenman, 'Folding in Time', in Lynn, ed., *Folding in Architecture*, op.cit., pp 22–7.

76 Rajchman, 'Out of the Fold', in Lynn, ed., *Folding in Architecture*, op.cit., p.61.

77 Hadid, 'Interview 2004', in Obrist, *Zaha Hadid: The Conversation Series*, op.cit., p.19.

78 See discussions of a differing consideration of the fold in Eisenman's Rebstockpark in Rajchman, 'Folding', in *Constructions*, op.cit., pp 18–19. Rajchman concludes that Eisenman's fold can be understood as 'visual origami' folded in three dimensions.

79 See discussion in Chapter 2, p.47ff.

80 Especially explained in *Malevich, Kasimir, From Cubism and Futurism to Suprematism: The New Painterly Realism*, 1915. See its inclusion in translation in Bowlt, John, ed., and trans., *Russian Art of the Avant Garde: Theory and Criticism, 1902–1934*, Viking Press, New York, 1976, p.132.

81 Hadid, 'Interview 2001', in Obrist, *Zaha Hadid: The Conversation Series*, op.cit., p.41.

82 Hadid, 'Interview 2001', ibid.

83 Hadid characterises the loss of painting in the AA Symposium, 'Rendering Speculations', an International Symposium at the Architectural Association, 7 May 2010, https://www.youtube.com/watch?v=63GbLuWNt_Q (accessed 13 September 2023).

## Conclusion
## Of Painting and Architecture

1 Steele, Brett, 'Anecdote as Evidence: Zaha's World', in Gad, Amira, and Gryczkowska, Agnes, eds, *Reflections on Zaha Hadid*, Serpentine Sackler Gallery, London, 2016, pp 131–45.

2 See Hadid, Zaha, *Recent Work*, lecture at the AA 25 November 1997, https://www.youtube.com/watch?v=ZcoY4i4P6n0 (accessed 9 October 2023). The image shown in the lecture was the 1983 version of the painting.

3 See Steele, Brett, 'Anecdote as Evidence', op.cit. I have italicised an addition that I included in the quote from her presentation *Recent Work*, op.cit.

4 See Hadid, *Recent Work*, op.cit.

5 It was titled *The World, 1983* and is first seen as a fully coloured painting in Futagawa, Yukio, ed., *GA Architect 5, Zaha M. Hadid*, A.D.A. Edita, Tokyo, 1986, p.112. Earlier publications of the image were grey tone with screened blue elements applied in the printing process. See Hadid, Zaha, and Boyarsky, Alvin, *Zaha Hadid: Planetary Architecture Two*, Architectural Association, London, 1983, loose folio.

6 This image is consistent with the printed grey-scale tonal values of the image as presented in Hadid and Boyarsky, *Zaha Hadid: Planetary Architecture Two*, ibid. While this publication gave the title *The Earth, London 1983*, the included image, *The World, The Eighty-nine Degrees*, was presented to Alvin Boyarsky on 26 March 1984. See Marjanović, Igor, and Howard, Jan, *Drawing Ambience: Alvin Boyarsky and the Architectural Association*, Mildred Lane Kemper Art Museum, St. Louis, Museum of Art, Rhode Island, and University of Chicago Press, Chicago, 2014, p.78.

7 Mostafavi, Mohsen, and Hadid, Zaha, 'Landscape as Plan', in Cecilia, Fernando, and Levene, Richard, eds, *El Croquis, Zaha Hadid 1983–2001*, Croquis Editorial, Madrid, 2004, pp 51–2.

8 This attribute is discussed in Chapter 2, p.47ff.

9 See Malevich, Kazimir, 'From Cubism and Futurism to Suprematism: The New Painterly Realism, 1915', in Bowlt, John, ed., and trans., *Russian Art of the Avant-Garde: Theory and Criticism 1902–1934*, Viking Press, New York, 1976, pp 116–35.

10 See Benjamin, Walter, 'The Rigorous Study of Art', in Jennings, M., et al., eds, *Walter Benjamin: Selected Writings*, trans. Livingstone, R., vol.2, Belknap Press of Harvard University, Cambridge, Mass., 1999, pp 669–70.

11 See Lyotard's catalogue entries for the room where Hadid's and Koolhaas's paintings were exhibited in Part 3, 'Introduction: Architecture's Mediated Presence', *Les Immatériaux, Inventaire*, Centre de Création Industrielle, Centre Pompidou, Paris, 1985, pp 4–5. See also Evans, Robin, 'Translation from Drawing into Building', *AA Files*, no.12, Summer 1986, pp 3–18. Reprinted as Evans, Robin, 'Translation from Drawing into Building', in *Translation from Drawing to Building and Other Essays*, Architectural Association, London, 1997, pp 160ff. Both these ideas are discussed in Chapter 4, p.88ff.

12 Hadid, *Recent Work*, op.cit.

13 See the larger colour version of the painting first explained in Futagawa, *GA Architect 5, Zaha M. Hadid*, op.cit., p.113.

## Selected Bibliography

Alberti, Leon Battista, *On the Art of Building in Ten Books*, trans., Rykwert, Joseph, Leach, Neil, and Tavernor, Robert, The MIT Press, Cambridge, Mass., 1988.

Alberti, Leon Battista, *On Painting*, trans., Spencer, John R., Yale University Press, New Haven, Conn., 1966.

Andersen, Troels, ed., *K.S. Malevich, Essays on Art, 1915–1933*, trans., Glowacki-Prus, Xenia, and McMillin, Arnold, Rapp & Whiting, London, 1968.

Andersen, Troels, ed., *K.S. Malevich, The World as Non-Objectivity: Unpublished Writings 1922–25*, trans., Glowacki-Prus, Xenia, and Little, Edmund, T., Borgen, Copenhagen, 1976.

Anon., 'Grand Exits, a Selection of the 278 Failed Schemes Submitted to the Grand Buildings Competition', *Architects' Journal*, vol.182, no.34/35, 21–28 August 1985, pp 20–25.

Anon., 'Zaha Hadid, Office Building in Berlin', *AA Files*, no.12, Summer 1986, pp 29–34.

Barthes, Roland, 'Sémiologie et Urbanisme', *Architecture d'Aujourd'hui*, no.153, December 1970/January 1971, pp 11–13.

Beck, Haig, ed., and Graves, Michael, guest ed., *Roma Interrotta, Architectural Design Profile 20 (AD)*, vol.49, no.3–4, 1979.

Benjamin, Andrew, 'Malevich and the Avant-Garde', *Malevich: Art and Design Profile 15 (AD)*, vol.5, no.5/6, 1989, pp 55–7.

Benjamin, Walter, 'The Rigorous Study of Art', in Jennings, M., et al., eds, *Walter Benjamin: Selected Writings*, trans., Livingstone, R., vol.2, Belknap Press of Harvard University, Cambridge, Mass., 1999, pp 669–70.

Blistène, Bernard, 'A Conversation with Jean-François Lyotard', *Flash Art*, vol.121, 1985, pp 32–5.

Bois, Yve-Alain, 'Lissitzky, Malevich, and the Question of Space', *Suprematisme*, Gallery Jean Chauvin, Paris, 1977, pp 29–43.

Bowlt, John, ed., and trans., *Russian Art of the Avant-Garde: Theory and Criticism 1902–1934*, Viking Press, New York, 1976.

Boyarsky, Alvin, and Hadid, Zaha, 'Interview, Alvin Boyarsky Talks with Zaha Hadid (October and December 1987)', in Celant, Germano, and Ramirez-Montagut, Mónica, eds, *Zaha Hadid*, Guggenheim Museum Publications, New York, 2006, pp 45–52.

Brown, Linda, and Sudjic, Deyan, eds, *Metropolis: New British Architecture and the City*, Belmont Press, London, 1988.

Buchanan, Peter, and Davis, Colin, 'Ambience and Alchemy, Alvin Boyarsky Interviewed', *Architectural Review*, vol.174, October 1983, pp 27–31.

Burns, Karen, and Morgan, Paul, 'Interview with Zaha Hadid', *Transition*, vol.20, May 1987, pp 17–21.

Calnek, Anthony, et al., eds, *The Great Utopia: The Russian and Soviet Avant-Garde, 1915–1932*, Guggenheim Museum, et al., New York, 1992.

Carpo, Mario, *The Digital Turn in Architecture 1992–2012*, John Wiley & Sons, West Sussex, 2013.

Cecilia, Fernando, and Levene, Richard, eds, *El Croquis: Zaha Hadid 1983–2001*, El Croquis Editorial, Madrid, 2004.

Cook, Peter, 'Reviews of AA Exhibitions: Larger than Life Cedric Price: The Home / Zaha Hadid: 59 Eaton Place', *AA Files*, no.3, January 1983, pp 78–83.

Dalrymple Henderson, Linda, *The Fourth Dimension and Non-Euclidean Geometry in Modern Art*, The MIT Press, Cambridge, Mass., 2013.

Davidson, Peter, and Bates, Don, guest eds, *Architecture After Geometry, Architectural Design (AD)*, vol.67, no.5/6, May/June 1997.

De Certeau, Michel, *The Practice of Everyday Life*, trans., Rendell, Steven, University of California Press, Berkeley, Calif., 1984.

Deleuze, Gilles, *The Fold: Leibniz and the Baroque*, trans., Conley, Tom, Athlone Press, London, 1993.

Deleuze, Gilles, *Francis Bacon: The Logic of Sensation*, trans., Smith, Daniel W., University of Minnesota Press, Minneapolis, Minn., 2005.

Deleuze, Gilles, and Guattari, Félix, *A Thousand Plateaus: Capitalism and Schizophrenia*, trans., Massumi, Brian, University of Minnesota Press, Minneapolis, Minn., 1987.

De Michelis, Marco, et al., eds, *La Ricostruzione dell Città: Berlino – IBA 1987*, XVII Trienalle di Milano and Electa, Milan, 1987, © 1985.

Derrida, Jacques, 'Point de Folie – Maintenant l'Architecture. Bernard Tschumi: La Case Vide – La Villette, 1985', *AA Files*, no.12, 1986, pp 65–75.

Dietsch, Deborah, 'Beyond the Peak', *Architectural Record*, June 1987, pp 120–29.

Eisenman, Peter, *Unfolding Frankfurt*, Aedes and Ernst & Sohn, Berlin, 1991.

Elkins, James, *The Poetics of Perspective*, Cornell, Ithaca, N.Y., 1994.

Evans, Robin, '1975–1980 Projects: From Axes to Violins', *AA Files*, no.1, Winter 1981–82, pp 115–20.

Evans, Robin, 'Translations from Drawing to Building', *AA Files*, no.12, Summer 1986, pp 3–18.

Evans, Robin, 'Architectural Projection', in Blau, Eve, and Kaufman, Edward, eds, *Architecture and its Image: Four Centuries of Architectural Representation, Works from the Canadian Centre for Architecture*, CCA and The MIT Press, Montreal and Cambridge, Mass., 1989, pp 18–35.

Evans, Robin, *Translations from Drawing to Building and Other Essays*, Architectural Association, London, 1997.

Fialová, Irena, ed., *Frank Gehry, Vlado Milunić: Dancing Building*, Zlaty rez, Prague, 2003.

Frampton, Kenneth, 'Two or Three Things I Know About Them: A Note on Manhattanism', *OMA, Architectural Design (AD)*, vol.47, no.5, 1977, pp 315–25.

Frampton, Kenneth, and Kolbowski, Silvia, eds, *Ivan Leonidov*, IAUS and Rizzoli, New York, 1981.

Futagawa, Yukio, ed., *GA Architect 5, Zaha M. Hadid*, A.D.A. Edita, Tokyo, 1986.

Futagawa, Yukio, ed., *Zaha M. Hadid: GA Document Extra 03*, Global Architecture, A.D.A Edita, Tokyo, 1995.

Gad, Amira, and Gryczkowska, Agnes, eds, *Zaha Hadid: Early Paintings and Drawings*, Serpentine Galleries and Koenig Books, London, 2016.

Gad, Amira, and Gryczkowska, Agnes, *Reflections on Zaha Hadid*, Serpentine Galleries and Koenig Books, London, 2016.

Golding, John, 'The Black Square', *Studio International Journal of Modern Art*, March/April 1975, pp 96–106, https://archive.studiointernational.com/SI1975/march-april/vol189-no974.html#p=96.

Hadid, Zaha, *Zaha M. Hadid: Planetary Architecture, Projects 77–81*, Galerie van Rooy, Amsterdam, 1981.

Hadid, Zaha, 'Dynamiser L'Urbain, Concours pour Trafalgar Square, London', *Architecture d'Aujourd'hui*, no.242, December 1985, pp 4–11.

Hadid, Zaha, 'The Calligraphy of the Plan', in Middleton, Robin, ed., *Architectural Associations: The Idea of the City*, Architectural Association and The MIT Press, London and Cambridge, Mass., 1996, pp 64–85.

Hadid, Zaha, 'Plane Sailing', *The Royal Academy of the Arts Magazine*, 22 July 2014, https://www.royalacademy.org.uk/article/zaha-hadid-ra-on-the-influence-of.

Hadid, Zaha, and Boyarsky, Alvin, *Zaha Hadid: Planetary Architecture Two*, Architectural Association, London, 1983, loose folio.

Hadid, Zaha, and Boyarsky, Alvin, 'Post Peak Conversations with Zaha Hadid, 1983 & 1986', in Futagawa, Yukio, ed., *GA Architect 5, Zaha M. Hadid*, A.D.A. Edita, Tokyo, 1986, pp 8–23.

Hadid, Zaha, and Futagawa, Yoshio, 'Zaha Hadid interviewed by GA', in Futagawa, Yukio, ed., *Zaha M. Hadid: GA Document Extra 03*, Global Architecture, A.D.A Edita, Tokyo, 1995, pp 12–21.

Hadid, Zaha, and Schumacher, Patrik, 'Latent Utopias', *Latent Utopias: Experiments with Contemporary Architecture*, Steirischer Herbst, Springer Verlag, Vienna, 2002.

Hadid, Zaha, and Schumacher, Patrik, *Zaha Hadid and Suprematism*, Hatje Cantz, Zurich, 2012.

Holl, Steven, 'New Journey into Space, to Zaha Hadid 31 October 1950 - 31 March 2016', in Gad, Amira, and Gryczkowska, Agnes, eds, *Reflections on Zaha Hadid*, Serpentine Galleries and Koenig Books, London, 2016, pp 54–67.

Hudek, Anthony, 'From Over- to Sub-Exposure: The Anamnesis of Les Immatériaux', *Tate Papers*, Tate's Online Research Journal, no.12, 2009, https://www.tate.org.uk/research/tate-papers/12/from-over-to-sub-exposure-the-anamnesis-of-les-immateriaux.

Jay, Martin, 'Scopic Regimes of Modernity', in Foster, Hal, ed., *Vision and Visuality*, Bay Press, Seattle, Wash., 1988, pp 3–27.

Jencks, Charles, 'Nonlinear Architecture: New Sciences = New Architecture', in Jencks, Charles, ed., *New Science = New Architecture, Architectural Design Profile 129 (AD)*, vol.67, September/October 1997, pp 6–9.

Jencks, Charles, and Baird, George, *Meaning in Architecture*, Braziller, New York, 1970.

Jodidio, Philip, *Zaha Hadid: Complete Works 1979–2009*, Taschen, Hong Kong, 2009.

Johnson, Philip, and Wigley, Mark, *Deconstructivist*

*Architecture*, Museum of Modern Art, New York, 1988.

Kauffman, Jordan, *Drawing on Architecture: The Object of Lines, 1970–1990*, The MIT Press, Cambridge, Mass., 2018.

Kemp, Martin, *The Science of Art: Optical Themes in Western Art from Brunelleschi to Seurat*, Yale University Press, New Haven, Conn., 1990.

Koolhaas, Rem, 'Ivan Leonidov's Dom Narkomtjazjprom, Moscow', *Oppositions*, no.2, 1974, pp 96–102.

Koolhaas, Rem, 'Life in the Metropolis or The Culture of Congestion', *OMA, Architectural Design*, vol.47, no.5, 1977, pp 319–25.

Koolhaas, Rem, *Delirious New York*, Oxford University Press, New York, 1978.

Kosloff, Max, 'Malevich as a Counterrevolutionary (East and West)', *Artforum International*, January 1974, pp 30–38.

Krier, Léon, 'Houses, Palaces, Cities', *Architectural Design*, vol.54, no.7/8, 1984.

Krier, Léon, *Léon Krier: Architecture & Urban Design 1967–1992*, Academy Editions, London, 1992.

Krier, Léon, et al., *Rational Architecture Rationelle: The Reconstruction of the European City*, Archives d'Architecture Moderne, Brussels, 1978.

Kries, Mateo, ed., *The Vitra Campus: Architecture Design Industry*, Vitra Design Museum, Weil am Rhein, 2013.

Levene, Richard, and Cecilia, Fernando, eds, *El Croquis 52: Zaha Hadid 1983/1991*, El Croquis Editorial, Madrid, 1991.

Lodge, David, 'Deconstruction: Will Deconstruction be the Architectural "ism" of the 1990s?', *The Guardian* (London), 8 April 1988, p.25.

Lynn, Greg, 'Multiplicitous and Inorganic Bodies', *Assemblage*, no.19, December 1992, pp 32–49.

Lynn, Greg, guest ed., *Folding in Architecture, Architectural Design Profile* (*AD*), no.102, 1993.

Lynn, Greg, *Animate Form*, Princeton Architectural Press, New York, 1999.

Lyotard, Jean-François, *The Postmodern Condition, A Report on Knowledge*, 1979 in French, trans. Bennington, Geoffrey, and Massumi, Brian, University of Minnesota Press, Minneapolis, 1984.

Lyotard, Jean-François, *Les Immatériaux*, 28 March to 15 July 1985, Centre de Création Industrielle, Grande Gallerie du Centre national d'art et la culture George Pompidou, https://www.centrepompidou.fr/fr/programme/agenda/evenement/cRyd8q.

Lyotard, Jean-François, 'After Six Months of Work … (1984)', in Hui, Yuk, and Broeckmann, Andreas, eds, *30 Years After Les Immatériaux: Art, Science, and Theory*, Meson Press, Hybrid Publishing, Lüneburg, 2015.

Lyotard, Jean-François, and Roberts, Mark, 'Plastic Space and Political Space', *Boundary 2*, vol.1/2, no.14, Autumn 1985 / Winter 1986, pp 211–23.

McDowell, Tara, 'Les Immatériaux: A Conversation with Jean-François Lyotard and Bernard Blistène', *e-flux Criticism*, https://www.e-flux.com/criticism/235949/les-immatriaux-a-conversation-with-jean-franois-lyotard-and-bernard-blistne.

Marjanović, Igor, and Howard, Jan, *Drawing Ambience: Alvin Boyarsky and the Architectural Association*, Mildred Lane Kemper Art Museum, St. Louis, Museum of Art, Rhode Island, and University of Chicago Press, Chicago, 2014.

Molteni, Enrico, 'Architettura per tutti gli usi: la collezione Vitra a Weil am Rhein' ('Architecture for a Multitude of Uses: The Vitra Campus in Weil am Rhein'), *Casabella*, vol.74, no.788, April 2010, pp 16–37 and 107–9.

Mostafavi, Mohsen, in conversation with Hadid, Zaha, 'Landscape as Plan' (2001), in Cecilia, Fernando, and Levene, Richard, eds, *El Croquis: Zaha Hadid 1983–2001*, El Croquis Editorial, Madrid, 2004, pp 40–69.

Nägeli, Walter, ed., *Zaha Hadid: Vitra Fire Station*, Aedes, Berlin, 1992.

Nakov, Andrei, *Tatlin's Dream: Russian Suprematist and Constructivist Art 1910–1923*, Fischer Fine Art Limited, 1973.

Nakov, Andrei, *Avant-Garde Russe*, Universe Books, New York, 1986.

Noever, Peter, ed., *Architecture in Transition: Between Deconstruction and New Modernism*, Prestel Verlag, Munich, 1991.

Noever, Peter, *Weiner Architektur-gespräche*, Ernst & Sohn, Berlin, 1991.

Norris, Christopher, and Benjamin, Andrew, *What is Deconstruction?*, Academy Editions/St. Martin's Press, London, 1988.

Obrist, Hans Ulrich, 'Philippe Parreno in interview with Hans Ulrich Obrist', in *Gasthof 2002 Städelschule Frankfurt/M*, Staatliche Hochschule, Städelschule, Frankfurt am Main, 2003, pp 98–106.

Obrist, Hans Ulrich, *Zaha Hadid: The Conversation Series*, Verlag der Buchhandlung Walther König, Cologne, 2007.

Obrist, Hans Ulrich, 'Zaha Hadid in Conversation', in Hadid, Zaha, and Schumacher, Patrik, *Zaha Hadid and Suprematism*, Hatje Cantz, Zurich, 2012, pp 43–7.

Panofsky, Erwin, *Perspective as Symbolic Form*, trans., Wood, Christopher S., Zone, New York, 1997.

Papadakis, Andreas, 'Architectural Design Project Awards', *British Architecture 1982, Architectural Design* (*AD*), Academy Editions, London, 1982.

Papadakis, Andreas, ed., *Deconstruction in Architecture, Architectural Design* (*AD*), vol.58, no.3/4, 1988.

Papadakis, Andreas, Cooke, Catherine, and Benjamin, Andrew, eds, *Deconstruction Omnibus Volume*, Academy Editions, London, 1989.

Petranzan, Margherita, with Coppola, Mario, eds, *Zaha Hadid Architects: MAXXI*, Antifone e Zeto, Padova, 2018.

Phillips, Patricia C., 'Zaha Hadid', *Artforum International*, vol.26, no.2, October 1987, https://www.artforum.com/print/reviews/198708/zaha-hadid-61905.

Pozzo, Andrea, *The Rules and Examples of Perspective Proper for Painters and Architects*, John James, Greenwich, 1707.

Racana, Gianluca, and Janssens, Manon, eds, *MAXXI: Zaha Hadid Architects*, Skira, New York, 2010.

Rajchman, John, *Constructions*, The MIT Press, Cambridge, Mass., 1998.

Rajchman, John, 'Jean-François Lyotard's Underground Aesthetics', *October*, no.86, Autumn 1998, pp 3–18.

Rossi, Aldo, *The Architecture of the City*, trans., Girardo, Diane, and Ockman, Joan, The Graham Foundation for Advanced Studies in the Fine Arts, The Institute for Architecture and Urban Studies, and The MIT Press, Chicago, New York, and Cambridge, Mass., 1982.

Rowe, Colin, and Koetter, Fred, *Collage City*, The MIT Press, Cambridge, Mass., 1978.

Rykwert, Joseph, *On Adam's House in Paradise: The Idea of the Primitive Hut in Architectural History*, The MIT Press, Cambridge, Mass., 1972 and 1981.

Rykwert, Joseph, *The Idea of a Town: The Anthology of Urban Form in Rome, Italy and the Ancient World*, Princeton University Press, Princeton, N.J., 1976.

Schumacher, Patrik, *Digital Hadid: Landscapes in Motion*, Birkhäuser, Basel, 2004.

Schumacher, Patrik, 'The Place of MAXXI in the Œuvre of Zaha Hadid', in Ciorra, Pippo, and Guccione, Margherita, eds, *Zaha Hadid in Italy*, Quodlibet, Rome, 2017, pp 32–7.

Sharma, Suresh, et al., eds, *Vision, Architecture + Design*, vol.1, no.4, April 1983.

Shatskikh, Aleksandra, 'Malevich, Curator of Malevich', in Petrova, Yevgenia, ed., *The Russian Avant-Garde: Representation and Interpretation*, Palace Editions, St Petersburg, 2001.

Steele, Brett, 'Anecdote as Evidence: Zaha's World', in Gad, Amira, and Gryczkowska, Agnes, eds, *Reflections on Zaha Hadid*, Serpentine Sackler Gallery, London, 2016, pp 131–45.

Sunwoo, Irene, 'Between the "Well Laid Table" and the "Marketplace": Alvin Boyarsky's Experiments in Architectural Pedagogy', a dissertation presented to Princeton University, 2013, UMI 3604509.

Szacha, Léa-Catherine, 'Roma Interrotta: Postmodern Rome as the Source of Fragmented Narratives', in Holdaway, Dom, and Trentin, Felippo, eds, *Rome, Postmodern Narratives of a Cityscape*, Routledge, London, 2015, pp 155–69.

Tupitsyn, Margarita, 'Fragmentation versus Totality: The Politics of (De)framing', in Solomon R. Guggenheim Museum, et al., *The Great Utopia: The Russian Avant-Garde, 1915–1932*, Guggenheim Museum, et al., New York, 1992, pp 482–96.

Van Schaik, Martin, and Máčel, Otaker, eds, *Exit Utopia: Architectural Provocations 1956–76*, Prestel Verlag, Munich, 2005.

Venturi, Robert, *Complexity and Contradiction in Architecture*, MOMA Art Papers, New York, 1966.

Venturi, Robert, Scott-Brown, Denise, and Izenour, Steven, *Learning from Las Vegas*, The MIT Press, Cambridge, Mass., 1977.

Viollet-le-Duc, Eugène-Emmanuel, *Histoire d'un dessinateur: comment on apprend à dessiner* (*Learning to Draw: or The Story of a Young Designer*), J. Hetzel, Paris, *ca*.1880. See it translated in Hearn, Millard Fillmore, *The Architectural Theory of Viollet-le-Duc: Readings and Commentary*, The MIT Press, Cambridge, Mass., 1992, pp 127–39.

Virilio, Paul, 'The Overexposed City', in Crary, Jonathan, et al., eds, *Zone 1:2*, Urzone, New York, 1986, pp 15–31.

Wigley, Mark, 'Postmortem Architecture, the Taste of Derrida', *Perspecta*, vol.23, 1987, pp 156–72.

Wilson, Peter, 'The Park and the Peak – Two International Competitions', *AA Files*, no.4, July 1983, pp 76–87.

Wittkower, Rudolph, *Architectural Principles in the Age of Humanism*, Academy Editions, London, 1973.

Wong, Tony, et al., eds, *Ubiquitous Urbanism, Total Architecture: The Tokyo Experiment: A Studio in Global Master Planning with Zaha M. Hadid at Columbia University Graduate School *of Architecture, Planning and Preservation*, Columbia Books of Architecture, New York, 1994.

Woods, Lebbeus, 'Zaha Hadid: The Tension Builds at Max Protetch Gallery', *A+U Architecture and Urbanism*, vol.9, no.204, 1987, pp 4–8.

Woods, Lebbeus, 'Drawn into Space: Zaha Hadid', *Architectural Design (AD) Special Issue: Protoarchitecture: Analogue and Digital Hybrids*, vol.78, no.4, July/August 2008, pp 28–35.

Zaha Hadid Architects and Betsky, Aaron, 'Project Information', *Zaha Hadid: The Complete Buildings and Projects*, Thames and Hudson and Rizzoli, London and New York, 1998.

'Zaha Hadid and Suprematism: Tate Talks', a discussion between multiple award-winning architect Zaha Hadid and Achim Borchardt-Hume, Head of Exhibitions at Tate Modern and curator of Malevich Exhibition, 30 October, 2014, https://www.youtube.com/watch?v=GF_qPKnrrHo.

Zenghelis, Elia, 'Text and Architecture: Architecture as Text', in van Schaik, Martin, and Máčel, Otaker, eds, *Exit Utopia: Architectural Provocations 1956–76*, Prestel Verlag, Munich, 2005, pp 255–276.

# Index

Numbers in italics indicate illustrations. Numbers in italics preceded by '*n*' or '*nn*' indicate the relevant endnote (or endnotes) numbers on the given page. See 'Hadid, Zaha' entry for list of works by Zaha Hadid included and see also 'drawings, woodblock and etching', 'painting' and 'photography' entries for works by other artists.

Aedes Gallery and Architectural Forum
    Berlin 37, 76, 78, 99, 108, *109*, 113, 146 *n13*, 148 *n30*, 149 *n18*
aesthetic values in architecture and art 20, 27, 69, 70, 88, 96, 103, 114,
Ahrends Burton Koralek 59
Alberti, Leon Battista 27, 65, 141 *n44*, 144 *n44*
Amsterdam 19, 37, 140 *n23*
    anatomy (as applied in architecture) 85–86, 121, 147 *n65*
    Koolhaas' usage 17
    skin and bones analogy 85–86, 94
apprehension of architecture through traditions of drawing technique 9, 10, 11, 12, 22, 23, 24, 30–35, 48, 65, 71, 74, 78, 83, 86–89, 93, 103, 105, 115, 135, 138, 139, 141 *n30*, 143 *n63*
Architectural Association School of Architecture, London (AA) 9, 10, 11, 15, 17, 19, 37, 38, 40, 42, 44, 45, *49*, 52, 54, 57, 58, 60, 67, 73, 76, 77, 78, 81, 85, 88, 94, 110, 121, 137, 140 *n7*, 141 *nn 25, 33, 50*, 142 *nn 46, 50*, 143 *nn 65, 96*, 144 *n12*, 146 *nn 35, 48, 65*, 147 *n74*, 148 *n77*, 150 *n 83*, *2*
    *Larger than Life: Cedric Price: The Home / Zaha Hadid 59 Eaton Place*, 1982 19
    *Planetary Architecture Two*, 1983 *9*, 37, 44, 49, 99, 100, 140 *n7*, 142 *n6*
    AADRL (Design Research Lab) 121, 149 *n23*
Association of Commissioned Officers
    *Nine-Lens Photograph of New York City*, U.S. Coast and Geodetic Survey, 1938 *45*
Austrian Museum of Applied Arts / Contemporary Art Vienna (MAK) 96, 99, 106, 148 *n34*
axonometric projection 9, 17, 23, 24, 86, 131, 140 *n6*, 141 *nn 31, 34*, 150 *n65*
    El Lissitzky, *Axonometric Projection of the Proun Room Installed at the Greater Berlin Art Exhibition*, 1923 *24*

Balla, Giacomo 94
    *Dinamismo di un cane al guinzaglio (Dynamism of a Dog on a Leash)* 1912 *94*
Bann, Stephen 95
Baroque 11, 117–118, 120, 128, 129
Barthes, Roland 58, 144 *n8*
Benjamin, Andrew 95, 97, 105, 108, 109, 114
Benjamin, Walter 15, 86, 89, 103, 139, 140 *nn 7, 1*
Bennington, Geoffrey 95,
Berlin 10, 13, 23, 37, 75, 76, 99, 110–113, 146 *n14*
Bois, Yve-Alain 23
Boyarsky, Alvin 37, 39, 41, 42, 52, 58, 60, 61, 67, 72, 77, *80*, 81, 88, 96, 137, 141 *n 33*
Boyarsky, Nicholas 142 *n18*, 146 *n51*
Borromini, Francesco 13, 128, 130
    *Plan, site plan and photograph* of San Carlo alle Quattro Fontane, Rome, 1646 *129, 130*
Bramante, Donato 13, 128, 130
    Tempietto, San Pietro in Montorio, Rome, 1502 *128*
Brislin, Paul 123, 125

Cartesian/Euclidean geometry 12, 13, 26, 27–28, 47, 65, 104, 114, 115, 117–122, 127–130, 131, 135, 138
Centre Georges Pompidou (Centre Pompidou)
    *Les Immatériaux* 12, 61, 73, 74, 75, 86, 141 *n50*, 144 *nn 6, 39*
    *Les Immatériaux*, exhibition at Centre Pompidou, Grande Galerie, Paris, 1985 *73*, *89*
Cesariano, Cesare 44
    *The Congress of Man, Di Lucio Vitruvio Pollione de architectura libri dece*, 1521 *44*
Chaput, Thierry 61, 73, 75
    *Les Immatériaux*, exhibition at Centre Pompidou, Grande Galerie, Paris, 1985 *73*, *89*
Charles III, formerly HRH Prince of Wales 57, 59, 73
Church of Sant'Ignazio di Loyola, Rome 28
city as organism 17, 71–72, 75
colour's effect (in painting and especially architectural painting) 9, 10, 11, 15, 17–19, 20–24, 27, 28, 29, 30, 33, 34, 39–40, 41, 42, 47–49, 52, 61, 65, 76–77, 79, 83–86, 88, 100, 102, 103, 105, 123, 134, 139, 141 *n32*
computer software (approaches and use) 77, 115, 117, 118, 122, 148 *n5*, 149 *n40*
Cousins, Nicola 39, 76, 99, 100
Crawford, Charles 76
Cubism 46–47, 93
    Synthetic Cubism 71

Daghini, Giairo 75
Dali, Salvador 26, 33
    *Le rêve de Vénus (The Dream of Venus)*, 1939 *32*
    *The Temptation of St. Anthony*, 1946 *26*
Debord, Guy 58
De Certeau, Michel 58, 68, 70, 105
deconstruction in architecture 13, 77, 95–97, 105, 109, 110, 114, 127, 128, 147 *nn 4, 8, 9*
    *Deconstructivist Architecture* (MOMA New York, June 23 to August 30 1988) 13, 77, 95, 127, 147 *n7*
    *Deconstruction in Art and Architecture* (Symposium at the Tate London 1988) 95, 147 *nn 3, 8*
Deleuze, Gilles 117–118, 120, 129, 132, 134
De Michelis, Marco 110, 112
Derrida, Jacques 13, 58, 95–97, 114
Descartes, Rene 97, 105, 108, 109, 147 *n21*
De Stijl 46
Dietsch, Deborah 76
Douglas, Charlotte 81
drawings, woodblock and etching (not by Zaha Hadid, ZHA)
    *Axonometric Projection of the Proun Room* El Lissitzky 1923 *24*
    *De humani corporis fabrica* John Stephen Calcar (sculptor) 1555 *86*
    *Draughtsman Making a Perspective Drawing of a Reclining Woman* Albrecht Dürer c. 1600 *26*
    *Frontispiece, Marc-Antoine Laugier, Essai sur l'architecture* Charles-Dominique-Joseph Eisen (engraver) 1755 *45*
    *Perspective of Burlington Arcade* Robert Blemmell Schnebbelie 1827 *27*
    *Plan of Rome, La nuova topografia di Roma, Alla Santità Di Nostro Signore Papa Benedetto XIV La Nuova Topografia Di Roma Ossequiosamente Offerisce e Dedica l'Umilissimo Servo Giambattista Nolli Comasco / Nuova pianta di Roma* Giambattista Nolli 1748 *112*
    *Radial and Spline Geometry* Greg Lynn 1999 *120*
    *San Carlo alle Quattro Fontane, site plan showing radial geometries* Francesco Borromini 1646 *129, 130*
    *Suprematism 34 Drawings* Kazimir Malevich 1920 *48*
    *Suprematist Construction No. 118* Kazimir Malevich 1917–18 *48*
    *The Congress of Man, from Vitruvius, Di Lucio Vitruvio Pollione de architectura libri dece* Cesare Cesariano 1521 *44*
    *Unexecuted competition design for the National Gallery Extension project, Hampton site, Trafalgar Square, London: perspective view of Trafalgar Square, including the church of St Martin-in-the-Fields and Nelson's Column, from the proposed extension, London* Skidmore Owings & Merrill 1982 *67*
Duchamp, Marcel 77, 92, 94
Dunn, Jonathan 20, 38, 39
Dürer, Albrecht 26
    *Draughtsman Making a Perspective Drawing of a Reclining Woman*, ca.1600 *26*

Eames, Charles and Ray 98
Eisenman, Peter 23, 58, 73, 77, 97, 112, 118, 141 *nn 30, 31, 33, 34*
Elkins, James 28, 141 *n40*
Enlightenment 9, 85, 147 *n65*
    rational/irrational beauty 24, 26, 44, 45, 67, 72, 74, 75, 83–85, 86, 92, 94, 103, 104, 108–109, 114, 121, 130
    reason/chance 46, 97, 98, 108, 138
Escher, M. C. 22, 141 *n31*
Evans, Robin 88–89, 139

Fehlbaum, Rolf 98, 114
fictionalise the historic city (its application to new architecture) 109, 113
field (in architectural drift) 110, 131–132, 135
    anti-gravitational field 33, 43
    force-field 118
    pictorial field 22, 30, 81, 103
    visual field 49, 80, 81
figure-ground 108–113, 127, 129
Fischer Fine Art Gallery, *Tatlin's Dream, Russian Suprematist and Constructivist Art 1910–1923* 17
Foucault, Michel 58
Futurism 11, 38, 46–47, 93–94

GA Gallery Tokyo, *The Architecture of Zaha M. Hadid*, 1985 61
Galway, Wendy 39
Galerie Gmurzynska, *Zaha Hadid and Suprematism*, 2010 81
Galerie van Rooy Amsterdam, *Planetary Architecture*, 1981 19, 37
Gehry, Frank 98, 108, 114, 118
Girard, Alexander 98
Gomersall, David 39, 49, 76, 77, 99, 106, 122, 123
graft (spatial grafting elements in painting and architecture) 12, 15, 17–18, 42, 49, 50, 142 *n46*
gravity (anti-gravitational force of painting and architecture) 33, 47–50, 52, 55, 67, 79, 102, 135, 137
Grimshaw, Nicholas 98, 114
Guattari, Félix 117, 132, 134
Guggenheim Museum *see* Solomon Guggenheim Museum, New York

Hadid, Foulath 19
Hadid, Zaha
    animation techniques 92, 122
    Architectural Association 1972-1977 as a student 11, 12, 15–19, 77, 110, 140 *n2*, 141 *nn 33, 4*, 142 *nn 46, 48*, 146 *n48*
    Architectural Association 1978-1984 as a tutor 57, 58–59, 61, 94, 88, 142 *nn 16, 27*, 146 *n35*
    architectural 'drift' 126, 127, 129, 130–132, 134, 135
    deconstruction 13, 77, 95–97, 105, 109, 110, 114, 128
    exhibitions
        *Architectural Drawings,* Austrian Museum of Applied Arts / Contemporary Art Vienna (MAK) 99
        *British Architecture 1982*, RIBA London 19, 141 *n26*
        *Deconstructivist Architecture,* MOMA New York 13, 95–97
        *Entwurf Zaha M. Hadid at the Aedes, Gutachten Kurfürstendamm 70/ Adenauerplatz,* Aedes Galerie Berlin 76, 78
        *La Riconstruzione della città: Berlino Triennale of Milan 1985,* Milan 110
        *Larger than Life: Cedric Price: Home / Zaha Hadid: 59 Eaton Place,* Architectural Association London 19, 54, 141 *n25*
        *Latent Utopias*, Graz 115, 117, 131
        *Les Immatériaux*, Centre Pompidou Paris 12, 61, 73, 74, 77, 82, 86, 88 132, 150 *n11*
        *Planetary Architecture,* Galerie van Rooy Amsterdam 37, 39
        *Planetary Architecture Two,* Architectural Association, London 19, 44, 49, 99, 100
        *Retrospective, Zaha Hadid, the Complete Buildings and Works,* San Francisco Museum of Modern Art, San Francisco 140 *n7*
        *Sparkling Metropolis,* Solomon R. Guggenheim Museum, New York 37, 141 *n4*
        *The Great Utopia,* Solomon R. Guggenheim Museum, New York 146 n 47
        *The Peak Competition Exhibition,* Far East Exchange Building, Hong Kong 142 *n12*
        *Zaha Hadid and Suprematism,* Galerie Gmurzynska, Zurich 81
        *Zaha Hadid Early Paintings and Drawings,* Serpentine Gallery, London 141 *n24*, 142 *n25*
        *Zaha Hadid: the Tension Builds,* Max Protetch Gallery, New York 11, 76
        *Zaha Hadid: Vitra Fire Station,* Aedes Galerie, Berlin 99
        *Zaha M. Hadid,* GA Gallery, Tokyo 61

gravity (defying gravity, liberation from gravity) 47, 48, 49, 50, 52, 67, 102, 135
London (critique) 12–13, 15, 17–18, 20, 22, 38, 57–63, 67, 70–74, 77, 95, 99, 110, 112, 138
Malevich's approach to pictorial space 46–49, 52, 54, 105, 113, 129–130, 134, 138
metropolis 12, 45, 48, 49, 50, 55, 59, 71, 75, 82, 110, 144 *n14*
movement as a force in architecture 22, 33, 46–49, 50, 52, 81, 92–94, 100, 106, 115, 117, 118, 120, 128; in relation to spline geometry 118–121; cinematic movement 125; flipbook 92
narrative force in painting 10, 20, 33, 48–49, 50, 62-63, 78–79, 85, 92–94, 104, 106, 114, 126,
pictorial depth 33, 46
pictorial ground (foreground/background, figure-ground) 18, 20, 22, 23, 26–28, 33, 34, 41, 46–49, 63, 65, 66, 69, 79, 83, 92, 100, 103, 108–109, 110–113, 126, 127, 129, 131, 134, 135
pictorial surface 18, 29, 33, 47, 130, 135, 138
political in architecture (as idea) 59–61, 69–74
subjective response to architecture (idea of) 22, 35, 55, 58, 68, 70–71, 72, 73, 74, 75, 78, 94, 104, 106, 138, 139
Rodchenko's politicising of the gaze 68–74
    camera's gaze 69
Rome's architectural geometry 128–129, 131, 132, 134, 135
sensation 12–13, 26, 28, 34, 46–50, 52, 54, 55, 58, 70, 73, 78, 79, 80–82, 85, 92, 94, 126, 139
spatial layering 33, 40, 54, 65, 96–97, 102
    in painting 10, 24, 49, 74, 83, 86, 92, 100, 102, 104, 105, 108, 109, 126, 128–129, 134, 138
subjective gaze and its relation to time and sensation 13, 73–74, 92–93
temporality (idea of) 10, 12, 52, 78–80, 85, 94, 106, 110
urban grid and Cartesian geometry in the city 45–46, 115, 117, 122, 129–131, 135, 138
viewer engagement with architecture through painting 11, 12, 15, 18, 19, 22–23, 24, 26–35, 37, 40–42, 44, 48, 50, 52, 62, 65, 67, 70, 71, 74, 75, 78, 80–86, 92–94, 103–105, 106, 114, 125, 126, 129, 137, 138, 139
weave, idea of woven space 130–135
Hadid, Zaha and Zaha Hadid Architects painted and contextual works
    *59 Eaton Place, Plot of Internal Elements* 1981 *21, 22, 23*
    *59 Eaton Place, Aerial Perspective of the Master Bedroom and Library* 1981 *25*
    *59 Eaton Place, Three Towers: the Flamboyant, the Suprematist, the Clinical* 1981 *31, 33*
    *Grand Buildings, Trafalgar Square, End Elevation Towards Trafalgar Square* 1985 *63*
    *Grand Buildings, Trafalgar Square, Inside Podium: Lobbies and Towers* 1985 *64*
    *Grand Buildings, Trafalgar Square, Interior of Office Scape in the Slab-tower, Floor Planes* 1985 *66*
    *Grand Buildings, Trafalgar Square, View from Trafalgar Square* 1985 *63*
    *Grand Buildings, Trafalgar Square, View of Site with London Skyline* 1985 *56*
    *Grand Buildings, Trafalgar Square, Worm's Eye View with Ramp and Towers* 1985 *64*
    *Horizontal Tektonik, Malevich's Tektonik* 1977 *6*
    *Malevich's Tektonik* 1976 *16*
    *Malevich's Tektonik, Axonometric* 1977 *16*
    *Malevich's Tektonik, Presentation Title Page* 1976–77 *14*

*MAXXI: Museum of XXI Century Arts, Composite Aerial View* 1999 *124, 127*
*MAXXI: Museum of XXI Century Arts, Computer Model from Above* 1999 *116*
*MAXXI: Museum of XXI Century Arts, Sketch* 1999 *121*
*MAXXI: Museum of XXI Century Arts, Sketch Painting* 1999 *133*
*MAXXI: Museum of XXI Century Arts, Stage Two, Competition Panel 1* 1999 *119, 126*
*Metropolis* 1988 *110*
*Office Building on Kurfürstendamm 70, Movement Sequence* 1986 *90–91, 93*
*Office Building on Kurfürstendamm 70, Red Painting* 1986 *84*
*Office Building on Kurfürstendamm 70, Section/ Perspective with Curtain Wall Detail* 1986 *87*
*Office Building on Kurfürstendamm 70, The Major Facade* 1986 *79*
*Office Building on Kurfürstendamm 70, View from Kurfürstendamm* 1986 *80*
*'Tektonik in Thames',* (detail) *Architectural Association School of Architecture, Projects Review 1975–76* 1976 *17*
*The Peak, Blue Slabs* 1983 *42, 43*
*The Peak, Confetti – Suprematist Snowstorm* 1983 *50, 51*
*The Peak, Divers* 1983 *2, 52*
*The Peak, Elements of Void* 1983 *53, 54*
*The Peak, Exploded Isometric* 1983 *36, 41*
*The World, The Eighty-nine Degrees* 1984 *137*
*Vitra Fire Station, Aerial Painting* 1990 *107*
*Vitra Fire Station, Concept Drawings* 1990 *109*
*Vitra Fire Station, Landscape study* 1990 *103*
*Vitra Fire Station, Plan and Aerial Perspective of Overall Scheme,* 1990 *101, 102, 103*
Hadid, Zaha and Zaha Hadid Architects realised buildings
    Vitra Fire Station, Weil am Rhein 10, 13, 95, 97, 98, 99, 105, 106, 108, 110, 113, 114, 115
    Museo Nazionale delle arti del XXI secolo (MAXXI), Rome 10, 13, 115, 117, 121, 122, 123, 125–135, 149 *n9*
Hitchcock, Alfred 10
Hitchcock, Henry-Russell 95
Ho, Kar Hwa 61, 99
Holl, Steven 117, 149 *n10*
Hong Kong 10, 12, 37, 38–42, 44, 45, 48, 49, 50, 52, 55, 60, 95, 110, 141 *n1*, 142 *nn 10, 11, 12, 13*, 143 *n61*

isometric projection 9, 20–24, 30, 38, 40, 41, 42, 44, 45, 50,
exploded isometric 30, 40–48, 100
Izenour, Steven 82, 127

Jay, Martin 26
Jencks, Charles 95
Johnson, Philip 77, 95, 96
Jung, Carl 45

Kemp, Martin 26
Kipnis, Jeffrey 73
Klotz, Heinrich 76
Koetter, Fred 58, 71, 112, 113, 127
Koolhaas, Rem 12, 15, 17, 34, 37, 44–45, 52, 57, 73, 75, 76, 77, 86, 88, 94, 139
Krier, Léon 57, 58, 59, 60, 67, 68, 71–73, 110, 143 *n5*

155

Laugier, Marc-Antoine 44
  *Frontispiece, Essai sur l'architecture*, second edition, 1755 *45*
Le Corbusier (Charles-Édouard Jeanneret) 17, 18, 128, 129
  *Voisin Plan for Paris*, 1925 *17*
Lee, Nan 19, 39, 40, 41
Lefebvre, Henri 58
*Les Immatériaux* (Centre Pompidou, Grande Galerie, Paris, 28 March 1985 to 15 July 1985) 73, 89, 145 *n84*
Libeskind, Daniel 37, 44-45
Lissitzky, El (Lazar) 23, 24, 46, 83, 102
  *Axonometric Projection of the Proun Room Installed at the Greater Berlin Art Exhibition*, 1923 *24*
London 10, 11, 12, 13, 15, 17-19, 20, 22, 27, 37, 38, 57-63, 67, 70-74, 76, 77, 95, 99, 110, 112, 122, 138
Lynn, Greg 117-118, 120-121, 128-129, 130
  'Radial and Spline Geometry', from *Animate Form*, 1999 *120*
Lyotard, Jean-Françoise 12, 61, 70, 73, 75-76, 77, 78, 82, 86, 88, 89, 94, 132, 139
  *Les Immatériaux*, Centre Pompidou, Grande Galerie, Paris, 28 March 1985 to 15 July 1985 73, 89, 145 *n84*

Mach, Ernst 81
Malevich, Kazimir 12, 15, 17, 18, 24, 33, 40, 46-49, 50, 52, 54, 58, 81-82, 83, 85, 94, 102, 113, 126, 129, 134, 135, 138
  sensation 46-48, 50
  gravity 47, 48, 49, 102
  intuitive reason 47, 138
  *Arkhitekton in Front of a Skyscraper*, 1924 *18*
  *House Under Construction*, 1915-16 *47*
  *Landscape with a Yellow House (Winter Landscape)*, 1906 *47*
  *Suprematism: 34 Drawings*, 1920 *48*
  *Suprematist Composition (with Yellow, Orange and Green Rectangle)*, 1915-16 *104*
  *Suprematist Construction No. 118*, 1917-18 *48*
  *Suprematist Painting (with Black Trapezium and Red Square)*, 1915 *49*
  *Yellow Plane in Dissolution*, 1917-18 *81*
Ma Siy, Brian 61, 99, 106
Max Protetch Gallery, New York 11, 37, 76
  *Zaha Hadid, the Tension Builds*, 1987 11, 76, 146 *n 14*
Modernism 19, 37, 38, 59, 65, 69, 70, 85, 95, 96, 114, 141 *n2*, 144 *nn 8, 41*
Molteni, Enrico 98
Mondrian, Piet 33, 46
  *Composition with Large Red Plane, Yellow, Black, Grey and Blue*, 1921 *46*
movement (sensation of movement in painting and architecture) 22, 33, 46-49, 50, 52, 77, 81, 92-94, 100, 106, 110, 114, 115, 117, 125, 128, 134, 138
  filmic movement 33, 41, 92, 93, 115, 134, 147 *n79*
  linear and spatial movement in spline geometry 118-120
  nomadic sense of time and space 134
Museum of Modern Art (MoMA) New York, *Deconstructivist Architecture* Exhibition 13, 77, 95, 127

Nakov, Andréi 81, 83, 85
Nelson, George 98
New York 11, 13, 17, 37, 41, 44-45, 57, 76, 77, 95, 121, 140 *n 15*

Nicolin, Pierluigi 110
Noever, Peter 96, 102, 104
Nolli, Gianbattista 113, 127
  Plan of Rome, La nuova topografia di Roma, Alla Santità Di Nostro Signore Papa Benedetto XIV La Nuova Topografia Di Roma Ossequiosamente Offerisce e Dedica l'Umilissimo Servo Giambattista Nolli Comasco / Nuova pianta di Roma, 1748 *112*
Norris, Christopher 68, 95

Obrist, Hans Ulrich 68
Oechslin, Werner 110
Oldenburg, Claes 98, 114
Office for Metropolitan Architecture (OMA) 37, 38, 45, 57, 86, 141 *n1*
  *Sparkling Metropolis* 37
  *Boompjes Tower Slab*, triptych, 1982 *88*
  orthographic drawing 9, 20, 38, 83, 85, 115
  plan 9, 20, 22, 23, 26, 30, 42, 48, 77, 104, 113, 127, 128
  elevation 9, 20, 22, 83, 86, 92
  section 9, 20, 30, 86, 131

paintings (works other than those by Zaha Hadid, ZHA; *see also* Hadid, Zaha)
  *Composition – Flying Shape*, Alexander Rodchenko 1918-19 81
  *Composition with Large Red Plane, Yellow, Black, Grey and Blue*, Piet Mondrian 1921 46
  *Dynamism of a Dog on a Leash*, Giacomo Balla 1912 94
  *House Under Construction*, Kazimir Malevich 1915-16 47
  *Je vous attends*, Yves Tanguy 1934 32
  *Landscape with a Yellow House*, Kazimir Malevich 1906 47
  *Le rêve de Vénus*, Salvador Dalí 1939 32
  *Removal of the Body of Saint Mark*, Jacopo Tintoretto 1562-66 28
  *Suprematist Composition (with Yellow, Orange and Green Rectangle)*, Kazimir Malevich 1915-16 104
  *Suprematist Painting*, Kazimir Malevich 1915 49
  *The Marriage of the Virgin*, Raphael 1504 128
  *The Temptation of St. Anthony*, Salvador Dalí 1946 26
  *Yellow Plane in Dissolution*, Kazimir Malevich 1917-18 81
Palme, Madelaine 61-62
Panofsky, Erwin 65
Panton, Verner 98
Parc de la Villette 52, 57, 58, 141 *n1*, 144 *nn 6, 7*
Paris 12, 17, 57, 61, 73, 75, 86, 88, 118, 142 *n22*, 144 *nn 6, 39*, 147 *n74*
perspective projection (perspectival geometries) 9, 12, 24, 26, 27, 28, 29, 33, 38, 47, 62, 65-70, 71, 74, 76, 78, 83, 85, 86, 92, 100, 103, 106, 115, 123, 125, 128-129
photographs
  *Arkhitekton in Front of a Skyscraper*, Kazimir Malevich 1924 8
  *Church of Sant'Ignazio di Loyola Nave interior*, Rome 29
  *Experiment 28, Myasnitskaya Street Balconies*, Alexander Rodchenko 1925 69
  *Foto-vopros Пионер (Pioneer)*, Alexander Rodchenko 1933 69
  *Nine-Lens Photograph of New York City*, U.S. Coast and Geodetic Survey, 1938 45

*Novyi LEF* (cover) no. 9, Alexander Rodchenko 1928 68
*Hong Kong 4000' 3.2.1983*, Survey Division Lands Department, Hong Kong 1983 46
*Les Immatériaux*, exhibition at the Centre Pompidou, Paris 1985 73, 89
*MAXXI: Museum of XXI Century Arts, Model from Above*, ZHA 1999 116
*MAXXI: Museum of XXI Century Arts, Sketch*, Zaha Hadid 1999 121
*Tempietto*, Rome Bramante 128
*San Carlo alle Quattro Fontane, dome interior*, Rome 129
*Viewers at the exhibition Zaha Hadid*, Palazzo Franchetti, Venice, Billy Feuerman, 2016 44
*Voisin Plan for Paris*, Le Corbusier 1925 17
*Zaha Hadid portraits* (AA and Simon Koumjian III) 8, 49
*Zambullida (The Diver)*, Alexander Rodchenko 1934 52
photography 11, 18, 44-46, 50, 67, 68-70, 74, 78, 117, 122, 125, 140 *n7*, 145 *n57*
photo still (Rodchenko's approach to photography) 12, 50, 68-70, 145 *n57*
pictorial space 9, 12, 46-49, 52, 54, 105, 113, 126, 129-130, 134, 138
Piranesi, Gianbattista 113
Pierce, Gareth 61
Podro, Michael 95
Postmodernism in architecture 37, 44, 65, 73, 95, 96
  postmodern condition in society 77
Pozzo, Andrea 28,
  Central Nave, Sant'Ignazio di Loyola, fresco ceiling, Rome, 1685 29
Price, Cedric 19, 54, 141 *n25*
program (program/programme, in architecture) 12, 13, 18, 40, 41, 48, 50, 52, 54-55, 59, 60, 61, 71, 96-97, 98, 102-105, 106, 108, 109, 110, 112, 113, 114, 118, 132, 134, 135, 139
Prouvé, Jean 98

Rajchman, John 134
Raphael 128
  *The Marriage of the Virgin*, 1504 *128*
Renaissance 11, 26, 27, 65, 85, 128, 141 *n40*
Revolutionary Society of Proletarian Photographers (ROPF) 70
Rodchenko, Alexander 12, 50, *52*, 68-70, 71, 72, 74, 81, 143 *n82*
  'Foto-kadry' 69, 71, 72, 74
  *Composition – Flying Shape*, 1918-19 *81*
  'Experiment 28', Myasnitskaya Street balconies, Moscow, 1925 69
  'Foto-vopros', Пионер (Pioneer), no.13, p.4, July 1933 69
  *Novyi LEF*, no.9, (cover), 1928 *68*
  *Zambullida (The Diver)*, 1934 *52*
Rome 10, 13, 28, 113, 115, 117, 123, 125-132, 134, 135
Rossi, Aldo 58, 71-72
Rowe, Colin 58, 71, 72, 112-113, 127, 129, 132
Royal Institute of British Architects (RIBA) 9, 19, 59
  *British Architecture exhibition* 1982 19
Russian Avant Garde 10, 15, 96, 126, 141 *n50*
Russian Constructivism 17, 38
Rykwert, Joseph 44, 48, 85, 88

San Carlo alle Quattro Fontane Rome 128-129
Sartogo, Piero 112,
Schnebbelie, Robert Blemmell 27

156   Index

*Perspective of Burlington Arcade, London*, 1827 *27*
sculpture
    *Balancing Tools* Claes Oldenburg and Coosje van Bruggen, 1984 98, 114
Schumacher, Patrik 99, 115–117, 121–122, 126, 127, 130
    *Latent Utopias* 115
SCI-Arc School of Architecture Los Angeles 102
Scott Brown, Denise 82, 127
sensation (spatial sensation in painting and architecture) 12, 13, 26, 28, 34, 46–49, 50, 52, 54, 55, 58, 70, 72, 73, 75–82, 85, 92, 94, 126, 139
Siu, Alfred 38, 142 *nn 10, 12*
Skidmore Owings and Merrill (SOM) 67, 68, 143 *n5*
    *Unexecuted competition design for the National Gallery Extension project*, 1982 *67*
Smerin, Piers 12, 39, 61, 76, 77, 92
software *see* computer software
Solà-Morales, Manuel de 112
Solomon Guggenheim Museum, New York
    *Malevich as a Counterrevolutionary* 17
    *Sparkling Metropolis* 37, 57
    Guggenheim Museum, Bilbao 118
subjective time 71, 74, 80, 94
subjectivity 69, 73, 78, 92, 132
spatial networks including distortion/illusion, effect/affect 9–12, 20–24, 26, 27–29, 33–35, 41, 45–49, 52–55, 60, 62, 65, 67, 70–71, 72, 73–74, 75–76, 83, 85, 86, 97, 102, 104–105, 106, 108, 109, 113–114, 118, 122, 123, 126, 127, 128–131, 134–135, 138, 139
Standing, Alistair 38, *49*
Steele, Brett 76, 77, 121, 137
Suprematism 10, 11, 12, 15, 17, 18, 23, 33, 34, 40, 42, 45–49, 50, 58, 61, 68, 77, 78, 81, 82, 96, 102–103, 105, 113, 134, 135, 138
    Dynamic Suprematism 33, 34
Surrealism (Surrealist practices, surreal imagery) 11, 15, 33, 41
Survey Division Lands Department, Hong Kong Government
    *Hong Kong 4000' 3.2.1983*, 1983 *46*
Szacka, Léa-Catherine 73

Tanguy, Yves 33
    *Je vous attends (I Await You)*, 1934 *32*
Tate Gallery (Tate Britain) 77, 79
    *Deconstruction in Art and Architecture* 77, 95, 97
time, temporality (as relational in architecture) 46–52, 55, 71, 74, 80–81, 82, 94, 105, 114, 115, 129, 131, 134
    bullet time 115,
tectonics in architecture 20, 44, 48, 49, 78, 89, 96, 104, 131, 138
Tektonik 10, 11, 12, 15, 17, 18, 34, 140 *nn 6, 7*
Tempietto, Rome (Bramante) 128
The National Gallery, London 57, 59, 63, 67, 70, 71, 72, 143 *n5*, 144 *n24*, 145 *n53*
Tintoretto (born Jacopo Robusti) 28
    *Removal of the Body of Saint Mark*, 1562–66 *28*
traditional techniques of architectural drawing 9, 11, 15–19, 23, 24, 26–27, 30, 34–35, 67, 76, 83, 86, 88–89, 94, 100, 103, 115, 138–139, 140 *n1*, 146 *n63*, 148 *nn 34, 65*; in relation to the elevation 9, 20, 22, 83, 86, 92; in relation to Lissitzky's axonometric 23–24, 143 *n90*; in relation to perspective technique 26–29, 65–70, 115; in relation to the plan 20–23, 26, 77, 104, 128; Grimshaw masterplan 98, 106–108, 114; in relation to the section 30, 86; orthography 9, 20, 38, 83, 85, 115; in relation to the axonometric and isometric projection 9, 17, 20, 22–24, 30, 38, 41, 45, 50, 131, 140 *n6*, 141 *n31, 34*, 150 n 65
Trafalgar Square, London 10, 13, 57, 59–63, 71, 145 *n53*
Tschumi, Bernard 37, 52, 54, 57, 58, 97
    *Paris Biennale*, 1980 57

urban politics 59, 67, 72–73, 138
Utopia, utopianism, utopian scenography 68, 70, 71, 105, 115, 117, 122, 131, 141 *n30*, 143 *n82*, 146 *n47*

Van der Waals, Marian 38
Vesalius, Andreas 85–86
    *De humani corporis fabrica libri septem (On the Fabric of the Human Body in Seven Books)*, 1555 *86*
Venturi, Robert 82, 127
Virilio, Paul 13, 75, 76, 77, 78, 82, 93, 94, 105
Vitruvius 44, 131
Vriesendorp, Madelon 35, 40

Wachowski, Lana and Lilly (*The Matrix*) 115
Ween, Camilla 38
Weil am Rhein 10, 98, 106–109, 110, 113, 148 *n26*
Werner, Frank 110
whoosh 39, 40, 41, 76, 79–81, 92, 100, 102, 125, 126
Wigley, Mark 77, 95, 96, 127, 128
Wolfson, Michael 38, 39, *49*, 61, 76, 140 *n9*
Woods, Lebbeus 9, 79

Zenghelis, Elia 12, 15, 17, 34, 35, 37, 52, 60, 61
Zenghelis, Zoe 35, 40

## Picture Credits

All efforts have been made to gain copyright licences for images published within this book.

All works by Zaha Hadid and Zaha Hadid Architects are © Zaha Hadid Foundation unless otherwise stated.

Zaha Hadid Foundation
Cover, frontispiece and figure: 1, 3, 4, 5, 9, 10, 11, 13, 19, 22, 23, 24, 25, 26, 39, 40, 41, 43, 44, 45, 46, 47, 48, 49, 50, 57, 58, 61, 63, 66a, 66b, 68, 69, 70, 71, 73, 74 a-c, 75, 77, 78, 80, 81, 82, 83, 84, 90, 91.

Those paintings by Zaha Hadid and Zaha Hadid Architects owned by individual galleries and archives have joint copyright of images. These holdings have been listed within image captions. See figures 1 and 75 © San Francisco Museum of Modern Art, San Francisco; figures 58 and 91 © Alvin Boyarsky Archive; figures 66a and 66b © Deutsches Architekturmuseum, Frankfurt; figure 73 © MAK – Museum of Applied Arts, Vienna.

Where original paintings by Zaha Hadid and Zaha Hadid Architects have not been located nor suitable digital images held by ZHF, digital images have been sought from secondary sources and copyright licence agreements gained. See figure 46 image supplied by Brian Ma Siy, © GA Photographs; figure 49 image supplied by Finn Marchant, © GA Photographs; figure 63 image supplied by Finn Marchant © Architectural Record; figure 68 image supplied and © Taschen; figure 74 a-c image supplied by Brian Ma Siy © Aedes Gallery, Berlin.

Supply of images through Scala Archives Florence:

© Cameraphoto Scala Archives: figure 14 © Musees Royaux des Beaux Arts, Brussels, Belgium; figure 17 © Gallerie dell'Academia, Venice courtesy of the Ministero Beni e Att. Culturali e del Turismo; figure 18 © White Images; figure 21 © Los Angeles County Museum (LACMA) Los Angeles; figure 32 © Kunstmuseum Den Haag, Netherlands; figure 34 © Russian State Museum, St. Petersburg; figure 35 © The Museum of Modern Art, New York; figure 37 Stedelijk Museum, Amsterdam; figure 52 © The Museum of Modern Art, New York; figure 86 © Pinacoteca di Brera, Milan, courtesy of the Ministero Beni e Att. Culturali e del Turismo; figure 87 © White Images.

Images supplied direct from Galleries:
Selections from figures 2, 7, 38 © The Architectural Association, London, with top left and bottom right images for figure 2 supplied by Finn Marchant.
Figure 6 © Fondation Le Corbusier, Paris.
Figure 8 © Getty Research Institute, Los Angeles.
Figures 12, 28, 29 © Centre Canadien d'Architecture: Canadian Centre for Architecture, Montreal.
Figures 15, 62 © The Metropolitan Museum, New York.
Figure 16 © Drawing Matter Collections, Sommerset.
Figure 20 © Hiroshima Prefectural Art Museum, Hiroshima.
Figure 30 © *Life Magazine*, image supplied by Finn Marchant.
Figure 31 © Survey Division, Lands Department, Hong Kong Government, Hong Kong, image supplied by ZHA.
Figure 33 © The National Gallery of Australia, Canberra.
Figures 36, 59, 72 © Stedelijk Museum, Amsterdam.
Figure 42 © Museum of Fine Arts, Boston.
Figure 51 © Royal Institute of British Architects, London.
Figure 67 © Buffalo AKG Art Museum, Buffalo, New York.
Figure 76 © Bibliotheca Hertziana, Rome.
Figures 88, 89 © Albertina Museum, Vienna.
Figures 55, 56, 65 © Centre Pompidou, Paris

Copyright of paintings ADAGP, ARS, and Copyright Agency Australia:
Figure 6 Fondation Le Corbusier; figure 20 The Dali Archive; figure 21 The Estate of Yves Tanguy; figure 67 The Estate of Giacomo Balla.

Copyright of photographs by Alexander Rodchenko: Images supplied or approved by Alexander Lavrentiev for the © Estate of Alexander Rodchenko, figures 42, 52, 53, 54, 60.

Photographer/copyright permissions:
Figure 79 © Greg Lynn, image supplied by author.
Figure 2 left bottom, top right, mid right supplied and © Simon Koumjian III.
Figure 27 supplied and © Billy Feuerman.
Figure 67 © Tom Loonan and Brenda Bieger.
Figure 80 © Luke Hayes.
Figure 85 supplied and © Leo Campbell.

'Around ten years since the death of Zaha Hadid, I am deeply touched to hold Desley Luscombe's publication on Zaha's drawings in my hands. These marvellous drawings, which once caused a sensation at the beginning of her career, were initially recognized by the architectural world as the work of a great artist, but definitely not that of an architect. But Zaha convinced everyone of the opposite.

'She was one of the few female architects of her time and played a key role in shaping the image of women in architecture. What is particularly impressive is how she asserted herself in London's male-dominated architecture scene and ultimately established a place for herself. Her path was by no means easy, and she had to fight hard to realize her visions and to be accepted. At her very first exhibition *The Peak Competition Exhibition*, Hong Kong, 1983, which we showed at Aedes, the visitors' reactions were characteristic: 'Oh, she can build too.' From artistic drawings to realized architecture, Zaha showed that she was not only capable of creating beautiful images, but that these could also serve as the basis for innovative and groundbreaking buildings. Whether working in two or three dimensions, she showed that her art and her architecture were intrinsically linked.

'In Zaha Hadid, the world lost an outstanding personality, a genius and an inspirational mind who constantly pushed the boundaries of architecture. Her spectacular drawings and pioneering architecture are an impressive testimony to her uniqueness and visionary spirit. She left behind a legacy that continues to inspire architects and artists around the world and has permanently changed the way we perceive space and structure. This publication is not only a tribute to Zaha Hadid's extraordinary career, but also an invitation to revisit her work and appreciate its importance to contemporary architecture drawings. These are more than just working sketches; they are an expression of her deep, theoretical reflections and her tireless search for new forms and spaces. Zaha Hadid's work remains a shining example of the transformative power of art and architecture.'

**Dr.h.c. Kristin Feireiss**, Director of Aedes Architecture Forum, Berlin


'Desley Luscombe's important book, structured through a sequence of case studies, explores the paintings of Zaha Hadid and the contexts within which they were produced and circulated. We learn about how they were made and their complex relationship with the projects, of which they are instantiations rather than depictions. Through its detailed discussion and extensive visual documentation, this excellent study expands, renews and refines our understanding of Hadid's remarkable body of work.'

**Mark Dorrian**, Forbes Chair in Architecture, University of Edinburgh and Editor-in-Chief, *Drawing Matter Journal*

'Desley Luscombe's book is extremely well informed and is based on multiple interviews with Hadid's colleagues who were instrumental in producing the paintings. Her perceptive and insightful readings of individual paintings trace how painting evolved as one of Hadid's critical design tools, a tool that Luscombe argues was both reflective and projective. The book brilliantly captures and evokes the intellectual, cultural and creative milieu of London and the AA in the 1970s and 80s. Drawing on the debates and dramas of the times and documenting the intense speculation and hard work by Zaha and her teams of collaborators, this is a compelling and authentic narrative of the formative years of one of our greatest architects.'

>   **Nicholas Boyarsky**, Professor of Architecture, RMIT University and Director, Boyarsky Murphy Architects

'Zaha Hadid endures as one of the great architects of the postwar period. Her work while positioned within the digital turn that occurred in the 1990s retains a singularity that continues to define it beyond the now perceived restrictions of that turn. Part of the singularity can be found in the array of prompts engendering it. Equally, it can be located in the modes of experimentation that occasioned it. Fundamental to the latter was painting. Hadid's own paintings functioned as *loci* of experimentation. It was in the paintings that spatial relations, colour and the possible overcoming of restrictive geometries were first worked out. The unique role of painting as experimentation in her work has not been analysed until now. Desley Luscombe's ground-breaking study of the role of painting in Hadid's practice gives rise to a radical reassessment of Hadid's work. Luscombe's book combines scrupulous analysis of the paintings, traces their history with meticulous detail and shows the differing way in which they figure within subsequent drawings and projects. This is a book of profound importance. It will alter the way drawing and painting are understood as part of architecture's experimental practice.'

>   **Andrew Benjamin**, Honorary Professorial Fellow, Faculty of Arts University of Melbourne